Governing
Lethal Behavior
in Autonomous
Robots

Governing Lethal Behavior in Autonomous Robots

Ronald Arkin

CRC Press
Taylor & Francis Group
Boca Raton London New York

CRC Press is an imprint of the
Taylor & Francis Group, an **informa** business

A CHAPMAN & HALL BOOK

Chapman & Hall/CRC
Taylor & Francis Group
6000 Broken Sound Parkway NW, Suite 300
Boca Raton, FL 33487-2742

First issued in hardback 2017

© 2009 by Taylor & Francis Group, LLC
Chapman & Hall/CRC is an imprint of Taylor & Francis Group, an Informa business

No claim to original U.S. Government works

ISBN-13: 978-1-4200-8594-5 (pbk)
ISBN-13: 978-1-138-43582-7 (hbk)

Library of Congress Cataloging-in-Publication Data

Arkin, Ronald C., 1949-
    Governing lethal behavior in autonomous robots / author, Ronald Arkin.
       p. cm.
    Includes bibliographical references and index.
    ISBN 978-1-4200-8594-5 (pbk. : alk. paper)
       1. Military robots--Moral and ethical aspects. 2. Autonomous robots--Moral and ethical aspects. 3. Robots--Control systems. 4. Robotics--Military applications. 5. Robotics--Moral and ethical aspects. 6. Military ethics. 7. War--Moral and ethical aspects. I. Title.

UG479.A74 2009
172'.42--dc22   2009011782

Visit the Taylor & Francis Web site at
http://www.taylorandfrancis.com

and the CRC Press Web site at
http://www.crcpress.com

To those whose lives were lost unjustly in war, whether friend, foe, or civilian.

Table of Contents

Preface

[N.B.] State a moral case to a ploughman and a professor. The former will decide it as well, and often better than the latter, because he has not been led astray by artificial rules.*

THOMAS JEFFERSON, 1787

One might wonder why a scientist having no military service would write a book on military robots capable of lethality; it certainly is a fair question. Some background on the author may help provide such a basis. Every since I was young I longed to study science, driven by an innate curiosity to understand what is going on in the world and why it happens. As a result my career led me to first study chemistry and applied mathematics (which then also included computer science), after which, in a somewhat serendipitous manner, I entered into the field of robotics. Curiosity-driven research, nonetheless, remained a mainstay as is the case for most scientists.

In the early days of robotics it was remarkable if one could accomplish anything with these sensory and computationally limited machines. Expectations were quite low. However, as time went on, and a series of successful accomplishments were achieved within the field, it became apparent, and often fueled by Hollywood imagery and science fiction, that now accompanying the job of a responsible roboticist was the role of expectation management. We now needed to convince people that they were *not* capable of doing everything imaginable, certainly in the near term.

---

* ME 6:257, Paper 12:15 as reported in [Hauser 06, p. 61].

In the United States there has been a long tradition of applying innovative technology in the battlefield that has often translated into military success. The Department of Defense (DOD) naturally extended this approach to robotics. Primary motivators for the use of intelligent robotic or unmanned systems in the battlefield include:

- *Force multiplication*—where fewer soldiers are needed for a given mission, and where an individual soldier can now do the job of what took many before.

- *Expand the battlespace*—where combat can be conducted over larger areas than was previously possible.

- *Extending the warfighter's reach*—to allow an individual soldier to act deeper into the battlespace; for example, seeing farther or striking farther.

- *Casualty reduction*—removing soldiers from the most dangerous and life-threatening missions.

Up to this time there was no mention of the use of robotics to reduce the number of ethical infractions that could potentially lead to a reduction in *noncombatant* fatalities.

For the reasons above and others, the United States Department of Defense has supported robotics researchers at numerous U.S. universities, industries, and government laboratories for decades towards achieving these ends. I myself have been involved in a number of such sponsored programs. They include:

1. As part of the Defense Advanced Research Projects Agency (DARPA):

   - **The Autonomous Land Vehicle (ALV) Program,** designing visual navigation algorithms and a software architecture in support of autonomous navigation (1985–87).

   - **The Unmanned Ground Vehicle (UGV) Demo II Program,** developing formation control and premission specification systems for teams of UGVs conducting military scouting missions (1993–97).

   - **The Tactical Mobile Robotic Program,** developing behaviors for robots capable of conducting interior building missions for urban combat (1998–2000).

- **The Mobile Autonomous Robotics Software Program,** providing intelligent learning mechanisms for military robotics applications (1999–2003).

- **The Unmanned Ground Combat Vehicle Program,** a joint effort led by SAIC to design a multiton weaponized unmanned platform (2001–2).

- **The Future Combat Systems (FCS) Communications Systems, Integration, and Demonstration Program,** a joint effort led by TRW to design an FCS surrogate robot to test communications capabilities for battlefield scenarios (2001–3).

- **The Mobile Autonomous Robotics Software Vision 2020 Program,** a joint program with the University of Pennsylvania, the University of Southern California, and BBN, to develop teams of heterogeneous robots conducting surveillance operations in an urban setting while effectively managing inter-robot communication (2002–5).

2. As part of the U.S. Army's Research and Development Programs:

- **For the U.S. Army Applied Aviation Directorate,** to develop visual tracking algorithms for an unmanned rotorcraft (1994–96).

- **For the Army Research Institute,** in a joint effort led by SoarTech, to design mission planning systems capable of terrain understanding and interpretation in support of unmanned vehicle navigation (2004–5).

- **For the Army Research Office,** to develop an architecture capable of ethically constraining the application of lethality in autonomous systems (2006–9). (This is the research that serves as the basis for this book.)

- **For the Army Research Laboratory,** in a joint effort led by BAE Systems, to develop complex mission planning and control software architectures for teams of micro-robots capable of flying and walking (2008–13).

3. As part of the U.S. Navy's Research and Development Programs:

- **For the NavAir Intelligent Autonomy Program,** to develop mission-specification and machine learning tools for heterogeneous teams of robots operating in littoral broad area environments (2005–7).

- **For the Office of Naval Research,** a joint program with the University of Pennsylvania, the University of California at Berkeley, and others, using biological and human organizational metaphors for the design of complex intelligent robot teams (2008–13).

4. As a private consultant for various defense industry contractors including Lockheed-Martin, Foster-Miller, and SRS Technologies on related robotics and unmanned systems research.

So while I have not served in uniform, I have been highly active in military robotics for 25 years. All of my research has been unclassified, as I feel it is important, as a Professor, to be able to publish our results openly and freely—an academic tradition. As a citizen of our nation, which unfortunately finds itself at war more often than it should, I personally feel a responsibility to support our young men and women in the battlefield with the best technology available including intelligent robotics and unmanned systems.

After working for nearly two decades in the field, it finally became clear to me that the impact of these robotic systems in warfare was going to be sooner rather than later. This was not really a surprise given the high level of funding that the Pentagon was according robotics research. Several extramural events occurred in the first few years of the twenty-first century that made me think long and hard about the ethical consequences of the research that we as a community and that I personally are conducting. An epiphany is too strong a phrase, but an awakening is not, regarding the realization of the consequences of the research I had and was continuing to conduct. Several specific events, all occurring within a few years of each other, helped provide this clarion call. They include the following:

- A general rising into my consciousness of the reality of these systems moving out from their ivy tower laboratories into the real-world military-industrial complex prior to their actual deployment. This, when accompanied by the realization that weaponization of these platforms was inevitable if unchecked, gave me pause. It became clear that these systems were not simply academic forays into the understanding of intelligence, but rather that they are moving down the pathway of becoming killing machines fully capable of taking human life, perhaps indiscriminately. This forced upon me a further responsibility to inform my colleagues of the consequences of their and our research and to strive to ensure that adequate discussion regarding the use of these systems was initiated at all levels.

- A watershed event in robot ethics that I had the privilege to partici-pate in was the first Robot and Ethics Symposium, held in January 2004 at Villa Nobel in San Remo, Italy, where Alfred Nobel spent his last years of life. This was not only an opportunity to present my own thoughts but also to be present at eye-opening presentations by (1) representatives from the Geneva Convention, who informed and surprised me regarding the technical details involving the velocity and caliber of bullets that are considered ethical to use to kill people during armed conflict; (2) the Pugwash Institute, which recounted the process whereby the Russell-Einstein Manifesto was created as a warning against the use of nuclear weapons; and (3) the Vatican, which expressed their opinion regarding appropriate human use of robotic technology including humanoids. Follow-up meetings in similar symposia continued to broaden my view, introducing me to the ethical perspectives of pacifists, philosophers, social scien-tists, ethicists, and many others through numerous enriching talks, debates, and discussions.

- Subsequently, I undertook positions of responsibility within the major robotics professional society's ethical committees, serving as co-chair of both the Technical Committee on Roboethics (2004-present) and the Standing Committee on Human Rights and Ethics for the IEEE Robotics and Automation Society (2006–9). I also serve as their liaison to the IEEE Social Implications of Technology Society (2006–9).

- I was further inspired to create a course that I teach annually at Georgia Tech titled "Robots and Society." The interaction with our students has been invaluable in shaping and honing my opinions on robot ethics.

- A tipping point for me, perhaps, was the viewing of an unscheduled video entitled "Apache Rules the Night" at a small DOD workshop I attended. This moved me into an activist stance and spurred me to think of potential research solutions to violations of the Laws of War. It now serves as a test scenario of how unmanned robotic systems should not perform, and it is described later in the book in Chapter 11. To avoid redundancy, I defer further discussion until then.

All of this has brought me into contact with many intellectual communities I would not have likely have otherwise encountered, all of whom have sharpened and annealed the ideas that are embodied in this volume and, perhaps, the robots of the future. The numerous points raised on my controversial approach deserved to be challenged and they were and are. These contrarian viewpoints are, I believe, fairly represented in the early chapters of what follows.

This pressing question captures my revelation: Is it not our responsibility as scientists to look for effective ways to reduce man's inhumanity to man through technology? It is my belief that research in *ethical* military robotics can and should be applied toward achieving this end. But how can this happen? Where does humanity fit on the battlefield? Extrapolating these questions further, we ask the following:

Should soldiers be robots?

Isn't that largely what they are trained to be?

Should robots be soldiers?

Could they be more humane than humans?

This sort of thinking resulted in my generating a relatively modest proposal to the United States Army Research Office, entitled "An Ethical Basis for Autonomous System Deployment." This effort has an overarching goal of producing an "artificial conscience," to yield a new class of robots termed *Humane-oids*—robots that can potentially perform more ethically in the battlefield than humans are capable of doing. The Army Research Office funded this three-year effort in 2006, and the results to date serve as the basis for this book.

The photograph of a Predator Unmanned Aerial Vehicle (UAV) shown in Figure P.1 that appeared in an article entitled "Robot Wars" in the June 7, 2007, *Economist* magazine was accompanied by the quip "Where do we plug in the ethics upgrade?", which at some level, despite its tongue-in-cheek flavor, captures the spirit of this research.

One lesson I have learned along the way is that roboticists should not run from the difficult ethical issues surrounding the use of their intellectual property that is or will be applied to warfare, whether or

FIGURE P.1   Predator unmanned aerial vehicle. (Super Nova Images/Alamy.)

not they directly participate. Wars unfortunately will continue and derivative technology from these ideas will be used. If your robotics research is of significance and it is published openly, it will be put to use in military systems by someone, somewhere, someday. Researchers are not immune from contributing to military applications by simply not accepting funds from the Department of Defense. To ensure proper usage of this technology, proactive management by all parties concerned is necessary. Complete relinquishment of robotics research as proposed by Bill Joy is the only alternative [Joy 00], but one I do not personally favor.

I remain active in my research for the DOD in battlefield applications of robotics for both the Army and Navy regarding the deployment of teams of robots, but it remains a personal goal that these systems and other related military research products will ultimately be ethically restrained by methods such as those described in this book, so they abide by the internationally agreed upon Laws of War. I also hope that this volume will spur others into not only considering this problem, but to help ensure that warfare is conducted justly even with the advent of autonomous robots, if international societies so deem it fit, and that those who step beyond those ethical bounds whoever they may be are successfully prosecuted for their war crimes. It is my conviction that when these weaponized autonomous systems appear in the battlefield, they should help to ensure that humanity, proportionality, responsibility, and relative safety are extended during combat not only to friendly forces, but equally to noncombatants and those who are otherwise *hors de combat.*

Acknowledgments

Many need to be thanked for helping, supporting, and inspiring this work. First my thanks to God and Jesus Christ for the will, ability, and calling to complete this work. My wife has put up with numerous sacrifices in both time and attention due to this endeavor; for that and everything else over our 35 years together, my gratitude and love are unending.

My colleagues in the military, past and present, who have supported my research on this controversial topic either through encouragement or sponsorship or both include Randy Zachery, Mark Swinson, Jon Bornstein, John Canning, Wesley Snyder, Jim Overholt, Norm Coleman, Alan Schultz, and Marc Steinberg. This research is funded under Contract #W911NF-06-0252 from the U.S. Army Research Office.

Those who have debated with me on this subject have only helped to sharpen my position, and for this I am indebted: Noel Sharkey, Peter Asaro, Shannon French, Jim Moor, and Rob Sparrow, among many others. This book would not have been possible without the support of the editors at Taylor & Francis, specifically, Randi Cohen and Jessica Vakili. And of course, the students who were involved in implementing the ideas contained herein are essential to its success as any senior faculty member knows; namely Lilia Moshkina, Patrick Ulam, Alan Wagner, Brittany Duncan, and Yoichiro Endo. Their significant contributions are manifested in Chapters 5 and 12.

Many have helped in providing the pictures and figures that help enliven the book. They include Kwanghak Huh of Samsung Techwin, Jerry Pratt and Jeff Bradshaw of the Institute for Human-Machine Cognition, Norm Coleman of Picatinny Arsenal, Mark Del Giorno of General Dynamics Robotics Systems, Charlie Vaida and Chris Jones of iRobot, Bart Everett, Hoa Nguyen, and Jake Deuel of Space and Naval Warfare Systems Center Pacific, Adam Gettings and Eric Ivers of RoboteX, John Clarke and Myron

Mills of Lockheed-Martin, Kishore Ramachandran and Hemanth Pai of Georgia Tech, and the photographic services of the Department of Defense, U.S. Army, and U.S Navy.

There are so many more that deserve credit that space and my memory prevents from being listed, but know that your influence appears throughout the pages of this book. I thank you all.

CHAPTER 1

Introduction

S INCE THE ROMAN EMPIRE, through the Inquisition and the Renaissance, until today, humanity has debated the morality of warfare [May et al. 05]. Although it is universally acknowledged that peace is a preferable condition to warfare, that has not deterred the persistent conduct of lethal conflict over millennia. Referring to the improving technology of the day and its impact on the inevitability of warfare, Clausewitz stated that "the tendency to destroy the adversary which lies at the bottom of the conception of war is in no way changed or modified through the progress of civilization" [Clausewitz 1832]. More recently, Cook observed, "The fact that constraints of just war are routinely overridden is no more a proof of their falsity and irrelevance than the existence of immoral behavior 'refutes' standards of morality: we know the standard, and we also know human beings fall short of that standard with depressing regularity" [Cook 04].

Saint Augustine is generally attributed, roughly 1,600 years ago, with laying the foundations of Christian Just War thought [Cook 04] and with introducing the idea that Christianity helped humanize war by refraining from unnecessary killing [Wells 96]. Augustine (as reported via Aquinas) noted that emotion can clearly cloud judgment in warfare:

> The passion for inflicting harm, the cruel thirst for vengeance, an unpacific and relentless spirit, the fever of revolt, the lust of power, and suchlike things, all these are rightly condemned in war. [May et al. 05]

Fortunately, these potential failings of man need not be replicated in autonomous battlefield robots.*

From the nineteenth century on, nations have struggled to create laws of war based on the principles of Just War Theory [Wells 96, Walzer 77]. These laws speak to both *Jus in Bello*, which applies limitations to the conduct of warfare, and *Jus ad Bellum*, which restricts the conditions required prior to entering into war, where both form a major part of the logical underpinnings of the Just War tradition.

The advent of autonomous robotics in the battlefield, as with any new technology, is primarily concerned with *Jus in Bello*, that is, defining what constitutes the ethical use of these systems during conflict, given military necessity. There are many questions that remain unanswered and even undebated within this context. At least two central principles are asserted from the Just War tradition: the principle of *discrimination* of military objectives and combatants from noncombatants and the structures of civil society; and the principle of *proportionality* of means, where acts of war should not yield damage disproportionate to the ends that justify their use. Noncombatant harm is considered only justifiable when it is truly collateral, i.e., indirect and unintended, even if foreseen. Combatants retain certain rights as well; for example, once they have surrendered and laid down their arms, they assume the status of noncombatant and are no longer subject to attack. *Jus in Bello* also requires that agents must be held responsible for their actions in war [Fieser and Dowden 07]. This includes the consequences for obeying orders when they are known to be immoral as well as the status of ignorance in warfare. These aspects also need to be addressed in the application of lethality by autonomous systems and, as we will see in Chapter 2, are hotly debated by philosophers.

The Laws of War† (LOW), encoded in protocols such as the Geneva Conventions, and Rules of Engagement (ROE) prescribe what is and what is not acceptable in the battlefield in both a global (standing ROE) and local (Supplemental ROE) context. The ROE are required to be fully compliant with the laws of war. Defining these terms [DOD 01]:

---

* That is not to say, however, they couldn't be. Indeed the Navy (including myself) has already conducted research on "Affect-Based Computing and Cognitive Models for Unmanned Vehicle Systems" [OSD 06], although clearly not designed for the condemned intentions stated by Augustine.

† The Laws of War (LOW) are alternatively referred to as the Laws of Armed Conflict (LOAC) in some literature.

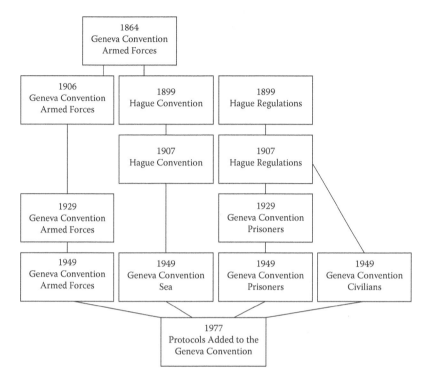

FIGURE 1.1 Development of Codified Laws of War. (Adapted from [Hartle 04].)

- Laws of War—That part of international law that regulates the conduct of armed hostilities.

- Rules of Engagement—Directives issued by competent military authority that delineate the circumstances and limitations under which United States forces will initiate and/or continue combat engagement with other forces encountered.

As early as 990, the Angiers Synod issued formal prohibitions regarding combatants' seizure of hostages and property [Wells 96]. Pope Gregory IX in the thirteenth century listed those who should be protected in war: priests and others of the cloth, pilgrims, travelers, merchants, peasant farmers, women, children, widows, and orphans. Animals, goods, and the lands of peasants and the naturally weak were also protected [Slim 08].

The Codified Laws of War have developed over centuries, with Figure 1.1 illustrating several significant landmarks along the way. Typical battlefield limitations, especially relevant with regard to the potential use of lethal autonomous systems, include [May et al. 05, Wikipedia 07a]:

- Acceptance of surrender of combatants and the humane treatment of prisoners of war.

- Use of proportionality of force in a conflict.

- Protecting of both combatants and noncombatants from unnecessary suffering.

- Avoiding unnecessary damage to property and people not involved in combat.

- Prohibition on attacking people or vehicles bearing the Red Cross or Red Crescent emblems, or those carrying a white flag and that are acting in a neutral manner.

- Avoidance of the use of torture on anyone for any reason.

- Nonuse of certain weapons such as blinding lasers and small caliber high-velocity projectiles, in addition to weapons of mass destruction.

- Mutilation of corpses is forbidden.

Walzer sums it up: "War is still, somehow, a rule-governed activity, a world of permissions and prohibitions—a moral world, therefore, in the midst of hell" [Walzer 77]. These laws of war continue to evolve over time as technology progresses, and any lethal autonomous system that attempts to adhere to them must similarly be able to adapt to new policies and regulations as they are formulated by international society.

Of course there are serious questions and concerns regarding the Just War tradition itself, often evoked by pacifists. Yoder questions the premises on which it is built and in so doing also raises some issues that potentially affect autonomous systems [Yoder 84]. For example, he questions, "Are soldiers when assigned a mission given sufficient information to determine whether this is an order they should obey? If a person under orders is convinced he or she must disobey, will the command structure, the society, and the church honor that dissent?" Clearly if we embed an ethical "conscience" into an autonomous system, it is only as good as the information upon which it functions. It is a working assumption, perhaps naïve, that the autonomous agent ultimately will be provided with an amount of battlefield information equal to or greater than a human soldier is capable of managing. This seems a reasonable assumption, however, with the advent of network-centric warfare and the emergence of the Global Information Grid (GIG) [DOD CIO 07]. It is also assumed in this work that if an autonomous agent refuses to conduct an unethical action, it will be able to explain to some degree its underlying logic for such a refusal. If commanders are provided with the authority by some means to override the autonomous system's resistance to executing an order that it deems unethical, he or she in so doing would assume responsibility for the consequences of such action. Chapters 10 and 11 discuss this in more detail.

On the other end of the spectrum is the evidence that occasioning civilian victimization historically increases the likelihood of victory for both asymmetric and interstate wars. "Targeting civilians seems to be at least as effective—and sometimes more effective—than conventional strategies" [Downes 08]. For some, this may argue that we should not restrain the military robots of the future by the Laws of War. Nonetheless if we, as a nation, intend not to descend into barbarity, it is our responsibility to ensure that our purported ideals are not only spoken of but also rigorously enacted within these autonomous battlefield systems, let alone our human warfighters.

These issues are but the tip of the iceberg regarding the ethical quandaries surrounding the deployment of autonomous systems capable of lethality. It is my contention, nonetheless, that if (or when) these systems will be deployed in the battlefield, it is the roboticist's duty to ensure they are as safe as possible to both combatant and noncombatant alike, as is prescribed by our society's commitment to International Conventions encoded in the Laws of War and other similar doctrine—for example, the Code of Conduct and Rules of Engagement. The research in this book operates upon these underlying assumptions.

CHAPTER 2

Trends toward Lethality

They don't get hungry. They're not afraid. They don't forget their
orders. They don't care if the guy next to them has just been shot.
Will they do a better job than humans? Yes.

Gordon Johnson of the U.S. Joint Forces Command at the
Pentagon Referring to Robot Soldiers in the
New York Times [Weiner 05]

T HERE IS ONLY MODEST evidence that the application of lethality
by autonomous systems is currently considered differently from
a research and development standpoint than any other weaponry. This
is typified by informal commentary where some individuals state that a
human will always be in the loop regarding the application of lethal force
to an identified target. Often the use of lethality in this context is considered more from a safety perspective [DOD 07a], rather than a moral
one. But if a human being in the loop is the flashpoint of this debate, the
real question is then, at what level is the human in the loop? Will it be
confirmation prior to the deployment of lethal force for each and every
target engagement? Will it be at a high-level mission specification, such as
"Take that position using whatever force is necessary"? Several military
robotic automation systems already operate at the level where the human
is in charge and responsible for the deployment of lethal force, but not
in a directly supervisory manner. Examples include the Phalanx system
for Aegis-class cruisers in the Navy "capable of autonomously performing its own search, detect, evaluation, track, engage and kill assessment

FIGURE 2.1 Phalanx close-in weapons system. (United States Navy photograph.)

functions" [U.S. Navy 08] (Figure 2.1), the MK-60 encapsulated torpedo (CAPTOR) sea mine system—one of the Navy's primary antisubmarine weapons capable of autonomously firing a torpedo, cruise missiles (Figure 2.2), Patriot antiaircraft missile batteries, "fire and forget" missile systems generally, or even (and generally considered as unethical due to their indiscriminate use of lethal force*) antipersonnel mines or alternatively other more discriminating classes of mines (e.g., antitank). These devices can even be considered to be robotic by some definitions, as they all are capable of sensing their environment and actuating, in these cases through the application of lethal force.

Congress in 2001 issued a mandate that stated that by 2010 one-third of all deep strike aircraft should be unmanned and by 2015 one-third of all ground vehicles should be likewise unmanned [Adams 02]. More recently, the United States Defense Department has issued in December of 2007, an Unmanned Systems Roadmap that spans 25 years, reaching until 2032 [DOD 07b]. It is very rare to see this sort of truly long-term planning in operation in any area, and it speaks to the commitment the DOD has made to this technology. The deputy director of Unmanned Aircraft

---

* Antipersonnel mines have been banned by the Ottawa Treaty, although as of the time of writing the U.S., China, Russia, and 34 other nations are not party to the agreement.

FIGURE 2.2 Tomahawk cruise missile on display. (United States Navy photograph.)

Systems, Dyke Weatherington, when speaking regarding the road map, stated the following:

> Continued development of artificial intelligence (robotics) technology may one day produce autonomous "thinking" unmanned systems that could, for example, be used in aerial platforms designed to suppress enemy air defenses… Certainly the roadmap projects an increasing level of autonomy … as the autonomy level increases, we do believe that will open the avenue for additional mission areas. [Gilmore 07]

An expert on military technologies, James Canton, at the Institute for Global Futures stated that "autonomy, even for armed robots is coming," including a machine that will hunt, identify, authenticate, and possibly kill a target without a human in the decision loop [Magnuson 07]. This trend is accelerating as evidenced by a funding shift in Future Combat Systems technology, suddenly moving away from developing new armored vehicles to now instead providing platoon-level UAVs and small UGVs faster to the battlefield [Pappalardo 08].

It is anticipated that teams of autonomous systems and human soldiers will work together on the battlefield, as opposed to the common science fiction vision of armies of unmanned systems operating by themselves. A Marine Corps reserves major, John Saitta, who served as a weapons and tactics instructor said "These armed robots [referring to the SWORDS platform described below] can be used as a force multiplier to augment an already significant force in the battlespace" [Magnuson 07]. As Adams succinctly stated regarding military applications of robotics, "The logic leading to fully autonomous systems seems inescapable" [Adams 02]. If the military keeps moving forward at its current rapid pace toward the deployment of intelligent autonomous robots, we must ensure that these systems be deployed ethically, in a manner consistent with standing protocols and other ethical constraints.

As early as the end of World War I, the precursors of autonomous unmanned weapons appeared in a project on unpiloted aircraft conducted by the U.S. Navy and the Sperry Gyroscope Company [Adams 02]. Multiple unmanned robotic systems are already being developed or are in use that employ lethal force such as the ARV (Armed Robotic Vehicle), a component of the Future Combat System (FCS); Predator UAVs (unmanned aerial vehicles) equipped with hellfire missiles, which have already been used in combat but under direct human supervision; and the development of an armed platform for use in the Korean Demilitarized Zone to name a few. Some particulars follow in the next two sections; the material presented is merely a sampling of representative armed robotic systems and it is by no means comprehensive.

2.1 WEAPONIZED UNMANNED GROUND VEHICLES

- The South Korean robot platform mentioned above (Figure 2.3) is intended to be able to detect and identify targets in daylight within a 4 km radius or at night using infrared sensors within a range of 2 km, providing for either an autonomous lethal or nonlethal response [Argy 07, Samsung Techwin 07]. Although a designer of the system states that "the ultimate decision about shooting should be made by a human, not the robot," the system does have an automatic mode in which it is capable of making the decision on its own [Kumagai 07]. This system is discussed further in Chapter 11 and provides the basis for one of the scenarios used to illustrate ethical control. In addition to this stationary board guard robotic platform, it has been reported that the Government's Agency Defense Funding is supporting the development of an 8-legged robot "armed with infrared sensors, pattern recognition cameras and an automatic rifle ... [that] will patrol the mountainous borderlands" [Card 07].

FIGURE 2.3   Samsung Techwin intelligent surveillance and security guard robot: *left*, prototype; *right*, newer model SGR-A1. (Courtesy of Samsung Techwin.)

- iRobot, the maker of the Roomba robotic home vacuum cleaner, is now providing versions of their Packbots capable of tasering enemy combatants (Figure 2.4) [Jewell 07]. This nonlethal response, however, does require a human-in-the-loop, unlike the South Korean robot under development. Vice Admiral Joe Dyer, the president of iRobot's

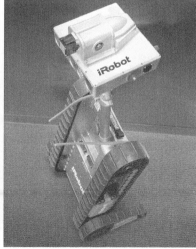

FIGURE 2.4   An iRobot Packbot equipped with a TASER X26 nonlethal weapon. (Courtesy of iRobot.)

Government and Industrial Robot Division, stated: "The addition of TASER technologies onto iRobot platforms will provide a critical tool for SWAT, law enforcement and military to handle a variety of dangerous scenarios" [iRobot 07]. Packbots have also recently been outfitted with weapon systems by third parties, notably Metal Storm Ltd. of Australia. This particular unit has a four-barrel lethal weapons pod, which was delivered to Dahlgren Naval Surface Weapons Center for evaluation [Shachtman 08].

- The TALON SWORDS platform (Figure 2.5) developed by Foster-Miller/QinitiQ has already been put to test in Iraq and Afghanistan and is capable of carrying lethal weaponry (M240 or M249 machine guns, or a Barrett .50-caliber rifle). Three of these platforms have already served for over a year in Iraq and as of April 2008 were still in the field at the time, contrary to some unfounded rumors [Foster-Miller 08].

FIGURE 2.5   Foster-Miller TALON SWORDS robot. (Department of Defense photograph.)

FIGURE 2.6 MAARS robot. Like SWORDS, it is not autonomous. (Courtesy of QinetiQ North America/Foster-Miller.)

- A newer version, referred to as MAARS (Modular Advanced Armed Robotic System), is ready to replace the earlier SWORDS platforms in the field (Figure 2.6). The newer robot can carry a 40 mm grenade launcher or an M240B machine gun in addition to various nonlethal weapons. The president of QinitiQ stated the purpose of the robot is to "enhance the warfighter's capability and lethality, extend his situational awareness and provide all these capabilities across the spectrum of combat" [QinetiQ 08].

- In 2007, Israel was developing stationary robotic gun-sensor platforms for deployment along its borders with Gaza in automated kill zones, equipped with .50-caliber machine guns and armored folding shields. Although currently intended to be only used in a remote controlled manner, an IDF division commander is quoted as saying "At least in the initial phases of deployment, we're going to have to keep a man in the loop," implying the potential for more autonomous operations in the future [Opall-Rome 07]. An Israeli scientist, Gal Kaminka at Bar-Ilan the head of Israel's largest robotics laboratory,

FIGURE 2.7 A physical model of the Lockheed-Martin MULE ARV–A (L) currently under development. (Courtesy of Lockheed-Martin.)

has said that "at this stage they are not yet shooting, but I am sure the army is also working on that" [Feldman 08]. Israel's Elbit Systems is also developing a small, portable, hunter-killer robot called the ViPer (Versatile, Intelligent, Portable Robot) for the Israel Defense Forces [Reuters 07]. Payloads include a 9 mm mini-Uzi and a grenade launcher.

- Lockheed-Martin, as part of its role in the Future Combat Systems program, is developing an Armed Robotic Vehicle-Assault (Light) MULE (Multifunction Utility/Logistics and Equipment) robot weighing in at 2.5 tons. It will be armed with a line-of-sight gun and an antitank capability to provide "immediate, heavy firepower to the dismounted soldier" [Lockheed-Martin 07]. A physical mock-up of the MULE is shown in Figure 2.7. Although this weaponized version of the MULE has not been completed at the time of writing, a functioning transport MULE version is in actual operation.

- The Gladiator Tactical Unmanned Ground Vehicle (TUGV) is being developed by BAE Systems and Carnegie-Mellon University for use by the Marine Corps (Figure 2.8). It will provide the ability to "rapidly detect, identify, locate, and neutralize a variety of threats" [CMU 07]. Six prototype vehicles were constructed and delivered for

FIGURE 2.8 Gladiator tactical unmanned ground vehicles. (Department of Defense photograph.)

operational evaluation by the Marines in 2006. It is equipped with a variety of mission payload modules, some of which can be used to lethal effect.

- In a joint program with West Virginia University, Picatinny Arsenal has exercised their weaponized Fire Ant Robot in a range of test events involving multiple aerial and ground unmanned systems [ARDEC-WVU 07]. The armed Fire Ant robot is shown in Figure 2.9. Demonstrated scenarios involving teleoperation of the Fire Ant platform include SUGV and SUAV (Small Unmanned Ground/Aerial Vehicle) target handoff and attack, manned unmanned/unmanned air/ground reconnaissance and target attack, and counter-sniper/counter-IED (Improvised Explosive Device) missions.

- Interestingly, Sandia National Laboratories also had an armed robot named Fire Ant developed in the early 1980s [Sandia 08]. It was equipped with an autonomous standoff mine system that used an explosively formed projectile. It was used to destroy a teleoperated tank that moved through its field of regard. The robot itself was not autonomous but the firing system was. The Fire Ant was teleoperated to a position overlooking a road, where the operator aimed the antitank weapon for the video motion tracking algorithm, thus lying in wait for a moving target. When the tank appeared, Sandia's Fire Ant autonomously fired, destroying the tank (Figure 2.10) and itself in the process.

26× Optical Color Camera
Stabilization; Daylight or IR

Color Digital Daylight or IR Scope

Pan Tilt

Weapon Payload with
Dynamic Stabilization

Inertial Navigation Unit
with GPS

Articulated Tracks
Front and Rear

Driving Camera

Laser Scanner

FIGURE 2.9   Picatinny Arsenal Fire Ant. (Courtesy of Picatinny Arsenal.)

- In a program for the U.S. Army's Tank Automotive Research, Development and Engineering Center (TARDEC), General Dynamics Robotic Systems (GDRS) demonstrated an autonomous Stryker unmanned vehicle with a Javelin missile system mounted on it (Figure 2.11). Although the vehicle used autonomous GPS waypoint

FIGURE 2.10   Sandia's Fire Ant robot: *left*, deployed by the roadside in wait for a target; *right*, the results of the Fire Ant's weapons discharge, destroying a tank. (Courtesy Sandia National Laboratories.)

FIGURE 2.11   GDRS Stryker Robotic Stryker equipped with Javelin Missile. (Courtesy of GDRS.)

following to move from one location to the next, the oversight and control of the missile system was completely in the hands of a remote soldier, fully in-the loop observing the target and issuing the firing command sequence. Under these conditions it did fire its weapons using remote control during an exercise at Ft. Bliss in Texas, under the watchful eye of numerous range safety officers [Thiesen 04, Del Giorno 08].

- At the Space and Naval Warfare Systems Center Pacific (SPAWAR Pacific), early groundbreaking research was conducted on teleoperated weaponized robotic platforms, focusing on operator aspects. Figure 2.12 shows a teleoperated dune buggy, circa 1982–85, equipped with an antiarmor rocket launcher [Hightower et al 86]. The GATERS (Ground-Air Telerobotic Systems) platform was developed shortly afterward (1985–89) and is shown in Figure 2.13 firing a Hellfire missile [Aviles et al 90]. This research continues to this day with one the most recent experiments involving a Mobile Detection Assessment and Response System (MDARS) Patrol Unit

FIGURE 2.12 Teleoperated dune buggy (1985) equipped with an antiarmor rocket launcher. (Courtesy Space and Naval Warfare Systems Center Pacific.)

FIGURE 2.13 GATERS UGV (1989) launching a Hellfire missile by remote command from an operator located several kilometers away. (Courtesy Space and Naval Warfare Systems Center Pacific.)

FIGURE 2.14   MDARS with PUV equipped with less-than-lethal weapons systems. (Courtesy Space and Naval Warfare Systems Center Pacific.)

Vehicle (PUV) equipped with less-than-lethal weapons (Figure 2.14) [SPAWAR 08].

• RoboteX, a Silicon Valley start-up company is developing armed robotics for the military, with a target price of between $30,000 and $50,000 [O'Brien 07]. An early version, Model AH (Figure 2.15A), can be equipped with a pair of specialized Atchisson-Assault 12 shotguns, capable of firing miniature grenades, bullets, and nonlethal Tasers. This system and their MH Tactical robot equipped with a single shotgun, which are under teleoperated and not autonomous control, are intended for urban warfare and perimeter defense. The company's follow-on concept vehicle is under development and is called the Infantry Replacement Vehicle (Figure 2.15B).

• The Institute for Human-Machine Cognition in Pensacola, Florida has recently applied for a patent for a weapons-bearing robot with a unique mobility system (Figure 2.16). The robot can also carry a camera for teleoperation and is able to switch between a tracked, four-wheel and two-wheel modes of operation. "The two-wheel high profile mode allows the robot to place its camera or weapon system at a high perch, thereby seeing over obstacles" [U.S. Patent Office 08].

(A)

(B)

FIGURE 2.15 RoboteX armed robots. (Courtesy of RoboteX.) (*A*) RoboteX AH-1 in a test firing exercise. (*B*) Computer-generated model of the Infantry Replacement Robot under development at RoboteX.

FIGURE 2.16 IHMC armed robot concept. (Courtesy of IHMC.)

2.2 WEAPONIZED UNMANNED AERIAL VEHICLES

It is interesting to note that soldiers have already surrendered to UAVs even when the aircraft has been unarmed. The first documented instance of this in history occurred during the 1991 Gulf War. An RQ-2A Pioneer UAV (Figure 2.17), used for battle damage assessment for shelling originating from the USS *Wisconsin*, was flying toward Faylaka Island, when several Iraqis hoisted makeshift white flags to surrender, thus avoiding another shelling from the battleship [Maksel 08]. Anecdotally, most UAV units during this conflict experienced variations of attempts to surrender to the Pioneer. A logical assumption is that this trend will only increase as UAVs direct response ability and firepower increases.

- The U.S. Air Force has created their first hunter-killer UAV, named the MQ-9 Reaper (Figure 2.18). According to USAF General Moseley, the name Reaper is "fitting as it captures the lethal nature of this new weapon system." It has a 64 foot wingspan and carries 15 times the ordnance of the smaller Predator UAV (Figure 2.19), flying nearly three times the Predator's cruise speed. As of September 2006, seven were already in the inventory of the U.S. Air Force with more on the way [Air Force 06]. The Reaper has served in Afghanistan

FIGURE 2.17   RQ-2A Pioneer UAV on its launch truck. (U.S. Marine Corps photograph.)

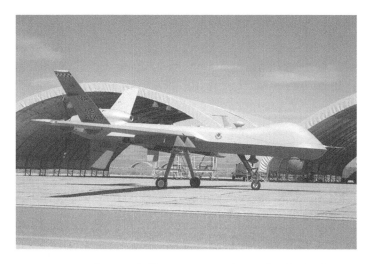

FIGURE 2.18 Reaper hunter-killer unmanned aerial vehicle. (Department of Defense photograph.)

since September 2007 and has conducted over 480 sorties through July 2008. It has been reported that Reapers have been conducting missions in Iraq since July 2008 and are piloted by UAV operators located in Creech Air Force Base in Nevada [*Air Force Times* 2008]. On August 16, 2008, a Reaper destroyed a car bomb using a GBU-12 laser-guided weapon, where officers were quoted as saying this "marked one of the first weapons engagements for the unmanned aircraft system... We searched for, found, fixed, targeted and destroyed a target with just one aircraft" [*World Tribune* 08].

FIGURE 2.19 Armed Predator UAV. (Department of Defense photograph.)

- The Predator UAV has been used in Bosnia for surveillance and reconnaissance for over 600 NATO missions. The first Predator Hellfire laser-guided missile launch was logged on February 16, 2001, against a stationary tank, marking the first time a UAV successfully fired a missile [Lazarski 02]. It was reported in early 2007 that 153 Predators had been delivered to Iraq of which 40% had been lost [Vanden Brook 07]. The number of attacks with Predators in Iraq has also steadily increased, reaching 11 total in April 2008 alone [Vanden Brook 08]. The United Kingdom also has at least two Reapers in operation [Hoyle 08]. Numerous enemy engagements have been reported for both the Predator [AFP 08] and the MQ-9 Reaper [Koehl 07, Loyd 08, Hussain and Dreazen 08].

- The U.S. Navy is requesting funding for the acquisition in 2010 of armed Firescout UAVs (Figure 2.20), a vertical-takeoff-and-landing tactical UAV that will be equipped with kinetic weapons. The system has already been tested with 2.75-inch unguided rockets. The UAVs are intended to deal with threats such as small swarming boats. As of this time the commander will determine whether a target should be struck [Erwin 07].

FIGURE 2.20 Navy Firescout UAV, planned to be armed by 2010. (Department of Defense photograph.)

FIGURE 2.21   UCAS concept. (U.S. Navy graphic.)

- The Unmanned Combat Air System (UCAS) (Figure 2.21) is being developed for the Navy by Northrop-Grumman under a $635 million contract awarded in August 2007 [Jean 07]. It will be about the size of a jet fighter plane, equipped with stealth technology. Potential missions include hunter-killer operations, suppression of enemy targets, close-air support, and interdiction. It is intended to complement manned aircraft operations. A surrogate UCAS vehicle, the X-47A, has already undergone flight testing, with the X-47B under development. The Navy is seeking to field an unmanned combat squadron of UCAS aircraft by 2025 [Butler and Wall 08].

- More autonomous armed flying weapons systems are also being deployed. One such platform is Lockheed-Martin's LOCAAS (Low Cost Autonomous Attack System) (Figure 2.22). It is only 36 inches long, weighs approximately 90 pounds, and is equipped with a miniature jet engine. It has a range of 100 nautical miles and has sophisticated laser radar sensing that can autonomously identify the target, aim the warhead, and determine the correct warhead mode. It loiters over a battlefield at an altitude of 750 feet traveling at a speed of 200 knots to cover an area of 25 square nautical miles. LOCAAS carries a multimode explosively formed penetrator warhead. Its greatest value is in situations where target locations are not known, searching for

FIGURE 2.22 Lockheed-Martin LOCAAS: *left*, flight configuration; *right*, stowed for launching. (Courtesy of Lockheed-Martin.)

missile launchers for example. These autonomous weapons can be carried by conventional fighters such as F-16s or the F-22 Raptor. Collaborative targeting is currently maintained using a data link to "sustain 'man-in-the-loop' capability especially against moving targets" [Defense Update 04].

Lockheed-Martin is also developing a NLOS-LAM (Non–Line of Sight, Loitering Attack Munition) hunter-killer system (Figure 2.23) that is a ground-launched autonomous munition intended to provide support for U.S. Army troops and is transportable by a HMMWV (High Mobility, Multipurpose Wheeled Vehicle). It is an expendable munition that is 7.5 inches square and weighs approximately 120 pounds. It uses a laser radar in the same manner that the LOCAAS system, described earlier does, for targeting, aiming, and engagement. It uses a micro-turbojet and can loiter

FIGURE 2.23 Lockheed-Martin NLOS-LAM: *left*, flight configuration; *right*, munitions being launched. (Courtesy of Lockheed-Martin.)

for up to 30 minutes searching for targets over a large area with its warhead payload [Lockheed-Martin 06].

The United States should not think itself alone in the development of armed unmanned aerial vehicles. For example:

- A European consortium (France, Greece, Italy, Spain, Sweden, and Switzerland) is headed by Dassault Aviation, under 405 million Euros funding. They are developing the Neuron Unmanned Combat Air Vehicle (UCAV) demonstrator, which is slated to fly by 2011 and capable of dropping two precision guided bombs from an internal bomb bay [Tran 08].

- South Korea has expressed an interest in developing their own UCAV with foreign partners [Sung-ki 08].

- Russia has produced a mock-up of a UCAV stealth bomber called the Skat, which it claims will be able to attack land and sea targets even under heavy antiaircraft fire over a range of up to just under 2500 miles [AFP 07].

- China has also shown a concept unmanned combat aircraft named "Anjian" or Invisible Sword [People Daily 06].

- Israel has developed the Harpy UAV, a fire-and-forget autonomous weapon system designed to suppress surface-to-air missiles and enemy radar. It weighs in at 135 kg, is 2.1 meters long with a 2.7-meter wingspan, and is ground truck launched. It has been in operation as early as the late 1990s and has been exported to the Turkish, Korean, Chinese, and Indian armies [Defense Update 08].

This no doubt is but a mere sample of armed UAVs being developed around the world by other nations.

2.3 PROSPECTS

An even stronger indicator regarding the future role of autonomy and lethality appears in a recent U.S. Army Solicitation for Proposals [U.S. Army 07], which states:

> Armed UMS [Unmanned Systems] are beginning to be fielded in the current battlespace, and will be extremely common in the Future Force Battlespace... This will lead directly to the need

for the systems to be able to operate autonomously for extended periods, and also to be able to collaboratively engage hostile targets within specified rules of engagement … with final decision on target engagement being left to the human operator…. *Fully autonomous engagement without human intervention should also be considered, under user-defined conditions, as should both lethal and non-lethal engagement and effects delivery means.* [Italics added for emphasis]

There is some evidence of restraint, however, in the use of unmanned systems designed for lethal operations, particularly regarding their autonomous use. A joint government–industry council has generated a set of Design Safety Precepts (DSP) [DOD 07a] that bear this hallmark:

DSP-6: The UMS [UnManned System] shall be designed to prevent uncommanded fire and/or release of weapons or propagation and/or radiation of hazardous energy.

DSP-13: The UMS shall be designed to identify to the authorized entity(s) the weapon being released or fired, but prior to weapon release or fire.

DSP-15: The firing of weapon systems shall require a minimum of two independent and unique validated messages in the proper sequence from authorized entity(ies), each of which shall be generated as a consequence of separate authorized entity action. Both messages should not originate within the UMS launching platform.

In the next chapter, we consider the strengths of autonomous battlefield weaponry in contrast to the shortcomings of human warfighters.

CHAPTER 3

Human Failings
in the Battlefield

THE TREND IS CLEAR: Warfare will continue and autonomous robots will ultimately be deployed in its conduct. Given this, questions then arise regarding if and how these systems can conform as well or better than our soldiers with respect to adherence to the existing Laws of War. This book focuses on this issue directly from a design perspective.

This is no simple task however. In the fog of war it is hard enough for a human to be able to effectively discriminate whether or not a target is legitimate. Fortunately, it may be anticipated, despite the current state of the art, that in the future autonomous robots may be able to perform better than humans under these conditions for the following reasons:

1. The ability to act conservatively: That is, they do not need to protect themselves in cases of low certainty of target identification. Autonomous armed robotic vehicles do not need to have self-preservation as a foremost drive, if at all. They can be used in a self-sacrificing manner if needed and appropriate without reservation by a commanding officer.

2. The eventual development and use of a broad range of robotic sensors better equipped for battlefield observations than humans currently possess.

3. They can be designed without emotions that cloud their judgment or result in anger and frustration with ongoing battlefield events.

In addition, "Fear and hysteria are always latent in combat, often real, and they press us toward fearful measures and criminal behavior" [Walzer 77]. Autonomous agents need not suffer similarly.

4. Avoidance of the human psychological problem of "scenario fulfillment" is possible, a factor believed partly contributing to the downing of an Iranian Airliner by the USS Vincennes in 1988 [Sagan 91]. This phenomenon leads to distortion or neglect of contradictory information in stressful situations, where humans use new incoming information in ways that only fit their pre-existing belief patterns, a form of premature cognitive closure. Robots need not be vulnerable to such patterns of behavior.

5. They can integrate more information from more sources far faster before responding with lethal force than a human possibly could in real-time. These data can arise from multiple remote sensors and intelligence (including human) sources, as part of the Army's network-centric warfare concept [McLoughlin 06] and the concurrent development of the Global Information Grid [DARPA 07]. "Military systems (including weapons) now on the horizon will be too fast, too small, too numerous and will create an environment too complex for humans to direct" [Adams 02].

6. When working in a team of combined human soldiers and autonomous systems as organic assets, they have the potential capability of independently and objectively monitoring ethical behavior in the battlefield by all parties and reporting infractions that might be observed. This presence alone might possibly lead to a reduction in human ethical infractions.

Aside from these ethical considerations, autonomous robotic systems offer numerous other potential operational benefits to the military: faster, cheaper, better mission accomplishment; longer range, greater persistence, longer endurance, higher precision; faster target engagement; and immunity to chemical and biological weapons among others [Guetlein 05]. All of these can enhance mission effectiveness and serve as drivers for the ongoing deployment of these systems. But this book focuses on enhancing ethical benefits by using these systems, ideally without eroding mission performance when compared to human warfighters.

It is not my belief that an autonomous unmanned system will be able to be perfectly ethical in the battlefield, but I am convinced that they can perform more ethically than human soldiers are capable of. Unfortunately the trends in human behavior in the battlefield regarding adhering to legal and ethical requirements are questionable at best. "Armies, armed groups, political and religious movements have been killing civilians since time immemorial" [Slim 08]. Battlefield atrocities* are as old as warfare. "Atrocity … is the most repulsive aspect of war, and that which resides within man and permits him to perform these acts is the most repulsive aspect of mankind" [Grossman 95].

Man's propensity to wage war has gone unabated for as long as history has been recorded. One could argue that man's greatest failing is being on the battlefield in the first place. Immanuel Kant asserted "War requires no motivation, but appears to be ingrained in human nature and is even valued as something noble" [Kant 85]. Even Albert Einstein, who remained a pacifist well into his fifties, eventually acknowledged "as long as there will be man, there will be war" [Isaacson 07]. Sigmund Freud was even more to the point: "There is no likelihood of our being able to suppress humanity's aggressive tendencies" [Isaacson 07]. In this book, however, we are concerned for the large part with the shortcomings humanity exhibits during the conduct of war (*Jus in Bello*) as opposed to what brought us there in the first place (*Jus ad Bellum*).

"The emotional strain of warfare and combat cannot be quantified" [Bourke 99], but at least there has recently been a serious attempt to gather data on that subject. A recent report from the Surgeon General's Office [Surgeon General 06] assessing the battlefield ethics and mental health of soldiers and marines deployed in Operation Iraqi Freedom is disconcerting. The following findings are taken directly from that report:

1. Approximately 10% of soldiers and marines report mistreating noncombatants (damaged/destroyed Iraqi property when not necessary or hit/kicked a noncombatant when not necessary). Soldiers that have high levels of anger, experience high levels of combat or those who screened positive for a mental health problem were nearly twice as likely to mistreat noncombatants as those who had low levels of anger or combat or screened negative for a mental health problem.

2. Only 47% of soldiers and 38% of marines agreed that noncombatants should be treated with dignity and respect.

---

* *Atrocity* here is defined as the killing of a noncombatant: either a civilian or a former combatant who has attained *hors de combat* status by virtue of surrender or wound.

3. Well over a third of soldiers and marines reported torture should be allowed, whether to save the life of a fellow soldier or marine or to obtain important information about insurgents.

4. 17% of soldiers and marines agreed or strongly agreed that all non-combatants should be treated as insurgents.

5. Just under 10% of soldiers and marines reported that their unit modifies the ROE to accomplish the mission.

6. 45% of soldiers and 60% of marines did not agree that they would report a fellow soldier/marine if he had injured or killed an innocent noncombatant.

7. Only 43% of soldiers and 30% of marines agreed that they would report a unit member for unnecessarily damaging or destroying private property.

8. Less than half of soldiers and marines would report a team member for an unethical behavior.

9. A third of marines and over a quarter of soldiers did not agree that their NCOs and Officers made it clear not to mistreat noncombatants.

10. Although they reported receiving ethical training, 28% of soldiers and 31% of marines reported facing ethical situations in which they did not know how to respond.

11. Soldiers and marines are more likely to report engaging in the mistreatment of Iraqi noncombatants when they are angry and are twice as likely to engage in unethical behavior in the battlefield than when they have low levels of anger.

12. Combat experience, particularly losing a team member, was related to an increase in ethical violations.

This formal study, although at the very least disconcerting, is by no means the first report of battlefield atrocities. "Atrocious behavior was a feature of combat in the two world wars, as well as in Vietnam" [Bourke 99]. One sociological study of fighting in Vietnam pointed out that, for all men in heavy combat, one-third of men in moderate combat and 8% in light combat had seen atrocities or committed or abetted noncombatant murder [Strayer and Ellenhorn 75]. These numbers are staggering.

Possible explanations for the persistence of war crimes by combat troops are discussed elsewhere [Bill 00, Parks 76, Parks 76a, Danyluk 00, Slim 08]. These include the following:

- High friendly losses leading to a tendency to seek revenge.

- High turnover in the chain of command, leading to weakened leadership.

- Dehumanization of the enemy through the use of derogatory names and epithets.

- Poorly trained or inexperienced troops. This lack of training is not simply in being a good soldier, but also in understanding the Laws of War.

- No clearly defined enemy.

- The issuance of unclear orders where the intent of the order may be interpreted incorrectly as unlawful.

- Shortage of personnel has also been associated in producing stress on combatants that can lead to violations.

- Youth and immaturity of troops.

- An overpowering sense of frustration.

- Pleasure from the power of killing.

- External pressure—for example, for a need to produce a high body count of the enemy.

There is clear room for improvement, and autonomous systems may help.

Bourke points out that modern warfare enables violent acts in ways unlike before. Now, "Combatants were able to maintain an emotional distance from their victims largely through the application of … technology" [Bourke 99]. This portends ill for the reduction of atrocities by soldiers. We now have bombs being dropped in Afghanistan and Iraq by UAV operators from almost halfway around the world in Nevada [CNN 08]. This use of technology enables a form of "numbed killing." She further notes that there is now a "technological imperative" to make full use of the new equipment provided. Although technological warfare has reduced the overall number of soldiers required to wage war, the price is that technology, while increasing the ability to kill, decreases "the awareness that dead human beings were the end product." When killing at a maximum range, one can pretend they are not killing human beings, and thus experience no regret [Grossman 95]. This physical distance detaches the warfighter from the consequences of the use of their weaponry.

The psychological consequences on our servicemen and women in Afghanistan and Iraq have reached record levels. In 2007 alone, 115 soldiers committed suicide, up from 102 the previous year; 24% of the suicides were those on their first deployment, and 43% were those who had returned from deployment. The suicide rates of active duty soldiers as of August 2008 "were on pace to surpass both last year's numbers and the rate of suicide in the general U.S. population for the first time since the Vietnam war, according to U.S. Army officials" [Mount 08]. A statistically significant relationship has been established between the suicide attempts and the number of days spent deployed in Iraq or Afghanistan. To make matters worse, this is coupled with "a growing number of troops diagnosed with post traumatic stress disorder" [Sevastopulo 08].

These psychiatric casualties are quite significant and common [Grossman 95]: In World War II alone more than 800,000 men were classified unfit due to psychiatric reasons, but an additional 504,000 (approximately fifty divisions) were subsequently rendered unfit as a result of psychiatric collapse after induction. In the 1973 Arab-Israeli war, one-third of the Israeli casualties were psychiatric in origin, twice the number of dead troops. One WWII study showed that after 60 days of continuous combat, 98% of all surviving troops suffered psychiatric trauma of some sort [Swank and Marchand 46]. These long-term exposures to combat are a recent trend in battle, emerging in the twentieth century. The psychiatric damage can result in many forms: battlefield fatigue, conversion hysteria, confusional states, anxiety states, obsession and compulsive states, and character disorders [Grossman 95]. The overall effect on the ability to wage war is obvious, let alone the damage to a nation's surviving citizens.

Creating true warfighters in the first place is a daunting challenge. "No matter how thorough the training, it still failed to enable most combatants to fight" [Bourke 99]. In World War II most men simply did not kill. In one U.S. Army interview of 400 men, only 15% of the men had actually fired at enemy positions (at least once) during an engagement despite the fact that 80% had the opportunity to do so [Marshall 47]. There was no observed correlation between the experience, terrain, nature of the enemy, or accuracy of enemy fire on this percentage.

This applied to both land and air forces. One study of the Korean War indicated that 50% of F-86 pilots never fired their guns and only 10% of those had actually hit a target [Sparks and Neiss 56]. During World War II, most fighter pilots never even tried to shoot anyone down, let alone succeeding. Less than 1% of the pilots accounted for 30–40% of all downed enemy aircraft [Grossman 95].

One conclusion of this is that human soldiers, although not cowardly, lacked an "offensive spirit." One possible reason for this lack of aggressiveness centers on the use of long distance weapons making battlefields "lonely" and the feeling that the enemy was not real but a phantom. This dehumanization of the enemy also quells guilt in killing [Bourke 99].

The soldiers in the field are not alone in their complicity. "Atrocities are the dark secret of military culture" [Danyluk 00]. "Servicemen of all ranks were unperturbed by most of these acts of lawless killing" [Bourke 99]. In Vietnam, combat commanders viewed the Laws of War as "unnecessary" and "unrealistic" restraining devices that would decrease the opportunity for victory [Parks 76]. A lawyer, defending one General's decision not to initiate a court martial for suspected war crimes violations, stated "It's a little like the Ten Commandments—they're there, but no one pays attention to them" [Hersh 71].

Nonetheless our military aspires to higher ethical performance. General Douglas MacArthur stated:

> The soldier, be he friend or foe, is charged with the protection of the weak and unarmed. It is the very essence and reason for his being. When he violates this sacred trust, he not only profanes the cult, but threatens the very fabric of international society. [Hay 76]

In addition the impact of atrocities on public opinion, as clearly evidenced by the My Lai incident in the Vietnam War, and the consequent effect on troop morale are secondary reasons to ensure that events like these are prevented.

Civilians are unfortunately killed during war by other humans for manifold reasons [Slim 08]:

- Genocidal thinking—ethnic or racial cleansing of populations

- Dualistic thinking—separating the good from the bad

- Power dominance and subjugation—power lust and to exert force

- Revenge—emotional striking back for perceived wrongs

- Punishment and forced compliance—to shape the behavior of civilian populations

- Utility—it furthers the war strategically

- Asymmetrical necessity—tactical killing of civilians due to an inferior military position

- Profit—mercenary and looting activity

- Eradicating potential—preemptive removal of civilians that may become warfighters in the future

- Recklessness—shooting anything that moves, or other forms of indiscriminate killing

- Reluctant killing—through human error or accident, collateral damage

- Collective and sacrificial thinking—killing of groups rather than individuals, they must be sacrificed for a greater good

These forms of thinking are alien to current artificial intelligence efforts and likely are to remain so. Armed autonomous systems need not nor should be equipped with any of these forms of unacceptable human rationalization or action.

A primary conclusion is that it seems unrealistic to expect normal human beings by their very nature to adhere to the Laws of Warfare when confronted with the horror of the battlefield, even when trained. As a Marine Corps Reserves Captain commented: "If wars cannot be prevented, steps can be taken to ensure that they are at least fought in as ethical a manner as possible" [Danyluk 00]. One could argue that battlefield atrocities, if left unchecked, may become progressively worse, with the progression of standoff weapons and increasing use of technology. Something must be done to restrain the technology itself, above and beyond the human limits of the warfighters themselves. This is the rationale behind the approach embodied in this book.

CHAPTER 4

Related Philosophical Thought

W E NOW TURN TO several philosophers and practitioners who have specifically considered the military's potential use of lethal autonomous robotic agents. Many of them are vocal opponents of the deployment of autonomous battlefield robots. Some acknowledge that these systems will ultimately be deployed despite their reservations, whereas others are calling for an outright ban on the technology.

Interestingly the arguments against automated weaponry date back millennia. The crossbow was banned by Pope Innocent II in 1139 for use against Christians, due to its immoral point-and-click interface, which enabled killing at a distance [RUSI 08]. Most new weapons have similarly struggled into widespread use.

For autonomous lethal robots, we must be clear in our use of the term *autonomy*, as it becomes ambiguous when we cross intellectual disciplines. It is not used here in the strictly philosophical sense, which implies that the autonomous agent has free will. Here we refer to autonomy as being self-directed, and in specific regard to lethality Foss' definition seems apropos: "the ability to 'pull the trigger'—to attack a selected target without human initiation nor confirmation, both in case of target choice or attack command" [Foss 08]. This is restricted only in the same sense a soldier is restricted: the robot soldier must be given a mission to accomplish, and any lethal action must be conducted only in support of that mission. At the highest level, a human is still in the loop so to speak—commanders must define the mission for the autonomous agent whether it be a human soldier or a robot. The warfighter, robot or human, must then abide by the Rules of Engagement and Laws of War as prescribed from their training or encoding. Autonomy in this sense is limited when compared to a philosopher's point of view.

In a contrarian position regarding the use of battlefield robots, Sparrow argues that any use of "fully autonomous" robots is unethical due to the *Jus in Bello* requirement that someone must be responsible for a possible war crime [Sparrow 06]. His position is based upon deontological (rights-based) and consequentialist (outcome-based) ethical arguments. He asserts that while responsibility could ultimately vest in the commanding officer for the system's use, it would be unfair, and hence unjust, to both that individual and any resulting casualties in the event of a violation, due to the inability to directly control an autonomous robot. Nonetheless, due to the increasing tempo of warfare, he shares my opinion that the eventual deployment of systems with ever increasing autonomy is inevitable. Although I agree that it is necessary that responsibility for the use of these systems must be made clear, I do not agree that it is infeasible to do so. As described in Chapter 2, several existing weapons systems are in use that already deploy lethal force autonomously to some degree, and they (with the exception of antipersonnel mines, due to their lack of discrimination, not responsibility attribution) are not generally considered to be unethical.

Sparrow further draws parallels between robot warriors and child soldiers, both of which he claims cannot assume moral responsibility for their action. He neglects, however, to consider the possibility of the direct encoding of prescriptive ethical codes within the robot itself, which can govern its actions in a manner consistent with the Laws of War and Rules of Engagement. This would seem to significantly weaken the claim he makes.

Along other lines, Sparrow points out several clear challenges to the roboticist attempting to create a moral sense for a battlefield robot [Sparrow 07]:

- "Controversy about right and wrong is endemic to ethics."

    - Response: While that is true, we have reasonable guidance by the agreed upon and negotiated Laws of War as well as the Rules of Engagement as a means to constrain behavior when compared to ungoverned solutions for autonomous robots.

- "I suspect that any decision structure that a robot is capable of instantiating is still likely to leave open the possibility that robots will act unethically."

  - Response: Agreed—It is the goal of this work to create systems that can perform more ethically than human soldiers do in the battlefield, albeit they will still be imperfect. This challenge seems achievable. Reaching perfection in almost anything in the real world, including human behavior, seems beyond our grasp.

- While he is "quite happy to allow that robots will become capable of increasingly sophisticated behavior in the future and perhaps even of distinguishing between war crimes and legitimate use of military force," the underlying question regarding responsibility, he contends, is not solvable.

  - Response: It is my belief that by making the assignment of responsibility transparent and explicit, through the use of a responsibility advisor at all steps in the deployment of these systems, this problem is indeed solvable. This is further addressed in subsequent chapters.

Asaro similarly argues from a position of loss of attribution of responsibility, but does broach the subject of robots possessing "moral intelligence" [Asaro 06]. His definition of a moral agent seems applicable, where the agent adheres to a system of ethics, which it employs in choosing the actions that it either takes or refrains from taking. He also considers legal responsibility, which he states will compel roboticists to build ethical systems in the future. He notes, similar to what is proposed here, that if an existing set of ethical policy (e.g., LOW and ROE) is replicated by the robot's behavior, it enforces a particular morality through the robot itself. It is in this sense that we strive to create such an ethical architectural component for unmanned autonomous systems, where that "particular morality" is derived from international conventions.

Regarding *Jus in Bello*, Asaro reminds us that if an autonomous system is potentially capable of reducing collateral damage over previously existing methods of waging war, there is an argument that it is morally required, i.e., a responsibility, to use them [Asaro 07]. The Human Rights Watch group, for example, has stated that only precision-guided bombs should be used in civilian areas [Human Rights Watch 03]. By extension, if autonomous battlefield robots could reduce civilian casualties over those occasioned by conventional forces, we would be derelict in not using them. Simply stated, at least in some people's view, that if the goals of the research outlined in this book are achieved, i.e., to produce warfighting robots that are more ethical in the battlefield than are human soldiers, a moral imperative exists to deploy such autonomous robotic systems capable of lethal force.

One of the earliest arguments encountered based on the difficulty to attribute responsibility and liability to autonomous agents in the battlefield was presaged by [Perri 01]. He assumes "at the very least the rules of engagement for the particular conflict have been programmed into the machines, and that only in certain types of emergencies are the machines expected to set aside these rules." I personally do not trust the view of setting aside the rules by the autonomous agent itself, as it begs the question of responsibility if it does so, but it may be possible for a human to assume responsibility for such deviation if it is ever deemed appropriate (and ethical) to do so. Chapter 10 discusses specific issues regarding order refusal overrides by human commanders. Although Perri rightly notes the inherent difficulty in attributing responsibility to the programmer, designer, soldier, commander, or politician for the potential of war crimes by these systems, it is believed that a deliberate assumption of responsibility by human agents for these systems can at least help focus such an assignment when required. An inherent part of the architecture for the project described in this book is a responsibility advisor, which will specifically address these issues, although it would be naïve to say it will solve all of them. Often assigning and establishing responsibility for human war crimes, even through international courts, is quite daunting.

Some would argue that the robot itself can be responsible for its own actions. Sullins, for example, is willing to attribute moral agency to robots far more easily than most, including myself, by asserting that simply if it is (1) in a position of responsibility relative to some other moral agent, (2) has a significant degree of autonomy, and (3) can exhibit some loose sort of intentional behavior ("there is no requirement that the actions really are intentional in a philosophically rigorous way, nor that the actions are derived from a will that is free on all levels of abstraction"), that it can then be considered to be a moral agent [Sullins 06]. Such an attribution unnecessarily complicates the issue of responsibility assignment for immoral actions, and a perspective that a robot is incapable of becoming a moral agent that is fully responsible for its own actions in any real sense, at least under present and near-term conditions, seems far more reasonable. [Dennett 96] states that higher-order intentionality is a precondition for moral responsibility (including the opportunity for duplicity for example), something well beyond the capability of the sorts of robots under development in this book. [Himma 07] requires that an artificial agent have both free will and deliberative capability before he is willing to attribute moral agency to it. Artificial (nonconscious) agents, in his view, have behavior that is either fully determined and explainable or purely random in the sense of lacking causal antecedents. The bottom line for all of this line of reasoning, at least for our purposes, is (and seemingly needless to say): for the sorts of autonomous agent architectures described in this book, the robot is off the hook regarding responsibility. We will need to look toward humans for culpability for any ethical errors they make in the lethal application of force.

But responsibility is not the lone sore spot for the potential use of autonomous robots in the battlefield regarding Just War Theory. Asaro notes that the use of autonomous robots in warfare is unethical due to their potential lowering of the threshold of entry to war, which is in contradiction of *Jus ad Bellum* [Asaro 07]. He cites the 1991 Persian Gulf War, the 1999 war in Kosovo, and the 2003 invasion of Iraq as instances where technology made it easier for a nation's leaders and citizens to decide to undertake and support a new war effort. One can argue however, and Asaro does, that this is not a particular issue limited to autonomous robots, but is typical for the advent of any significant technological advance in weapons and tactics. A primary goal of military research is to provide technological tactical superiority over an opposing force. Thus the argument degenerates to the relinquishing of all military-related research, something that is not likely to happen. As autonomous robotic systems are not envisioned to pose threats similar to those associated with weapons of mass destruction (nuclear, biological, and chemical), it appears unlikely that associated research will be restrained in a similar manner by international convention. A potential arms race could possibly ensue, but again this is a problem for any form of military technology that provides an asymmetric advantage, not simply robotic.

Other *Jus ad Bellum* counterarguments could involve the resulting human-robot battlefield asymmetry as instead having a deterrent effect regarding entry into conflict by the state not in possession of the technology, which now might be more likely to sue for a negotiated diplomatic settlement. In addition, the potential for live or recorded data and video from gruesome real-time front-line conflict, possibly being made available to the media to reach into the living rooms of our nation's citizens, could lead to an even greater abhorrence of war by the general public rather than its acceptance*. Quite different imagery, one could imagine, as compared to the relatively antiseptic standoff precision high-altitude bombings often seen in U.S. media outlets.

Armstrong is concerned with the impact on the "hearts and minds" of the people in conflict and postconflict zones when and if autonomous robots are deployed [Armstrong 08]. He recalls numerous instances of positive human contact that have helped in reconciling the differences between different cultures, where the presence of robotic technology instead could create a vacuum. In contrast, however, we must note not only the good but also the poor performance of some of our contractors and soldiers in similar circumstances, who have certainly done damage to this cooperative spirit. In any case, a theme that will recur throughout this book is that robots of this sort will not be used in isolation, but rather as organic assets working alongside troops, and not simply replacing them in toto. Human-to-human contact opportunities will persist, just as they have, for example, with the use of canine assets operating side-by-side with soldiers.

Sharkey has been one of the most vocal opponents of autonomous lethal robots, going so far as to calling himself a Cassandra [Sharkey 07, Sharkey 08]. His concerns are manifold: it simply cannot be done correctly because of fundamental limits of artificial intelligence (AI) regarding reliability and discrimination; an echoing of the responsibility concerns voiced by Sparrow and others; the potential for risk-free warfare; and even the cynical point of view that the military will co-opt research such as described in this book "to allay opposition to the premature use of autonomous weapons." Much of his argumentation involves pathos (i.e., it is fear-based), and little logical or formal support is provided for his arguments on AI's limits. Simply because he "has no idea how this could be made to work reliably" does not mean it cannot. The issues surrounding risk-free warfare are addressed below. My personal experience with the integrity of the military allays my concerns regarding co-opting. Besides, the fielding of these systems is likely to proceed independently of whatever efforts are undertaken in regard to ethically embedding an "artificial conscience," no doubt by using more conventional approaches to manage the legality

---

* This potential effect was pointed out by BBC reporter Dan Damon during an interview in July 2007.

of this new class of weapons. Sharkey and I both agree, however, that the time has come to discuss these issues on an international scale, to determine what and if any limits should be applied to battlefield use of lethal autonomous systems.

Borenstein takes a more reasoned stance, revisiting some of the concerns already raised [Borenstein 08]. To those he adds the unforeseen problems associated with software glitches, some of which have already resulted in significant deaths. He cites software problems surrounding the death of 28 Americans when a missile defense system failed [GAO 92] and a South African automated antiaircraft system that went out of control resulting in the deaths of nine soldiers [Hosken et al. 07]. He also notes that humans have situational and instinctual knowledge to rely on that will be difficult to encode in a robotic system, well above and beyond the Laws of War. Although this is currently true, it may not be a limit of the future, but in any case it should not serve as a deterrent to restrain the use of force by autonomous systems provided with existing well-defined laws, as these systems are seemingly inevitably being deployed. Other concerns (e.g., technological vulnerability such as hacking) are more easily dismissed with the ongoing major efforts by the DOD in cybersecurity. Although Borenstein remains skeptical, he does cede that "If advances in AI do continue to move forward, reaching close to duplicating the human brain, some of the fears relating to AWS [Autonomous Weapons Systems] might conceivably lessen" [Borenstein 08]. Nonetheless, his *Jus ad Bellum* concerns regarding "escalation and removing potential deterrents to war" persist.

Sparrow has recently commented on the requirement that UV systems be designed to be ethical from the onset, focusing on the responsibility of the designer to ensure that these systems are built to be safe and to incorporate the Laws of War [Sparrow 08]. One key aspect is his focus on the design of an interface for operators that enforces morality, building ethics into the system directly. "The interface for an [Unmanned System] should facilitate killing where it is justified and frustrate it where it is not," a challenge, as he puts it, that is yet to be met. We share this concern and seemingly agree on the value of embedding ethics into both the robotic system itself and its operator interface.

Another often heard argument against the use of autonomous weapons is that they will be incapable of exhibiting mercy, compassion, and humanity [Davis 08]. Although substantial progress is being made in artificial intelligence on the use of emotions in robotic systems (e.g., [Fellous and Arbib 05]), and indeed guilt and remorse are recommended for implementation within the architecture presented in subsequent chapters, no current provision is made for these emotions at this time. The rationale is not because it is more challenging than other secondary emotions, but rather that humanity is legislated into the Laws of War, and as such if they are followed, the robot will exercise restraint consistent with societal norms. This may be inadequate to some, but the reduction of the inhumanity exhibited by a significant percentage of soldiers [Surgeon General 06] is believed to offset this loss and can potentially result in a fighting force that is more humane overall than an all-human one.

Potential proliferation of the underlying technology has also been expressed as a concern. Rear Admiral Chris Parry of the U.K. Royal Navy broached this subject at a recent workshop [Parry 08]. The ease with which unmanned drones can be made from hobby aircraft kits coupled with GPS and cell phone technology is just one example that would enable terrorists to easily manufacture buzz-bomb-type UAVs for use against events such as the upcoming Olympics in London. Frightening prospects indeed. It was reported that Hezbollah launched two attack UAVs against Israel on August 13, 2006, with at least one apparently armed with 30 kg of explosive that was recovered at the wreckage site [Eshel 06]. They were intercepted by the Israeli Air Force before they reached their target. Clearly, you need not be a major international power to take advantage of the underlying technology. These worrisome aspects of proliferation need ongoing attention.

One argument voiced by military personnel regarding the introduction of ethical autonomous robots into the battlefield is the potential for a deleterious effect on squad cohesion. This term refers to the "Band of Brothers" attitude formed by a small group of men in combat, who come to rely on and protect each other. If a robot that is capable of objectively monitoring the moral performance of team members is injected into the unit, it may seriously impede the effectiveness of the team due to a fracturing of trust. The concept of even "fragging" the robot has been mentioned, where it would be deliberately destroyed by squad members to prevent infractions from being reported. The counterargument for this possible effect may lie within the performance of the robot itself: if it is willing to go out in advance of my men, if it is willing to take a bullet for me, if it can watch my back better than a fellow human soldier could, then the omnipresent ethical monitoring might be a small price to pay in favor of my enhanced survival. Attention would need to be focused on how to establish this level of human-robot trust, but through experience and training it should be feasible to establish a meaningful bond between man and machine.

For example, consider one robot's story used for removing improvised explosive devices in Iraq:

> After several successful missions, the Packbot ... was destroyed. The operator brought it back to the makers and asked for it to be rebuilt. He didn't want a new one, he wanted it fixed. It was a good robot and they'd been through a lot together. [Bains 07]

The United States Navy is examining the legal ramifications of the deployment of autonomous lethal systems in the battlefield [Canninget al. 04], observing that a legal review is required of any new weapons system prior to its acquisition to ensure that it complies with the LOW and related treaties. To pass this review, it must demonstrate that it neither acts indiscriminately nor causes superfluous injury. In other words it must act with proportionality and discrimination, the hallmark criteria of *Jus in Bello*. The authors contend, and rightly so, that the problem of discrimination is the most difficult aspect of lethal unmanned systems, with only legitimate combatants and military objectives as just targets. They shift the paradigm for the robot to only identify and target weapons and weapon systems, not the individual(s) manning them, unless that individual poses a potential threat. While they acknowledge several significant difficulties associated with this approach (e.g. spoofing and ruses to injure civilians), another question is whether simply destroying weapons, without clearly identifying those nearby as combatants or a lack of recognition of neighboring civilian objects, is legal in itself (i.e., ensuring that proportionality is exercised against a military objective). Canning advocates the use of escalating force if a combatant is present, to encourage surrender over the use of lethality, a theme common to our approach as well.

Canning's approach poses an interesting alternative where the system "directly targets either the bow or the arrow, but not the archer" [Canning 06, Canning 08]. Concerns arise from current limits on the ability to discriminate combatants from noncombatants on the battlefield. Although we are nowhere near providing robust methods to accomplish this in the near-term, (except in certain limited circumstances with the use of friend-foe interrogation (FFI) technology), in my estimation, considerable effort can and should be made in this research area, and in many ways it already has begun, e.g., by using gait recognition and other patterns of activity to identify suspicious persons. These early steps, coupled with weapon recognition capabilities, could potentially provide even greater target discrimination than simply recognizing the weapons alone. Unique tactics (yet to be developed) by an unmanned system to actively ferret out the traits of a combatant by using direct approach by the robot or other risk-taking (exposure) methods can further illuminate what constitutes a legitimate target in the battlefield. This is an acceptable strategy by virtue of the robot's not needing to defend itself as a soldier would, perhaps even using self-sacrifice to reveal the presence of a combatant. There is no inherent need for the right of self-defense for an autonomous system. In any case, clearly this is not a short-term research agenda, and the ideas, design, and results presented in this book constitute only preliminary steps in that direction.

The elimination of the need for an autonomous agent's claim of self-defense as an exculpation of responsibility through either justification or excuse is of related interest, which is a common occurrence during the occasioning of civilian casualties by human soldiers [Woodruff 82]. Robotic systems need make no appeal to self-defense or self-preservation in this regard and thus can and should value civilian lives above their own continued existence. Of course there is no guarantee that a lethal autonomous system would be given that capability, but to be ethical I would contend that it must. This is a condition that a human soldier likely could not easily or ever attain to, and as such it would allow an ethical autonomous agent to potentially perform in a manner superior to that of a human in this regard. It should be noted that the system's use of lethal force does not preclude collateral damage to civilians and their property during the conduct of a military mission according to the Just War Principle of Double Effect*, only that no claim of self-defense could be used to justify any such incidental deaths. It also does not negate the possibility of the autonomous system acting to defend fellow human soldiers under attack in the battlefield.

We will strive to hold the ethical autonomous systems to an even higher standard, invoking the Principle of Double Intention [Walzer 77]. Walzer argues that the Principle of Double Effect is not enough; i.e., that it is inadequate to tolerate noncombatant casualties as long as they are not intended; they are not the ends or the means to the ends. He argues for a stronger

---

* The Principle (or Doctrine) of Double Effect, derived from the Middle Ages, asserts "that while the death or injury of innocents is always wrong, either may be excused if it was not the intended result of a given act of war" [Norman 95, Wells 96]. As long as the collateral damage is an unintended effect (i.e., innocents are not deliberately targeted), it is excusable according to the LOW even if it is foreseen (and that proportionality is adhered to).

stance—the Principle of Double Intention, which has merit for our implementation. It has the necessity of a good being achieved (a military end), the same as for the Principle of Double Effect, but instead of simply tolerating collateral damage, it argues for the necessity of intentionally reducing noncombatant casualties as far as possible. Thus the acceptable (good) effect is aimed to be achieved narrowly, and the agent, aware of the associated evil effect (noncombatant casualties), aims intentionally to minimize it, accepting the costs associated with that aim. This seems an altogether acceptable approach for an autonomous robot to subscribe to as part of its moral basis. This principle is captured in the requirement that "due care" be taken. The challenge is to determine just what that means, but any care is better than none. In our case, this can be in regard to choice of weaponry (e.g., rifle versus grenade), targeting accuracy (standoff distances) in the presence of civilian populations, or other similar criteria. Walzer does provide some guidance:

> Since judgments of "due care" involve calculations of relative value, urgency, and so on, it has to be said that utilitarian arguments and rights arguments (relative at least to indirect effects) are not wholly distinct. Nevertheless the calculations required by the proportionality principle and those required by "due care" are not the same. Even after the highest possible standards of care have been accepted, the probable civilian losses may still be disproportionate to the value of the target; then the attack must be called off. Or, more often … "due care" is an additional requirement [above the proportionality requirement]. [Walzer 77]

Anderson, in his blog, points out the fundamental difficulty of assessing proportionality by a robot as required for *Jus in Bello*, largely due to the "apples and oranges" sorts of calculations that may be needed [Anderson, K 07]. He notes that a "practice," as opposed to a set of decision rules, will need to be developed, and although a daunting task, he sees it in principle as the same problem that humans have in making such a decision. Thus his argument is based on the degree of difficulty rather than any form of fundamental intransigence. Research in this area can provide the opportunity to make this form of reasoning regarding proportionality explicit. Indeed, different forms of reasoning beyond simple inference will be required, and case-based reasoning (CBR) is just one such candidate to be considered [Kolodner 93]. We have already put CBR to work in intelligent robotic systems [Ram et al. 97,

Likhachev et al. 02], where we reason from previous experience using analogy as appropriate. It may also be feasible to expand its use in the context of proportional use of force.

Walzer comments on the issue of risk-free war-making, an imaginable outcome of the introduction of lethal autonomous systems. He states "there is no principle of Just War Theory that bars this kind of warfare" [Walzer 04]. Just War theorists have not discussed this issue to date, and he states it is time to do so. Despite Walzer's assertion, discussions of this sort could possibly lead to prohibitions or restrictions on the use of lethal autonomous systems in the battlefield for this or any of the other reasons above. For example, [Bring 02] states for the more general case, "An increased use of standoff weapons is not to the advantage of civilians. The solution is not a prohibition of such weapons, but rather a reconsideration of the parameters for modern warfare as it affects civilians." Personally, I clearly support the start of such talks at any and all levels to clarify just what is and is not acceptable internationally in this regard. In my view the proposition will not be risk-free, as teams of robots (as organic assets) and soldiers will be working side-by-side in the battlefield, taking advantage of the principle of force multiplication where a single warfighter can now project his presence as equivalent to several soldiers' capabilities in the past. Substantial risk to the soldier's life will remain present, albeit significantly less so on the friendly side in a clearly asymmetrical fashion.

I suppose a discussion of the ethical behavior of robots would be incomplete without some reference to Asimov's "Three Laws of Robotics"* [Asimov 50] (there are actually four [Asimov 85]). Needless to say, I am not alone in my belief that, while they are elegant in their simplicity and have served a useful fictional purpose by bringing to light a whole range of issues surrounding robot ethics and rights, they are at best a straw man to bootstrap the ethical debate and as such serve no useful practical purpose beyond their fictional roots. Anderson from a philosophical perspective similarly rejects them, arguing, "Asimov's 'Three Laws of Robotics' are an unsatisfactory basis for Machine Ethics, regardless of the status of the machine" [Anderson 07b]. With all due respect, I must concur.

---

* See http://en.wikipedia.org/wiki/Three_Laws_of_Robotics for a summary discussion of all four laws.

CHAPTER 5

What People Think

Opinions on Lethal Autonomous Systems

W E'VE HEARD FROM PHILOSOPHERS, social scientists, Just War theorists, and the military regarding their views on the future use of lethal autonomous systems. But these robots will potentially affect far more than these few. As part of our work for the Army Research Office, we conducted a survey to gauge the views of a broad range of people on lethal autonomous robots. Specifically, the goal was to establish opinion on the use of lethality by autonomous systems spanning the public, researchers, policymakers, and military personnel to ascertain the current point of view maintained by these various demographic groups on this subject.

Although it may be difficult to interpret some of these results, given the fact that these robotic systems are not yet in widespread use, the survey serves as a benchmark for future opinion and also provides insights into what people are concerned about now. One could imagine the difficulty in conducting a survey in the days of the Wright Brothers regarding whether people would support and use commercial aviation, and we face a similar problem of soliciting opinion in advance of the technological development and deployment of lethal autonomous system. Please keep this in mind while reading this chapter.

The rationale for the survey from the original proposal is as follows:

> In order to fully understand the consequences of the deployment of autonomous machines capable of taking human life under military doctrine and tactics, a systematic ethical evaluation needs to be conducted to guide users (e.g., warfighters), system designers, policy makers, and commanders regarding the intended future use of this technology. This study needs to be conducted prior to the deployment of these systems, not as an afterthought.

That intent serves as the basis for what follows.

5.1 SURVEY BACKGROUND

The survey was conducted online, hosted by a commercial survey company (*SurveyMonkey.com*), and was approved using formal Institute Review Board procedures for the use of human subjects. It was of the descriptive-explanatory type [Punch 03] and followed the recommendations and guidelines espoused for the preparation and conduct of internet surveys [Dillman 07, Best and Krueger 04]. In addition to developing a general picture of the public view on the matter, we studied the relationships among a number of other variables, described below. The survey instrument was prototyped and refined prior to release on the Internet to ensure that it was unambiguous, understandable, and easy to use.

As mentioned earlier, the target demographic populations were fourfold: robotics researchers, the military, policymakers, and the general public. These communities were reached with varying degrees of success given the limited available funding for this effort, with the robotic researcher community being the best responding group. We relied on respondent self-identification for demographic analysis. Special care was taken using e-mail registration and passwords to control potential abuse by malicious users.

The full survey structure, design, and results are reported in detail in a lengthy technical report [Moshkina and Arkin 08a]. This chapter only touches the surface. The first section (Questions 1–5) assessed some of the background knowledge of the respondents and then defined the terms used for the remainder of the survey, including the following:

1. **Robot:** An automated machine or vehicle, capable of independent perception, reasoning, and action.

2. **Robot as an extension of the warfighter**: A robot under the direct authority of a human, including authority over the use of lethal force.

3. **Autonomous robot**: A robot that does not require direct human involvement, except for high-level mission tasking; such a robot can make its own decisions consistent with its mission without requiring direct human authorization, including decisions regarding the use of lethal force.

The main section of the survey (Questions 6–22) then probed a number of ethical issues including:

1. Given that military robots follow the same laws of war and code of conduct as for a human soldier, in which roles and situations is the use of such robots acceptable?

2. What does it mean to behave ethically in warfare?

3. Should robots be able to refuse an order from a human, and what ethical standards should they be held to?

4. Who, and to what extent, is responsible for any lethal errors made?

5. What are the benefits and concerns for use of such robots?

6. Would an emotional component be beneficial to a military robot?

Note that these are not the actual questions that were presented to the respondents, just an abstraction of the general issues being probed (see [Moshkina and Arkin 08a] for the full survey details). In all cases, response choices were randomized to the extent possible to avoid order bias.

The last section of the survey (Questions 23–45) gathered demographic information such as age, gender, occupation, education, military experience, geographic information, level of spirituality, attitudes toward technology, robots and war in general, and so on.

5.2 RESPONSE

Subjects were recruited using a variety of means: flyers, Internet discussion/news groups, professional magazine survey announcements, publicity on the research in a number of popular press articles, announcements at various talks and conferences, and in some cases (policymakers) direct recruitment. Bulk e-mail (spam) was not used. Figure 5.1 shows the

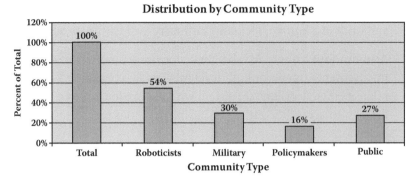

FIGURE 5.1 Distribution of survey participants by demographic group. (Note that a single respondent may be a member of more than one demographic group.)

distribution of the 430 participants who fully completed the survey. Given the large percentage of roboticists who responded, and the lack of potential coverage error due to our ability to reach this audience more effectively than the others, the responses for this group are the most reliable and can be quantitatively interpreted [Moshkina and Arkin 08b]. The other groups we must treat as descriptive, qualitative, and comparative.

5.3 COMPARATIVE RESULTS

Provided the caveat just mentioned, the distilled results for the multiple demographic groups are presented (for detailed analysis see [Moshkina and Arkin 08a]). We must first provide some additional information to help clarify these results. The terms in Table 5.1 are derived directly from the survey itself.

Now that the terminology is clear, the results can be summarized as follows:

1. Demographics

    a. A typical survey respondent was an American or western European male in his twenties or thirties, with higher education, significant computer experience, and positive attitude toward technology and robots.

    b. The participants ranged from under twenty-one to over sixty-six years old (all the participants were over 18); 11% of the participants were female; non-U.S. participants (45%) were from all over the world, including Australia, Asia, eastern Europe, and Africa.

TABLE 5.1   Survey Terms and Their Definitions

Roles	Reconnaissance
	Crowd/mob control
	Sentry/perimeter surveillance
	Prison guard
	Hostage rescue
	Direct combat
Situations	Open warfare with the war on foreign territory
	Open warfare with the war on home territory
	Covert operations on foreign territory
	Covert operations on home territory
Levels of autonomy	Human soldier
	Robot as an extension of the warfighter
	Autonomous robot
Community type	Roboticists
	Military
	Policymaker
	Public

2. Levels of Autonomy

a. With respect to levels of autonomy, regardless of roles or situations, the more the control shifts away from the human the less such an entity is acceptable to the participants; a human soldier was the most acceptable entity in warfare followed by a robot as an extension of the warfighter, with autonomous robot being the least acceptable.

b. There was a larger gap in terms of acceptability between a robot as an extension of the warfighter and autonomous robot than that between soldier and robot as an extension of the warfighter.

c. Taking human life by an autonomous robot in both open warfare and covert operations is unacceptable to more than half of the participants (56% disagreed or strongly disagreed), especially in the case of covert operations on home territory.

3. Comparison between Community Types

a. Regardless of roles or situations, in most cases the general public found the employment of soldiers and robots less acceptable than any other community type, and, conversely, those with military experience and policymakers found such employment more acceptable.

    b. More military and policymakers were in favor of the same ethical standards for both soldiers and robots than both the general public and roboticists, who were more in favor of higher standards for robots.

    c. When asked about the responsibility for any lethal errors, those with military experience attributed the least amount of blame to any of the responsible parties.

4. Roles

    a. The most acceptable role for using both types of robots (as an extension of the warfighter or autonomous) is reconnaissance; the least acceptable is for crowd control.

    b. Robots could be acceptably used for roles where less force is involved, such as a sentry and for reconnaissance, and should be avoided for roles where the use of force may be necessary, especially when civilian lives are at stake such as crowd control and hostage rescue.

5. Situations

    a. Covert operations were less acceptable to the entire set of participants than open warfare (whether on home or foreign territory).

6. Ethical Considerations

    a. The majority of participants, regardless of the community type, agreed that the ethical standards, namely the Laws of War, Rules of Engagement, Code of Conduct and Additional Moral Standards, do apply to both soldiers (84%) and robots (72%).

    b. The more concrete, specific, and identifiable ethical standards were, the more likely they were to be considered applicable to both soldiers and robots, with Laws of War being the most applicable, and Additional Moral Standards the least.

    c. 59% of the participants believed that an autonomous robot should have a right to refuse an order it finds unethical, thus in a sense admitting that it may be more important for a robot to behave ethically than to stay under the control of a human.

    d. 66% of the participants were in favor of higher ethical standards for a robot than those for a soldier.

    e. The majority of the participants (69%) believe that it would be easier to start wars if robots were employed in warfare.

7. Responsibility

    a. A soldier was the party considered the most responsible for both his/her own lethal errors and those using a robot as an extension under his/her control. Robots were the least blamed parties, although an autonomous robot was found responsible for erroneous lethal action twice as much as the robot as an extension of the warfighter. It is interesting that even though robots were blamed the least, 40% of the respondents still found an autonomous robot responsible for its errors to a very significant or significant extent.

    b. As the control shifts away from the soldier, the robot and its maker should take more responsibility for its actions, according to the participants. A robot designer was blamed 31% less for the mistakes of robot as an extension than for those of an autonomous robot.

8. Benefits and Concerns

    a. Saving lives of soldiers was considered the most clear-cut benefit of employing robots in warfare, and the main concern was that of risking civilian lives by their use.

    b. Saving soldiers' lives and decreasing psychological trauma to soldiers outweigh the risk to the soldiers the most. Decreasing cost and producing better battlefield outcomes were also viewed as benefits rather than concerns.

9. Emotion

    a. Sympathy was considered to be beneficial to a military robot by over half of the participants (59%), and guilt by just under a half (49%).

5.4 DISCUSSION

People are clearly concerned about the potential use of lethal autonomous robots. Despite the perceived ability to save soldiers' lives, there is clear concern for collateral damage, in particular civilian loss of life.

The *Jus ad Bellum* argument of lowering the threshold of entry into war by the introduction of these systems is also voiced by the majority. The concept of autonomy in the battlefield is not well accepted in general when compared to the other alternatives. This begs the question as to whether armed robots should be allowed in the battlefield in the first place—a valid discussion that must be continued through international discourse. Clearly there is concern.

Autonomous systems may have a place in warfare, according to the respondents, but it seems that it is preferred that they do not exhibit force. If they were armed and deployed, the majority feels that a robot should be able to refuse an unethical order (assuming that said order can be so adjudged). A significant number (well over 1/3) feel that an autonomous robot can be held responsible for its own actions, a surprising result, at least to me. An autonomous robot is also expected to be held to at least as high or a higher ethical standard than human soldiers.

Emotions may also have a place in the battlefield for these systems, sympathy in particular, to perhaps enhance the humaneness of such a weapon system. Guilt is also recommended by almost half, which indeed forms part of the ethical adaptor component of the ethical autonomous robot architecture presented in Chapter 10. The omission of sympathy in our approach may be considered a design flaw by some.

As stated earlier however, these results, while largely qualitative, must also be put in context with the current state of the art. There are no autonomous battlefield robots in the sense that most people envision. Thus human imagination is required to fill in the blanks. Robots in Western civilization have long engendered fear, as evidenced by Hollywood films such as *The Terminator*, and this fear is fueled by a so-called Frankenstein syndrome, where such human creations will ultimately turn on and destroy us [Perkowitz 04].

In any case, there is no doubt at the very least that we should proceed with caution as these systems inevitably move forward toward military use. We must ensure that lethal autonomous systems, when and if they are introduced into routine battlefield operations, behave in a manner consistent with international law.

CHAPTER 6

Formalization for Ethical Control

I N ORDER TO PROVIDE a basis for the development of autonomous systems architectures capable of supporting ethical behavior regarding the application of lethality in war, we now consider the use of mathematical formalization as a means to express first the underlying flow of control in the architecture itself and then how an ethical component can effectively interact with that flow. This approach is derived from the formal methods used to describe behavior-based robotic control as discussed in [Arkin 98] and that has been used to provide direct architectural implementations for a broad range of autonomous systems, including military applications (e.g., [MacKenzie et al. 97, Balch and Arkin 98, Arkin et al. 99, Collins et al. 00, Wagner and Arkin 04]).

Mathematical methods can be used to describe the relationship between sensing and acting using a functional notation:

$$\beta(\mathbf{s}) \rightarrow \mathbf{r}$$

where behavior β when given stimulus $\mathbf{s}$ yields response $\mathbf{r}$. In a purely reactive system, time is not an argument of β as the behavioral response is instantaneous and independent of the time history of the system. Immediately below we address the formalisms that are used to capture the relationships within the autonomous system architecture design that supports ethical reasoning described in Chapters 9 and 10. The issues regarding specific representational choices for the ethical component are presented in Chapter 8.

6.1 FORMAL METHODS FOR DESCRIBING BEHAVIOR

We first review the use of formal methods for describing autonomous robotic performance. The material in this subsection is drawn largely from [Arkin 98] and adapted as required.

A robotic behavior can be expressed as a triple (S,R,β) where S denotes the domain of all interpretable stimuli, R denotes the range of possible responses, and β denotes the mapping $\beta\!:\!S \to R$.

6.1.1 Range of Responses: R

An understanding of the dimensionality of a robotic motor response is necessary in order to map the stimulus onto it. It will serve us well to factor the robot's actuator response into two orthogonal components: strength and orientation.

- *Strength:* denotes the magnitude of the response, which may or may not be related to the strength of a given stimulus. For example, it may manifest itself in terms of speed or force. Indeed the strength may be entirely independent of the strength of the stimulus yet modulated by exogenous factors such as intention (what the robot's internal goals are) and habituation or sensitization (how often the stimulus has been previously presented).

- *Orientation:* denotes the direction of action for the response (e.g., moving away from an aversive stimulus, moving toward an attractor, engaging a specific target). The realization of this directional component of the response requires knowledge of the robot's kinematics.

The instantaneous response **r**, where $\mathbf{r} \in R$ can be expressed as an n-length vector representing the responses for each of the individual degrees of freedom (DOFs) for the robot. Weapons system targeting and firing are now to be considered within these DOFs, and considered to also have components of strength (regarding firing pattern, weapons selection, and proportionality) and orientation (target location).

6.1.2 The Stimulus Domain: S

S consists of the domain of all perceivable stimuli. Each individual stimulus or percept **s** (where $\mathbf{s} \in S$) is represented as a binary tuple (p,λ) having both a particular type or perceptual class p and a property of strength, λ, which can be reflective of its uncertainty. The complete set of all p over the domain S defines all the perceptual entities distinguishable to a robot, that is, those things that it was designed to perceive. This concept is loosely related to affordances [Gibson 79]. The stimulus strength λ can be defined in a variety of ways: discrete (e.g., binary: absent or present; categorical: absent, weak, medium, strong), or it can be real valued and continuous. λ, in the context of lethality, can refer to the degree of discrimination of a candidate combatant target; in our case it may be represented as a real-valued percentage between -1 and 1, with -1 representing 100% certainly of a noncombatant, $+1$ representing 100% certainty of a combatant, and 0% unknown. Other representational choices may be developed in the future to enhance discriminatory reasoning—for example, two separate independent values between [0,1], one each for combatant and noncombatant probability, which are maintained by independent ethical discrimination reasoners.

We define τ as a threshold value for a given perceptual class p, above which a behavioral response is generated. Often the strength of the input stimulus (λ) will determine whether or not to respond and the associated magnitude or type of the response, although other factors can influence this (e.g., habituation, inhibition, ethical constraints, etc.), possibly by altering the value of τ. In any case, if λ is positive, this denotes that the stimulus specified by p is present to some degree, whether or not a response is undertaken.

The primary p involved for this research in ethical autonomous systems involves the discrimination of an enemy combatant as a well-defined perceptual class. The threshold τ in this case serves as a key factor in providing the necessary discrimination capabilities prior to the application of lethality in a battlefield autonomous system, and both the determination of λ for this particular p (enemy combatant) and the associated setting of τ (threshold for engagement) provide some of the greatest challenges for the effective deployment of an ethical battlefield robot from a perceptual viewpoint.

It is important to recognize that certain stimuli may be of value to a behavior-based system in ways other than provoking a motor response. In particular they may have useful side effects upon the robot, such as inducing a change in a behavioral configuration even if they do not necessarily induce a motor response. Stimuli with this property will be referred to as perceptual triggers and are specified in the same manner as previously described (p,λ). Here, however, when p is sufficiently strong as evidenced by λ, the desired behavioral side effect, a state change, is produced rather than direct motor action. This may involve the invocation of specific tactical behaviors if λ is sufficiently low (uncertain) such as reconnaissance in force*, reconnaissance by fire†, changing formation, or other aggressive maneuvers such as purposely brandishing or targeting a weapon system (without fire) or putting the robot itself at risk in the presence of the enemy (perhaps by closing the distance with the suspected enemy or by exposing it in the open leading to increased vulnerability and potential engagement by the suspected enemy). This is all in an effort to increase or decrease the certainty λ of the potential target p, as opposed to directly engaging a candidate target with unacceptably low discrimination. This should include new deliberate tactics that are unavailable to human soldiers, especially those regarding increased risk exposure to a potential, but yet uncertain, enemy.

6.1.3 The Behavioral Mapping: β

Finally, for each individual active behavior we can formally establish the mapping between the stimulus domain and response range that defines a behavioral function β where:

$$\beta(\mathbf{s}) \rightarrow \mathbf{r}$$

β can be defined arbitrarily, but it must be defined over all relevant p in S. In the case where a specific stimulus threshold, τ, must be exceeded before a response is produced for a specific $s = (p,\lambda)$, we have

$$\beta\,(p,\lambda) \rightarrow \{\text{for all } \lambda < \tau \quad \text{then } \mathbf{r} = \emptyset \qquad\qquad \text{*no response*}$$

$$\text{else } \mathbf{r} = \text{arbitrary-function}\} \quad \text{*response*}$$

where $\emptyset$ indicates that no response is required given the current stimulus $\mathbf{s}$.

Associated with a particular behavior, β, there may be a scalar gain value g (strength multiplier) further modifying the magnitude of the overall response $\mathbf{r}$ for a given $\mathbf{s}$.

$$\mathbf{r}' = g\mathbf{r}$$

These gain values are used to compose multiple behaviors by specifying their strengths relative one to another. In the extreme case, g can be used

---

* Used to probe an enemy's strength and disposition, with the option of a full engagement or falling back.

† A reconnaissance tactic, where a unit may fire on likely enemy positions to provoke a reaction. The issue of potential collateral casualties must be taken into account before this action is undertaken. "Effective reconnaissance of an urban area is often difficult to achieve, thus necessitating reconnaissance by fire" [OPFOR 98].

to turn off the response of a behavior by setting it to 0, thus reducing **r'** to 0. Shutting down lethality can be accomplished in this manner if needed (e.g., by an operator override).

The behavioral mappings, β, of stimuli onto responses fall into three general categories:

- Null—the stimulus produces no motor response.

- Discrete—the stimulus produces a response from an enumerable set of prescribed choices where all possible responses consist of a pre-defined cardinal set of actions that the robot can enact. R consists of a finite set of stereotypical responses that is enumerated for the stimulus domain S and is specified by β. It is anticipated that all behaviors that involve lethality will fall in this category.

- Continuous—the stimulus domain produces a motor response that is continuous over R's range. (Specific stimuli **s** are mapped into an infinite set of response encodings by β.)

Obviously it is easy to handle the null case as discussed earlier: For all **s**, β:**s** → ø. Although this is trivial, there are instances (perceptual triggers) where this response is wholly appropriate and useful, enabling us to define perceptual processes that are independent of direct motor action.

For the continuous response space (which is less relevant for the direct application of lethality in the approach outlined in this book, although this category may be involved in coordinating a range of other normally active behaviors not involved with the direct application of lethality by the autonomous system), we now consider the case where multiple behaviors may be concurrently active with a robotic system. Defining additional notation, let:

- **S** denote a vector of all stimuli s_i relevant for each behavior β_i at a given time t.

- **B** denote a vector of all active behaviors β_i at a given time t.

- **G** denote a vector encoding the relative strength or gain g_i of each active behavior β_i.

- **R** denote a vector of all responses r_i generated by the set of active behaviors **B**.

S defines the perceptual situation that the robot is in at any point in time, i.e., the set of all computed percepts and their associated strengths.

Other factors can further define the overall situation such as intention (plans from the deliberative component of the architecture) and internal motivations (endogenous factors such as fuel levels, affective state, etc.).

A new behavioral coordination function, C, is now defined such that the overall robotic response ρ is determined by:

$$\rho = C(G * B(S))$$

or alternatively:

$$\rho = C(G * R)$$

where

$$R = \begin{pmatrix} \mathbf{r}_1 \\ \mathbf{r}_2 \\ \vdots \\ \mathbf{r}_n \end{pmatrix}, S = \begin{pmatrix} \mathbf{s}_1 \\ \mathbf{s}_2 \\ \vdots \\ \mathbf{s}_n \end{pmatrix}, G = \begin{pmatrix} g_1 \\ g_2 \\ \vdots \\ g_n \end{pmatrix} \quad \text{and} \quad B = \begin{pmatrix} \beta_1 \\ \beta_2 \\ \vdots \\ \beta_n \end{pmatrix}$$

and where $*$ denotes the special scaling operation for multiplication of each scalar component (g_i) by the corresponding magnitude of the component vectors ($\mathbf{r}_i$) resulting in a column vector $R' = (G * R)$ of the same dimension as R composed of component vectors $\mathbf{r}'_i$.

Restating, the coordination function C, operating over all active behaviors B, modulated by the relative strengths of each behavior specified by the gain vector G, for a given vector of detected stimuli S (the perceptual situation) at time t, produces the overall robotic response ρ.

6.2 ETHICAL BEHAVIOR

In order to concretize the discussion of what is acceptable and unacceptable regarding the conduct of robots capable of lethality and consistent with the Laws of War, we describe the set of all possible behaviors capable of generating a discrete lethal response ($\mathbf{r}_{\text{lethal}}$) that an autonomous robot can undertake as the set B_{lethal}, which consists of the set of all potentially lethal behaviors it is capable of executing $\{\beta_{lethal-1}, \beta_{lethal-2}, \ldots \beta_{lethal-n}\}$ at time t. Summarizing the notation used below:

- Regarding individual behaviors: β_i denotes a particular behavioral sensorimotor mapping that for a given $\mathbf{s}_j$ (stimulus) yields a particular response $\mathbf{r}_{ij}$, where $\mathbf{s}_j \in S$ (the stimulus domain), and $\mathbf{r}_{ij} \in R$

(the response range). $\mathbf{r}_{\text{lethal-ij}}$ is an instance of a response that is intended to be lethal that a specific behavior $\beta_{lethal-i}$ is capable of generating for stimulus $\mathbf{s}_j$.

- Regarding the set of behaviors that define the controller: $\mathbf{B}_i$ denotes a particular set of m active behaviors $\{\beta_1, \beta_2, \dots \beta_m\}$ currently defining the control space of the robot, that for a given perceptual situation $\mathbf{S}_j$ defined as a vector of individual incoming stimuli $(\mathbf{s}_1, \mathbf{s}_2, \dots \mathbf{s}_n)$, produces a specific overt behavioral response ρ_{ij}, where $\rho_{ij} \in P$ (read as capital rho), and P denotes the set of all possible overt responses. $\rho_{lethal-ij}$ is a specific overt response which contains a lethal component produced by a particular controller $\mathbf{B}_{\text{lethal-i}}$ for a given situation $\mathbf{S}_j$.

P_{lethal} is the set of all overt lethal responses $\rho_{lethal-ij}$. A subset $P_{l-ethical}$ of P_{lethal} can be considered the set of *ethical* lethal behaviors if for all discernible $\mathbf{S}$, any $\mathbf{r}_{\text{lethal-ij}}$ produced by $\beta_{lethal-i}$ satisfies a given set of specific ethical constraints C, where C consists of a set of individual constraints c_k that are derived from and span the LOW and ROE over the space of all possible discernible situations ($\mathbf{S}$) potentially encountered by the autonomous agent in a given mission context. If the agent encounters any situation outside of those covered by C, it cannot be permitted to issue a lethal response—a form of Closed World Assumption* preventing the usage of lethal force in situations which are not governed by (or are outside of) the ethical constraints.

The set of ethical constraints C defines the space where lethality constitutes a valid and permissible response by the system. Thus, the application of lethality as a response must be constrained by the LOW and ROE before it can be executed by the autonomous system.

A particular c_k can be considered either

1. a negative behavioral constraint (a prohibition) that prevents or blocks a behavior $\beta_{lethal-i}$ from generating $\mathbf{r}_{\text{lethal-ij}}$ for a given perceptual situation $\mathbf{S}_j$; or

2. a positive behavioral constraint (an obligation) that requires a behavior $\beta_{lethal-i}$ to produce $\mathbf{r}_{\text{lethal-ij}}$ in a given perceptual situational context $\mathbf{S}_j$.

---

* The Closed World Assumption, from artificial intelligence, presumes that whatever is not currently known to be true is false.

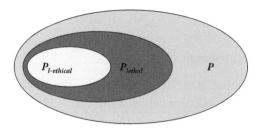

FIGURE 6.1   Behavioral action space ($P_{l\text{-}ethical} \subseteq P_{lethal} \subseteq P$).

Discussion of the specific representational choices for these constraints C is deferred until Chapter 10.

Now consider Figure 6.1, where P denotes the set of all possible overt responses ρ_{ij} (situated actions) generated by the set of all active behaviors $\mathbf{B}$ for all discernible situational contexts $\mathbf{S}$ for a given robot; P_{lethal} is a subset of P which includes all actions involving lethality, and $P_{l\text{-}ethical}$ is the subset of P_{lethal} representing all ethical lethal actions that the autonomous robot can undertake in all given situations $\mathbf{S}$. $P_{l\text{-}ethical}$ is determined by C being applied to P_{lethal}. For simplicity in notation the l-ethical and l-unethical subscripts in this context refer only to ethical *lethal* actions, and not to a more general sense of ethics.

$P_{lethal} - P_{l\text{-}ethical}$ is denoted as $P_{l\text{-}unethical}$, where $P_{l\text{-}unethical}$ is the set of all individual $\rho_{l\text{-}unethical\text{-}ij}$ unethical lethal responses for a given $\mathbf{B}_{lethal\text{-}i}$ in a given situation $\mathbf{S}_j$. These unethical responses must be avoided in the architectural design through the application of C onto P_{lethal}. $P - P_{l\text{-}unethical}$ forms the set of all permissible overt responses $P_{permissible}$, which may be lethal or not. Figure 6.2 illustrates these relationships.

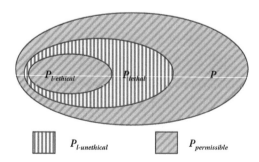

FIGURE 6.2   Unethical and permissible actions regarding the intentional use of lethality (compare to Figure 6.1).

The goal of the robotic controller design is to fulfill the following conditions:

1. *Ethical Situation Requirement:* Ensure that only situations S_j that are governed (spanned) by C can result in $\rho_{lethal\text{-}ij}$ (a lethal action for that situation). Lethality cannot result in any other situations.

2. *Ethical Response Requirement (with respect to lethality):* Ensure that only permissible actions $\rho_{ij} \in P_{permissible}$, result in the intended response in a given situation S_j (i.e., actions that either do not involve lethality or are ethical lethal actions that are constrained by C).

3. *Unethical Response Prohibition:* Ensure that any response $\rho_{l\text{-}unethical\text{-}ij} \in P_{l\text{-}unethical}$, is either:

   a. mapped onto the null action $\varnothing$ (i.e., it is inhibited from occurring if generated by the original controller);

   b. transformed into an ethically acceptable action by overwriting the generating unethical response $\rho_{l\text{-}unethical\text{-}ij}$, perhaps by a stereotypical nonlethal action or maneuver, or by simply eliminating the lethal component associated with it; or

   c. precluded from ever being generated by the controller in the first place by suitable architectural design through the direct incorporation of C into the design of **B**.

4. *Obligated Lethality Requirement:* In order for a lethal response $\rho_{lethal\text{-}ij}$ to result, there must exist at least one constraint c_k derived from the ROE that obligates the use of lethality in situation S_j.

5. Jus in Bello *Compliance:* In addition, the constraints C must be designed to result in adherence to the requirements of proportionality (incorporating the Principle of Double Intention) and the combatant/noncombatant discrimination requirements of *Jus in Bello*.

We will see that these conditions result in several alternative architectural choices for the design and implementation of an ethical lethal autonomous system (see Chapter 10 for an expanded discussion of each of these approaches):

1. *Ethical Governor:* which suppresses, restricts, or transforms any lethal behavior $\rho_{lethal\text{-}ij}$ (ethical or unethical) produced by the existing architecture so that it must fall within $P_{permissible}$ after it is initially

generated by the architecture (post facto). This means if $\rho_{l\text{-}unethical\text{-}ij}$ is the result, it must either nullify the original lethal intent or modify it so that it fits within the ethical constraints determined by C; that is, it is transformed to $\rho_{permissible\text{-}ij}$.

2. *Ethical Behavioral Control*: which constrains all active behaviors $(\beta_1, \beta_2, \ldots \beta_m)$ in **B** to yield **R** with each vector component $\mathbf{r}_i \in P_{permissible}$ set as determined by C; that is, only lethal ethical behavior is produced by each individual active behavior that involves lethality in the first place.

3. *Ethical Adaptor:* if a resulting executed lethal behavior is post facto determined to have been unethical, that is, $\rho_{ij} \in P_{l\text{-}unethical}$, then the system must use some means to adapt the system to either prevent or reduce the likelihood of such a reoccurrence and propagate it across all similar autonomous systems (group learning), for example, via an after-action reflective review or through the application of an artificial affective function (e.g., guilt, remorse, or grief).

These architectural design opportunities lie within both the reactive (ethical behavioral control approach) or deliberative (ethical governor approach) components of an autonomous system architecture. If the system verged beyond appropriate behavior, after-action review and reflective analysis can be useful during both training and in-the-field operations, resulting only in more restrictive alterations in the constraint set, perceptual thresholds, or tactics for use in future encounters. An ethical adaptor driven by affective state, also acting to restrict the lethality of the system, can fit within an existing affective component of a deliberative/reactive hybrid autonomous robot architecture such as AuRA [Arkin and Balch 97], similar to one under development in our laboratory referred to as TAME (for Traits, Attitudes, Moods, and Emotions) [Moshkina and Arkin 03, Moshkina and Arkin 05]. All three of these ethical architectural components are not mutually exclusive, and indeed can serve complementary roles.

In addition, a crucial design criterion and associated design component, the **Responsibility Advisor** (Chapter 10), should make clear and explicit as best as possible, just where *responsibility* vests, if: (1) an unethical action within the space $P_{l\text{-}unethical}$ be undertaken by the autonomous robot as a result of an operator/commander override; or (2) the robot performs an unintended unethical act due to some inadvertent or deliberate representational deficiency in the constraint set C or in the system's application outside of an appropriate mission context either by the operator or from within the architecture itself. To do so requires not only suitable training of operators and officers as well as appropriate architectural design, but also an on-line system that generates awareness to soldiers and commanders alike about the consequences of their deployment of a lethal autonomous system. The robot architecture must be capable to some degree of providing suitable explanations for its actions regarding lethality (including refusals to act).

Chapter 10 forwards architectural specifications for handling all these design alternatives above, and Chapter 12 presents some prototype implementation results driven from those specifications. One area not yet considered is that it is possible, although not certain, that certain sequences of actions when composed together may yield unethical behavior, when none of the individual actions by itself is unethical. Although the ethical adaptor can address these issues to some extent, it is still preferable to ensure that unethical behavior does not occur in the first place. Representational formalisms exist to accommodate this situation (finite state automata [Arkin 98]) but they will not be considered within this book, and it is left for future work.

CHAPTER 7

Specific Issues for Lethality

What to Represent

B ASED ON THE REQUIREMENTS of the formalisms derived in the previous chapter, we now need to determine how to ensure that only ethical lethal behavior is produced by a system that is capable of life-or-death decisions. This requires us to consider what constitutes the constraint set C as previously described, in terms of both what it represents and how to represent it in a manner that will ensure that unethical lethal behavior is not produced.

The primary question is how to operationalize information regarding the application of lethality that is available in the LOW and ROE, which prescribes the "what is permissible," and then to determine how to implement it within an intelligent robotic architecture, specifically a hybrid deliberative reactive one [Arkin 98]. Reiterating from the last chapter: the set of ethical constraints C defines the space where a lethal action constitutes a valid permissible or obligated response. The application of lethal force as a response *must* be constrained by the LOW and ROE before it can be employed by the autonomous system.

We are specifically dealing here with "bounded morality" [Allen et al. 06], a system that can adhere to its moral standards within the situations that it has been designed for, in this case specific battlefield missions and not in a more general sense. It is thus equally important to be able to represent these situations correctly to ensure that the system will indeed provide the appropriate response when it is encountered. This is further complicated by the variety of sensory and informational feeds that are available to a particular robotic implementation. Thus it is imperative that the robot be able to assess the situation correctly in order to respond ethically. A lethal response for an incorrectly identified situation is unacceptable. Clearly this is a nontrivial task. For the majority of this book, however, we will assume that effective situational assessment methods exist for certain missions, and then, given a particular battlefield situation, we examine how an appropriate response can be generated.

This requires determining at least two things: specifically *what* content we need to represent to ensure the ethical application of lethality (this chapter) and then *how* to represent it (Chapter 8). Chapters 9 and 10 address the issues regarding how to put this ethical knowledge to work from a robot architectural perspective once it has been embedded in the system. Clearly the representational choices that are made will significantly affect the overall architectural design.

7.1 WHAT IS REQUIRED

The application of lethality by a robot in one sense is no different than the generation of any particular robotic response to a given situation. In our view, however, we chose to designate the actions with potential for lethality as a class of special *privileged* responses which are governed by a set of external factors, in this case the Laws of War and other related ethical doctrine such as the Rules of Engagement.

Issues surround the underpinning ethical structure, i.e., whether a utilitarian approach is applied, which can afford a specific calculus for the determination of action (e.g., [Brandt 82, Cloos 05]), or a deontological basis that invokes a rights or duty-based approach (e.g., [Powers 05]). This will impact the selection of the representations to be chosen. Several options are described below in support of the decision regarding the representations employed in the prototype architecture described in Chapter 12.

While robotic responses in general can be encoded using either discrete or continuous approaches as mentioned in Chapter 6, for behaviors charged with the application of weapons they will be considered as a binary discrete response ($\mathbf{r}$), i.e., the weapon system is either fired with intent or not. There may be variability in a range of targeting parameters, some of which involve direct lethal intent and others that do not, such as weapon firing for warning purposes (a shot across the bow), probing by fire (testing to see if a target is armed or not), reconnaissance by fire (searching for responsive combatant targets using weaponry), wounding with nonlethal intent, or deliberate lethal intent. There may also be variations in the patterns of firing both spatially and temporally (e.g., single shot, multiple bursts with pattern, suppressing fire, etc.) but each of these will be considered as separate discrete behavioral responses r_{ij}, all of which, nonetheless, have the potential effect of resulting in lethality, even if unintended. The application of nonlethal weaponry—for example, Tasers, sting-nets, foaming agents—also can be considered as discrete responses, which although are technically designated as nonlethal responses can also potentially lead to unintentional lethality. They are sometimes referred to as less-lethal weapons, rather than nonlethal, for that reason.

7.2 LAWS OF WAR

But specifically what are we trying to represent within the architecture? Some examples can be drawn from the United States Army Field Manual FM 27-10 *The Law of Land Warfare* [U.S. Army 56], which states that the law of land warfare "is inspired by the desire to diminish the evils of war by

1. protecting both combatants and noncombatants from unnecessary suffering;

2. safeguarding certain fundamental human rights of persons who fall into the hands of the enemy, particularly prisoners of war, the wounded and sick, and civilians; and

3. facilitating the restoration of peace."

Although lofty words, they provide little guidance regarding specific constraints. Other literature can help us in that regard. Walzer recognizes two general classes of prohibitions that govern the "central principle that soldiers have an equal right to kill. ... War is distinguishable from murder and massacre only when restrictions are established on the reach of the battle" [Walzer 77]. The resulting restrictions constitute the set of constraints C we desire to represent.

The underlying principles that guide modern military conflict are [Bill 00]:

1. *Military Necessity:* One may target those things which are not prohibited by LOW and whose targeting will produce a military advantage. Military Objective: persons, places, or objects that make an effective contribution to military action.

2. *Humanity or Unnecessary Suffering:* One must minimize unnecessary suffering and incidental injury to people, and collateral damage to property.

3. *Proportionality:* The U.S. Army prescribes the test of proportionality in a clearly utilitarian perspective as "the loss of life and damage to property incidental to attacks must not be *excessive* in relation to the *concrete and direct* military advantage expected to be gained" [U.S. Army 56, para. 41, change 1].

4. *Discrimination or Distinction:* One must discriminate or distinguish between combatants and noncombatants, military objectives and protected people/protected places.

These restrictions determine *when and how* soldiers can kill and *who* they can kill. Specific U.S. Army policy assertions from Army headquarters Field Manual FM3-24 validate the concepts of lawful warfighting [U.S. Army 06]:

- Combat, including COIN [Counterinsurgency] and other irregular warfare, often obligates soldiers and marines to choose the riskier course of action to minimize harm to noncombatants.

- Even in conventional operations, soldiers and marines are not permitted to use force disproportionately or indiscriminately.

- As long as their use of force is proportional to the gain to be achieved and discriminate in distinguishing between combatants and noncombatants, soldiers and marines may take actions where they knowingly risk, but do not intend, harm to noncombatants. [Principle of Double Effect]

- Combatants must take all feasible precautions in the choice of means and methods of attack to avoid and minimize loss of civilian life, injury to civilians, and damage to civilian objects.

Drawing directly from the Laws of War, we now aggregate specific prohibitions, permissions, and obligations that the warfighter (and an ethical autonomous system) must abide by. It must be ensured that these constraints are effectively embedded within an autonomous robot potentially capable of lethal action for the specific battlefield situations that it will encounter.

Specific examples of prohibited acts include the following [U.S. Army 56]:

1. *It is especially forbidden*

    a. To declare that no quarter will be given the enemy.

    b. To kill or wound an enemy who, having laid down his arms, or having no longer means of defense, has surrendered at discretion.

    c. To employ arms, projectile, or material calculated to cause unnecessary suffering.

2. The pillage of a town or place, even when taken by assault, is prohibited.

3. The taking of hostages is prohibited (including civilians).

4. Devastation as an end in itself or as a separate measure of war is not sanctioned by the Laws of War. There must be some reasonably close connection between the destruction of property and the overcoming of the enemy's army.

Regarding lawful targeting (who can and cannot be killed and what can be targeted in warfare):

1. *Regarding combatants and military objectives*:

    a. Once war has begun, soldiers (combatants) are subject to attack at any time, unless they are wounded or captured. [Walzer 77]

    b. Targeting of enemy personnel and property is permitted unless otherwise prohibited by international law. [Bill 00]

    c. Attacks on military objectives which may cause collateral damage to civilian objects or collateral injury to civilians not taking a direct part in the hostilities are not prohibited (Principle of Double Effect). [Rawcliffe and Smith 06]

    d. Collateral/Incidental damage is not a violation of international law in itself (subject to the law of proportionality). [Bill 00]

    e. All reasonable precautions must be taken to ensure only military objectives are targeted, so damage to civilian objects (collateral damage) or death and injury to civilians (incidental injury) is avoided as much as possible. [Klein 03]

f. The presence of civilians in a military objective does not alter its status as a military objective. [Rawcliffe and Smith 06]

g. In general, any place the enemy chooses to defend makes it subject to attack. This includes forts or fortifications, places occupied by a combatant force or through which they are passing, and city or town with indivisible defensive positions. [Bill 00]

h. A belligerent attains combatant status by merely carrying his arms openly during each military engagement, and visible to an adversary while deploying for an attack. (The United States believes this is not an adequate test as it "diminishes the distinction between combatants and civilians, thus undercutting the effectiveness of humanitarian law"). [Bill 00]

i. Retreating troops, even in disarray, are legitimate targets. They could only be immunized from further attack by surrender, not retreat. [Dinstein 02]

j. Destroy, take, or damage property based *only* upon military necessity. [Bill 00]

k. A fighter must wear "a fixed distinctive sign visible at a distance" and "carry arms openly" to be eligible for the war rights of soldiers. Civilian clothes should not be used as a ruse or disguise. [Walzer 77]

l. [Dinstein 02] enumerates what he views as legitimate military objectives under the current *Jus in Bello:*

   1. Military facilities of all types including: fortifications, bases, barracks and installations, training and war-gaming facilities; depots, munitions dumps, warehouses or stockrooms for the storage of weapons, ordnance, military equipment and supplies; temporary military camps, entrenchments, staging areas, deployment positions, and embarkation points; military ports and docks, military airfields and missile launching sites; and military repair facilities.

   2. Military units and individual members of the armed forces.

   3. Weapon systems, military equipment and ordnance, armor and artillery; military vehicles; military aircraft and missiles; enemy warships; and enemy military aircraft.

4. Factories manufacturing of weapons, munitions, and military supplies.

5. Research and development facilities for new weapons and military devices.

6. Power plants serving the military.

7. Strategic transportation routes including railroads and rail yards, major motorways, navigable rivers and canals, and rail and road tunnels and bridges.

8. War operational command, control, and communication centers.

9. Intelligence-gathering centers, even if nonmilitary.

10. Enemy merchant vessels engaged directly in belligerent acts (e.g., laying mines or minesweeping); acting in support of the enemy (e.g., carrying troops, carrying military materials, or replenishing warships); engaging in reconnaissance or intelligence gathering; refusing an order to stop or resisting capture; armed where it can inflict damage on a warship; or traveling in a convoy escorted by warships.

11. Enemy civilian aircraft when flying within their own State, should enemy military aircraft approach and they do not make the nearest available landing; when flying within or near (outside of their own State) the jurisdiction of the enemy; or near land or sea military operations of the enemy (the right of prompt landing does not apply).

2. *Regarding noncombatant immunity*:

a. Civilians:

1. Individual civilians, the civilian population, and civilian objects are protected from intentional attack. [Rawcliffe and Smith 06]

2. Civilians are protected from being sole or intentional objects of a military attack, from an indiscriminate attack, or attack without warning prior to a bombardment [Bill 00] unless and for such time as he or she takes a direct part in hostilities. [Rawcliffe and Smith 06]

3. Launching attacks against civilian populations is prohibited [Klein 03]. Noncombatants cannot be attacked at any time or be the targets of military activity (noncombatant immunity). [Waltz 77]

4. There exists an obligation to take feasible measures to remove civilians from areas containing military objectives. [Bill 00]

5. It is forbidden to force civilians to give information about the enemy. [Brandt 72]

6. It is forbidden to conduct reprisals against the civilian population "on account of the acts of individuals for which they cannot be regarded as jointly and severally responsible." [Brandt 72]

7. Regarding treatment of civilians [Bill 00] (including those in conflict areas):

   a. No adverse distinction is to be made based upon race, religion, sex, and so on.

   b. No violence to life or person

   c. No degrading treatment

   d. No civilian may be the object of a reprisal

   e. No brutality

   f. No coercion (physical or moral) to obtain information

   g. No insults and exposure to public curiosity

   h. No general punishment for the acts of an individual, sub-group, or group

   i. Civilians may not be used as "human shields" in an attempt to immunize an otherwise lawful military objective. However, violations of this rule by the party to the conflict do not relieve the opponent of the obligation to do everything feasible to implement the concept of distinction (discrimination).

   j. Civilian wounded and sick must be cared for.

k. Special-needs civilians are defined as mothers of children under seven; wounded, sick, and infirm; aged; children under the age of fifteen; and expectant mothers, which results from the presumption that they can play no role in support of the war effort. Special-needs civilians are to be respected and protected by all parties to the conflict at all times. This immunity is further extended to ministers, medical personnel and transport, and civilian hospitals.

8. In order to ensure respect and protection of the civilian population and civilian objects, there exists a need to distinguish between the civilian population and combatants and between civilian objects and military objectives and accordingly direct operations only against military objectives [UN 48]. Specifically:

   a. Civilians may never be the object of attack.

   b. Attacks intended to terrorize the civilian population are prohibited.

   c. Indiscriminate attacks are prohibited. Indiscriminate is defined as:

      (1) Attacks not directed at a specific military objective, or employing a method or means of combat that cannot be so directed.

      (2) Attacks that employ a method or means of combat the effects of which cannot be controlled.

      (3) Attacks treating dispersed military objectives, located in a concentration of civilians, as one objective.

      (4) Attacks that may be expected to cause collateral damage excessive in relation to the concrete and direct military advantage to be gained (proportionality).

b. Prisoners of War (POWs) [Bill 00]:

   1. Surrender may be made by any means that communicates the intent to give up (there is no clear rule).

2. Onus is on the person or force surrendering to communicate their intent to surrender.

3. Captor must not attack, and must protect those who surrender (no reprisals).

4. A commander may not put his prisoners to death because their presence retards his movements or diminishes his power of resistance by necessitating a large guard ... or it appears that they will regain their liberty through the impending success of their forces. It is likewise unlawful for a commander to kill his prisoners on the grounds of self-preservation [U.S. Army 56].

c. Medical personnel, relief societies, religious personnel, journalists, and people engaged in the protection of cultural property shall not be attacked [Bill 00].

d. Passing sentences and carrying out [summary] executions without previous judgment of a regularly constituted court is prohibited at any time and in any place whatsoever [U.S. Army 04].

3. *Regarding nonmilitary objectives*:

a. A presumption of civilian property attaches to objects traditionally associated with civilian use (dwellings, schools, etc.) as contrasted with military objectives, i.e., they are presumed not subject to attack [Rawcliffe and Smith 06].

b. Undefended places are not subject to attack. This requires that all combatants and mobile military equipment be removed, no hostile use of fixed military installations, no acts of hostility, and no activities in support of military operations, excluding medical treatment and enemy police forces [Bill 00].

c. The environment cannot be the object of reprisals. Care must be taken to prevent long-term, widespread, and severe damage [Bill 00].

d. Cultural property is prohibited from being attacked, including buildings dedicated to religion, art, science, charitable purposes, and historic monuments. The enemy has a duty to mark them clearly with visible and distinctive signs. Misuse will make them subject to attack [Bill 00].

e. Works and installations containing dangerous forces should be considered to be immune from attack. This includes nuclear power plants, dams, dikes, etc. (This is not U.S. law, however, which believes the standard proportionality test should apply.)

f. It is prohibited to attack, destroy, remove, or render useless objects indispensable for survival of the civilian population, such as foodstuffs, crops, livestock, water installations, and irrigation works [Rawcliffe and Smith 06] unless these objects are used solely to support the enemy military [Bill 00].

g. There exists an obligation to take feasible precautions in order to minimize harm to nonmilitary objectives [Bill 00].

4. *Regarding use of arms*:

a. Cannot use lawful arms in a manner that causes unnecessary suffering or used with the intent to cause civilian suffering (humanity and proportionality). The test essentially is whether the suffering occasioned by the use of the weapon is needless, superfluous, or grossly disproportionate to the advantage gained by its use [Bill 00].

b. Indiscriminate attacks are prohibited. This includes attacks not directed against a military objective and a method of attack that cannot be effectively directed or limited against an enemy objective [Bill 00].

5. *Regarding war crime violations*:

a. All violations of the LOW should be promptly reported to a superior [U.S. Army 06, Rawcliffe and Smith 06].

b. Members of the armed forces are bound to obey only lawful orders [U.S. Army 04].

c. Soldiers must also attempt to prevent LOW violations by other U.S. soldiers [Rawcliffe and Smith 06].

d. (Troop Information) In the rare case when an order seems unlawful, don't carry it out right away but don't ignore it either; instead seek clarification of that order [Rawcliffe and Smith 06].

6. *Regarding definition of civilians*:

An important issue regarding discrimination is how to determine who is defined as a civilian to afford them due protection from war [Bill 00]. As late as 1949, the fourth Geneva Convention, which was primarily concerned with the protection of civilians, provided no such definition and relied on common sense, which may be hard to operationalize in modern warfare. The 1977 Protocol I commentary acknowledged that a clear definition is essential but used an awkward negative definition: anyone who does not qualify for prisoner of war (POW) status (i.e., does not have combatant status) is considered a civilian. This is clarified further by the following [U.S. Army 62]:

> The immunity afforded individual civilians is subject to an overriding condition, namely, on their abstaining from all hostile acts. Hostile acts should be understood to be acts which by their nature and purpose are intended to cause actual harm to the personnel and equipment of the armed forces. *Thus a civilian who takes part in armed combat, either individually or as part of a group, thereby becomes a legitimate target.*

Expanding further: "This 'actual harm' standard is consistent with contemporary U.S. practice, as reflected in ROE-based 'harmful act/harmful intent' test for justifying use of deadly force against civilians during military operations" [Bill 00].

Those civilians who participate only in a general sense in the war effort (nonhostile support, manufacturing, etc.) are excluded from attack [Bill 00, U.S. Army 56]: "According to Article 51(3) [Geneva Convention Protocol I of 1977], civilians shall enjoy the protection of this section (providing general protection against dangers arising from military operations) *unless and for such time as they take a direct part in hostilities,*" where "direct part" means acts of war which by their nature or purpose are likely to cause actual harm to the personnel and equipment of the enemy armed forces. Although the United States decided not to ratify Protocol I, there was no indication that this definition of "civilian" was objectionable.

Appendix A contains the specific language used in the U.S. military manual that describes these Laws of War in more detail. We will restrict ourselves in this research to those laws that are specifically concerned with the application of lethality in direct combat, but it is clear that a more expansive treatment of ethical behavior of autonomous systems should also be considered in the future.

7.3   RULES OF ENGAGEMENT

In order to provide more mission and context-sensitive guidance regarding the use of force in the battlefield, Rules of Engagement (ROE), Rules for the Use of Force (RUF), and General Orders are provided in advance of an engagement [U.S. Army 04]. "United States soldiers and marines face hard choices about what, when, and where they can shoot" [Martins 94]. ROE are concerned with when and where military force may be used and against whom and how it should be used. ROE are drafted in conjunction with judge advocates with the intent that they are legally and tactically sound, versatile, understandable, and easily executed [Berger et al. 04]. ROE are defined as follows:

> Directives issued by competent military authority that delineate the circumstances and limitations under which United States forces will initiate and/or continue combat engagement with other forces encountered. [DOD 02]

Two high-level functions of the ROE are to provide guidance from the President and Secretary of Defense to *deployed units* on the use of force and to act as a control mechanism for the transition from peacetime to war [Berger et al. 04]. Ten specific ROE function types include (from [Martins 94]):

1. **Hostility Criteria:** Provide those making decisions whether to fire with a set of objective factors to assist in determining whether a potential assailant exhibits hostile intent and thus clarify whether shots can be fired before receiving fire.

2. **Scale of Force or Challenge Procedure:** Specify a graduated show of force that ground troops must use in ambiguous situations before resorting to deadly force. Include such measures as giving a verbal warning, using a riot stick, perhaps firing a warning shot, or firing a shot intended to wound. This may place limits on the pursuit of an attacker.

3. **Protection of Property and Foreign Nationals:** Detail what and who may be defended with force, aside from the lives of U.S. soldiers and citizens. May include measures to be taken to prevent crimes in progress or the fleeing of criminals. May place limits on pursuit of an attacker.

4. **Weapon Control Status or Alert Conditions:** Announce, for air defense assets, a posture for resolving doubts over whether to engage. Announce, for units observing alert conditions, a series of measures designed to adjust unit readiness for attack to the level of the perceived threat. The measures may include some or all of the other functional types of rules.

5. **Arming Orders:** Dictate which soldiers in the force are armed and which have live ammunition. Specify which precise orders given by whom will permit the loading and charging of firearms.

6. **Approval to Use Weapons Systems:** Designates what level commander must approve use of particular weapons systems. Perhaps prohibits use of a weapon entirely.

7. **Eyes on Target:** Require that the object of fire be observed by one or more human or electronic means.

8. **Territorial or Geographic Constraints:** Create geographic zones or areas into which forces may not fire. May designate a territorial, perhaps political boundary, beyond which forces may neither fire nor enter except perhaps in hot pursuit of an attacking force. Include tactical control measures that coordinate fire and maneuver by means of graphic illustrations on operations map overlays, such as coordinated fire lines, axes of advance, and direction of attack.

9. **Restrictions on Manpower:** Prescribe numbers and types of soldiers to be committed to a theatre or area of operations. Perhaps prohibit use of United States manpower in politically or diplomatically sensitive personnel assignments requiring allied manning.

10. **Restrictions on Point Targets and Means of Warfare:** Prohibit targeting of certain individuals or facilities. May restate basic rules of the Laws of War for situations in which a hostile force is identified and prolonged armed conflict ensues.

7.3.1 Standing Rules of Engagement

There are both Standing Rules of Engagement (SROE), which are global in context, applying to all missions, and ROE, which are customized for the needs of the mission. All are intended to strictly adhere to the

LOW. The following definitions are used for the SROE (from [Berger et al. 04]):

1. **Hostile Act:** An attack or other use of force against the United States, U.S. forces, and, in certain circumstances, U.S. nationals, their property, U.S. commercial assets, and/or other designated non-U.S. forces, foreign nationals and their property. It is also force used directly to preclude or impede the mission and/or duties of U.S. forces, including the recovery of U.S. personnel and vital U.S. government property. A hostile act triggers the right to use *proportional force* in self-defense to deter, neutralize, or destroy the threat.

2. **Hostile Intent:** The threat of imminent use of force against the United States, U.S. forces, or other designated persons and property. It is also the threat of force used directly to preclude or impede the mission and/or duties of U.S. forces, including the recovery of U.S. personnel and vital U.S. government property. When hostile intent is present, the right exists to use *proportional force* in self-defense to deter, neutralize, or destroy the threat.

3. **Hostile Force:** Any civilian, paramilitary, or military force or terrorist(s), with or without national designation, that has committed a hostile act, exhibited hostile intent, or has been declared hostile by appropriate U.S. authority.

4. **Declaring Forces Hostile:** Once a force is declared to be "hostile," U.S. units may engage it without observing a hostile act or demonstration of hostile intent; that is, the basis for engagement shifts from conduct to status. The authority to declare a force hostile is limited.

5. **Necessity:** when a hostile act occurs or when a force or terrorists exhibits hostile intent.

6. **Proportionality:** Force used to counter a hostile act or demonstrated hostile intent must be reasonable in intensity, duration, and magnitude to the perceived or demonstrated threat based on all facts known to the commander at the time.

SROE focus on self-defense, i.e., "a commander may use the weapon of choice, unless specifically prohibited, tempered only by proportionality and necessity" [Womack 96]. Self-defense is considered in the context of the nation, collective (non-U.S. entities), unit, and individual. The SROE

Means of Self-Defense. All necessary means available and all appropriate actions may be used in self-defense. The following guidelines apply for individual, unit, national, or collective self-defense:

1. Attempt to De-escalate the Situation. When time and circumstances permit, the hostile force should be warned and given the opportunity to withdraw, or cease threatening actions.

2. Use Proportional Force—Which May Include Nonlethal Weapons—to Control the Situation. When the use of force in self-defense is necessary, the nature, duration, and scope of the engagement should not exceed that which is required to decisively counter the hostile act or demonstrated hostile intent and to ensure the continued protection of U.S. forces or other protected personnel or property.

3. Attack to Disable or Destroy. An attack to disable or destroy a hostile force is authorized when such action is the only prudent means by which a hostile act or demonstration of hostile intent can be prevented or terminated. When such conditions exist, engagement is authorized only while the hostile force continues to commit hostile acts or exhibit hostile intent.

Pursuit of Hostile Forces. Self-defense includes the authority to pursue and engage hostile forces that continue to commit hostile acts or exhibit hostile intent.

FIGURE 7.1   SROE permissible actions for self-defense [Berger et al. 04].

permissible actions for self-defense are stated clearly [Berger el al. 04], and the relevant ones are reproduced in Figure 7.1.

The Standing Rules of Engagement (SROE) provide for implementation and guidance on the right and obligation of self-defense and the application of force for mission accomplishment. "The SROE do not limit a commander's inherent authority and obligation to use all necessary means available to take all appropriate action in self-defense of the commander's unit and other U.S. forces in the vicinity" [AFJAGS 06]. Hot pursuit in self-defense is permissible, where an enemy force can be pursued and engaged that has either committed a hostile act or demonstrated hostile intent and remains an imminent threat [SROE 94].

7.3.2 Rules of Engagement (Non-SROE)

Supplemental ROE measures are applicable beyond the SROE.

The current SROE now recognizes a fundamental difference between the supplemental measures. Those measures that are reserved to the President or Secretary of Defense or Combatant Commander are generally **restrictive**; that is, either the President or Secretary of Defense or Combatant Commander must specifically permit the particular operation, tactic, or weapon before a field commander may utilize them. Contrast this with the remainder of the supplemental measures, those delegated to subordinate commanders. These measures are all **permissive** in nature, *allowing a commander to use any weapon or tactic available and to employ reasonable force to accomplish his mission*, without having to get permission first. Inclusion within the subordinate commanders' supplemental list does not suggest that a commander needs to seek authority to use any of the listed items. *SUPPLEMENTAL ROE RELATE TO MISSION ACCOMPLISHMENT, NOT TO SELF-DEFENSE, AND NEVER LIMIT A COMMANDER'S INHERENT RIGHT AND OBLIGATION OF SELF DEFENSE.* [Berger et al. 04]

We can use this notion of restrictive and permissive measures (instead using the stronger version of *obligated* instead of *permissive*) to advantage in the design of representations and architectural methods to be developed for use in lethal autonomous systems as described in subsequent chapters.

Every operations plan normally provides ROE as part of the mission. They are different for each operation, area, and can change as the situation changes. There are classified ROE documents that provide general guidance for specific air, land, and sea mission operations. There also exist Theater-Specific ROE for use by Combatant Commanders in the Area of Responsibility that address strategic and political sensitivities.

ROE are tailored to local circumstances, and the nature and history of the threat and must be dynamic and changing as the mission evolves [AFJAGS 06]. They do not limit a soldier's right to self-defense. "The ROE are frequently more restrictive than the Law of War, because they take into consideration the specifics of the operating environment, such as culture, religious sensitivities, geography, historical monuments, and so forth" [USM 07]. They are based on the LOW, U.S. foreign policy, U.S. domestic law and concerns, and operational matters. Military necessity for self-defense requires that a hostile act occur or the exhibition of hostile intent be present before armed force is permitted. Proportionality states that the force used must have intensity, duration, and magnitude that is reasonable based upon the information available at the time. No more force than is necessary is to be employed.

Sagan observes two types of ROE failures that can occur in their writing [Sagan 91]. An ROE *Weakness* error occurs when the rules are excessively tight, so a commander cannot effectively complete his mission or defeat an attack. An ROE *Escalatory* error occurs if the rules are excessively loose to the point where force may be used that is deemed undesirable by political authorities (it should never be so written that it is illegal). Great care should be taken in the writing of the ROE for lethal autonomous systems to avoid both failure types, but especially escalatory ones.

ROE can be in the form of a *command by negation* where a soldier can act on his own in this manner unless explicitly forbidden, or a positive command that can be taken only if explicitly ordered by a superior. ROE are deliberated upon well in advance of an engagement, may cover several scenarios, and have different rules for each [Wikipedia 07b].

Some of the basics of the ROE include (forming the RAMP acronym) [U.S. Army 04]:

- *Return Fire with Aimed Fire.* Return force with force. You always have the right to repel hostile acts with necessary force.

- *Anticipate* Attack. Use force if, but only if, you see clear indicators of hostile intent.

- *Measure* the amount of force that you use, if time and circumstances permit. Use only the amount of force necessary to protect lives and accomplish the mission.

- *Protect* with deadly force only human life, and property designated by your commander. Stop short of deadly force when protecting other property.

Example ROE Cards appear in Figure 7.2 to Figure 7.4 (from [Berger et al. 04]). These cards are intended to only serve as a reminder for the troops of the most salient features of the more detailed ROE applicable in their theater of operation. A more comprehensive list of ROE cards and vignettes is available in [CLAMO 00].

7.3.3 Rules for the Use of Force

The Rules for the Use of Force (RUF) provides rules for performing security duty *within the United States.* They are escalating rules used as a last resort, and provide for the use of lethal force in the following conditions [U.S. Army 04]:

- For immediate threat of death or serious bodily injury to self or others

- For defense of persons under protection

- To prevent theft, damage, or destruction of firearms, ammunition, explosives, or property designated vital to national security

DESERT STORM

RULES OF ENGAGEMENT

**ALL ENEMY MILITARY PERSONNEL AND VEHICLES
TRANSPORTING THE ENEMY
OR THEIR SUPPLIES MAY BE ENGAGED SUBJECT
TO THE FOLLOWING RESTRICTIONS:**

A. Do not engage anyone who has surrendered, is out of battle due to sickness or wounds, is shipwrecked, or is an aircrew member descending by parachute from a disabled aircraft.

B. Avoid harming civilians unless necessary to save U.S. lives. Do not fire into civilian populated areas or buildings that are not defended or being used for military purposes.

C. Hospitals, churches, shrines, schools, museums, national monuments, and other historical or cultural sites will not be engaged except in self-defense.

D. Hospitals will be given special protection. Do not engage hospitals unless the enemy uses the hospital to commit acts harmful to U.S. forces, and then only after giving a warning and allowing a reasonable time to expire before engaging, if the tactical situation permits.

E. Booby traps may be used to protect friendly positions or to impede the progress of enemy forces. They may not be used on civilian personal property. They will be recovered and destroyed when the military necessity for their use no longer exists.

F. Looting and the taking of war trophies are prohibited.

G. Avoid harming civilian property unless necessary to save U.S. lives. Do not attack traditional civilian objects, such as houses, unless they are being used by the enemy for military purposes and neutralization assists in mission accomplishment.

H. Treat all civilians and their property with respect and dignity. Before using privately owned property, check to see if publicly owned property can substitute. No requisitioning of civilian property, including vehicles, without permission of a company level commander and without giving a receipt. If an ordering officer can contract the property, then do not requisition it.

I. Treat all prisoners humanely and with respect and dignity.

J. ROE Annex to the OPLAN provides more detail. Conflicts between this card and the OPLAN should be resolved in favor of the OPLAN.

REMEMBER

1. FIGHT ONLY COMBATANTS.

2. ATTACK ONLY MILITARY TARGETS.

3. SPARE CIVILIAN PERSONS AND OBJECTS.

4. RESTRICT DESTRUCTION TO WHAT YOUR MISSION REQUIRES.

FIGURE 7.2   An example ROE card for *armed conflict* (war).

ROE Used for Operation United Shield

Nothing in these Rules of Engagement limits your right to take appropriate action to defend yourself and your unit.

a. You have the right to use deadly force in response to a hostile act or when there is a clear indication of hostile intent.

b. Hostile fire may be returned effectively and promptly to stop a hostile act.

c. When U.S. forces are attacked by unarmed hostile elements, mobs, and/or rioters, U.S. forces should use the minimum force necessary under the circumstances and proportional to the threat.

d. Inside designated security zones, once a hostile act or hostile intent is demonstrated, you have the right to use minimum force to prevent armed individuals/crew-served weapons from endangering U.S./UNOSOM II forces. This includes deadly force.

e. Detention of civilians is authorized for security reasons or in self-defense.

Remember:

1. The United States is not at war.

2. Treat all persons with dignity and respect.

3. Use minimum force to carry out mission.

4. Always be prepared to act in self-defense.

FIGURE 7.3 An ROE card for a marine *operation other than war* (OOTW) in an urban environment, in this case for the evacuation of U.N. peacekeeping troops in Somalia in 1995.

The escalation should adhere to the following pattern for security [U.N. Army 04]:

1. SHOUT—verbal warning to halt.

2. SHOVE—nonlethal physical force.

3. SHOW—intent to use weapon.

4. SHOOT—deliberately aimed shots until threat no longer exists.

   • Warning shots are not permitted.

KFOR RULES OF ENGAGEMENT FOR USE IN KOSOVO

MISSION

Your mission is to assist in the implementation of and to help ensure compliance with a Military Technical Agreement (MTA) in Kosovo.

SELF-DEFENSE

a. You have the right to use necessary and proportional force in self-defense.

b. Use only the minimum force necessary to defend yourself.

GENERAL RULES

a. Use the minimum force necessary to accomplish your mission.

b. Hostile forces/belligerents who want to surrender will not be harmed. Disarm them and turn them over to your superiors.

c. Treat everyone, including civilians and detained hostile forces/belligerents, humanely.

d. Collect and care for the wounded, whether friend or foe.

e. Respect private property. Do not steal. Do not take "war trophies."

f. Prevent and report all suspected violations of the Law of Armed Conflict to superiors.

CHALLENGING AND WARNING SHOTS

a. If the situation permits, issue a challenge:

  • In **English**: "NATO! Stop or I will fire!"

  • Or in **Serbo-Croat**: "NATO! Stani ili pucam!"

  • (Pronounced as: "NATO! Stani ili putsam!")

  • Or in **Albanian:** "NATO! Ndal ose une do te qelloj!"

  • (Pronounced as: "NATO! N'dal ose une do te chilloy!")

b. If the person fails to halt, you may be authorized by the on-scene commander or by standing orders to fire a warning shot.

FIGURE 7.4 An ROE card example for a *peacekeeping* mission in Kosovo.

OPENING FIRE

a. You may open fire only if you, friendly forces or persons or property under your protection are threatened with deadly force. This means:

  (1) You may open fire against an individual who fires or aims his weapon at, or otherwise demonstrates an intent to imminently attack, you, friendly forces, or Persons with Designated Special Status (PDSS) or property with designated special status under your protection.

  (2) You may open fire against an individual who plants, throws, or prepares to throw, an explosive or incendiary device at, or otherwise demonstrates an intent to imminently attack you, friendly forces, PDSS or property with designated special status under your protection.

  (3) You may open fire against an individual deliberately driving a vehicle at you, friendly forces, or PDSS or property with designated special status.

b. You may also fire against an individual who attempts to take possession of friendly force weapons, ammunition, or property with designated special status, and there is no way of avoiding this.

c. You may use minimum force, including opening fire, against an individual who unlawfully commits or is about to commit an act which endangers life, in circumstances where there is no other way to prevent the act.

MINIMUM FORCE

a. If you have to open fire, you must:

  • Fire only aimed shots; and

  • Fire no more rounds than necessary; and

  • Take all reasonable efforts not to unnecessarily destroy property; and

  • Stop firing as soon as the situation permits.

b. You may not intentionally attack civilians or property that is exclusively civilian or religious in character, except if the property is being used for military purposes or engagement is authorized by the commander.

FIGURE 7.4 *(Continued)*

7.3.4 ROE for Peace Enforcement Missions

Peace enforcement missions may have varying degrees of expanded ROE and may allow for the use of force to accomplish the mission (i.e., the use of force beyond that of self-defense.) For Chapter VI United Nations Peacekeeping operations, the use of deadly force is justified only under conditions of extreme necessity (typically self-defense) and as a last resort when all lesser means have failed to curtail the use of violence by the parties involved [Rawcliffe and Smith 06].

CHAPTER 8

Representational Choices

How to Represent Ethics in a Lethal Robot

A LTHOUGH "THERE IS EVERY reason to believe that ethically sensitive machines can be created" [Anderson et al. 04], there is also widespread acknowledgment, however, regarding the difficulty associated with machine ethics [Moor 06, McLaren 06]. There are several specific problems to point out [McLaren 05]:

1. The ethical laws, codes, or principles (i.e., rules) are almost always provided in a highly conceptual, abstract level.

2. Their conditions, premises, or clauses are not precise, are subject to interpretation, and may have different meanings in different contexts.

3. The actions or conclusions in the rules are often abstract as well, so even if the rule is known to apply, the ethically appropriate action may be difficult to execute due to its vagueness.

4. These abstract rules often conflict with each other in specific situations. If more than one rule applies, it is not often clear how to resolve the conflict.

First-order predicate logic and other standard logics based on deductive reasoning are not usually applicable in the general case as they operate from inference and deduction, not the notion of obligation. In addition, controversy exists about the correct ethical framework to use in the first place given the multiplicity of philosophies that exist: Utilitarian, Kantian, Social Contract, Virtue Ethics, Cultural Relativism, and so on.

It is my belief that battlefield ethics are more clear-cut and precise than everyday or professional ethics, ameliorating these difficulties somewhat, but not removing them. For this research effort, a commitment to a framework that is consistent with the LOW and ROE must be maintained, strictly adhering to the rights of noncombatants regarding discrimination (deontological), while considering similar principles for the assessment of proportionality based on military necessity and double intention (utilitarian). As stated earlier, it is no mean feat to be able to perform situational awareness in a manner to adequately support combatant/noncombatant discrimination. By starting, however, from a "first, do no harm" strategy, battlefield ethics may be feasible to implement, i.e., do not engage a target until obligated to do so consistent with the current situation, and there exists no conflict with the LOW and ROE. If no obligations are present or any potential violations of discrimination and proportionality exist, the system simply cannot fire. By conducting itself in this manner, it is believed that the ethically appropriate use of constrained lethal force can be achieved by an autonomous system.

This ethical autonomy architecture capable of lethal action will use an action-based approach, where ethical theory (as encoded in the LOW and ROE) informs the agent what actions to undertake. Action-based methods have the following attributes [Anderson et al. 06]:

1. Consistency—the avoidance of contradictions in the informing theory

2. Completeness—how to act in any ethical dilemma

3. Practicality—it should be feasible to execute

4. Agreement with expert ethicist intuition

None of these appear out of reach for battlefield applications. The LOW and ROE are designed to be consistent. They should prescribe how to act in each case, and when coupled with a "first, do no harm" as opposed to a "shoot first, ask questions later" strategy (ideally attacking surgically when so required, to further expand upon the medical metaphor of do no harm), the system should act conservatively in the presence of uncertainty (doubt) and not fire in the presence of a dilemma. Bounded morality ensures practicality, as it limits the scope of actions available and the situations in which it is permitted to act with lethal force. Agreement with an expert should be feasible assuming they subscribe to the existing International Protocols governing warfare. This expert agreement is also important for the attribution of responsibility and can play a role in the design of the responsibility advisor using methods such as case-based reasoning.

This chapter reviews the space of potential choices for representing the necessary constraints on lethal action derived from the LOW and ROE for use within the architecture. An overview of various methods already in use in the nascent field of machine ethics is provided, and they are assessed for utility within the lethal ethical autonomous robot architecture, leading to design commitments for the system as outlined in Chapters 10 and 12.

8.1 UNDERPINNINGS

Turilli describes a method by which ethical principles can be transformed into an ethically consistent protocol—that is, a process that produces the same ethical results independent of the actor (computational agents or human individuals) [Turilli 07]. In our case, his original process must be transformed somewhat (Figure 8.1), but it can still contribute to the correct development of the set of constraints C that are required for the ethical processing within our architecture.

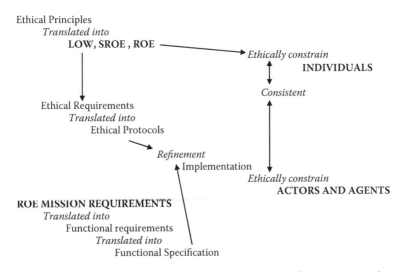

FIGURE 8.1 A process for deriving the constraint set C from LOW and ROE. (Adapted from [Turilli 07].)

Ethical judgments on action can be seen to take three primary forms: obligatory (the agent is required to conduct the action based on moral grounds), permissible (the action is morally acceptable but not required), and forbidden (the action is morally unacceptable). Hauser outlines the logical relationship between these action classes [Hauser 06]:

1. If an action is permissible, then it is potentially obligatory but not forbidden.

2. If an action is obligatory, it is permissible and not forbidden.

3. If an action if forbidden, it is neither permissible nor obligatory.

Lethal actions for autonomous systems can potentially fall into any of these classes. Certainly the agent should never conduct a forbidden lethal action, and although an action may be permissible, it should also be deemed obligatory in the context of the mission (military necessity) to determine whether it should be undertaken. So in this sense, I argue that any lethal action undertaken by an unmanned system must be obligatory and not solely permissible, where the mission ROE define the situation-specific lethal obligations of the agent and the LOW define absolutely forbidden lethal actions. Although it is conceivable that permissibility alone for the use of lethality is adequate, we will require the provision of additional mission constraints explicitly informing the system regarding target requirements (e.g., as part of the ROE) to define exactly what constitutes an acceptable action in a given mission context. This will also assist with the assignment of responsibility for the use of lethality (Chapter 10). Summarizing:

- Laws of War and related Rules of Engagement determine what are absolutely forbidden lethal actions.

- Rules of Engagement mission requirements determine what is obligatory lethal action, i.e., where and when the agent must exercise lethal force. Permissibility alone is inadequate.

Let us now relate this back to the set theoretic description depicted earlier in Figures 6.1 and 6.2.

- Obligatory lethal actions represent $P_{l\text{-}ethical}$ under these restrictions, i.e., the set of ethical lethal actions.

- Forbidden lethal actions are defined as $P_{l\text{-}unethical} = P_{lethal} - P_{l\text{-}ethical}$, which defines the set of unethical lethal actions.

- For a lethal response $\rho_{lethal\text{-}ij}$ to be an ethical lethal action $\rho_{l\text{-}ethical\text{-}ij}$ for situation **i**, it must not be forbidden by constraints derived from the LOW, and it must be obligated by constraints derived from the ROE.

It is now our task to:

1. determine how to represent the LOW as a suitable set of forbidding constraints $C_{Forbidden}$ on P_{lethal} such that any action $\rho_{lethal\text{-}ij}$ produced by the autonomous system is not an element of $P_{l\text{-}unethical}$; and

2. determine how to represent the ROE as a suitable set of obligating constraints $C_{Obligate}$ on P_{lethal} such that any action $\rho_{lethal\text{-}ij}$ produced by the autonomous system is an element of $P_{l\text{-}ethical}$.

Item 1 permits the generation of only nonlethal or ethical lethal (permissible) actions by the autonomous system and forbids the production of unethical lethal action. Item 2 requires that any lethal action must be obligated by the ROE to be ethical. This aspect of obligation will also assist in the assignment of responsibility, which will be discussed further in Chapter 10.

Regarding the representation for the ethical constraints C, where $C = C_{Forbidden} \cup C_{Obligate}$, there are at least two further requirements:

1. Adequate expressiveness for a computable representation of the ethical doctrine itself.

2. A mechanism by which the representation of the ethical doctrine can be transformed into a form usable within a robotic controller to suitably constrain its actions.

Recalling from Chapter 6, a particular c_k can be considered either:

1. a negative behavioral constraint (a prohibition) that prevents or blocks a behavior $\beta_{lethal\text{-}i}$ from generating $r_{lethal\text{-}ij}$ for a given perceptual situation S_j; or

2. a positive behavioral constraint (an obligation) which requires a behavior $\beta_{lethal\text{-}i}$ to produce $r_{l\text{-}ethical\text{-}ij}$ in a given perceptual situational context S_j.

It is desirable to have a representation that supports growth of the architecture, where constraints can be added incrementally. This means that we can initially represent a small set of forbidden and obligated constraints and test the overall system without the necessity of a fully complete set of representational constraints that captures the entire space of the LOW and ROE. An underlying assumption will be made that any use of lethality by the autonomous unmanned system is prohibited by default, unless an obligating constraint requires it and it is not in violation of any and all forbidding constraints. This will enable us to incrementally enumerate obligating constraints and be able to assess discrimination capabilities and proportionality evaluation in a step-by-step process. Keep in mind that this project represents only the most preliminary steps toward the design of a fieldable ethical system, and that substantial additional basic and applied research must be conducted before any such system can even be considered for use in a real-world battlefield scenario. But baby steps are better than no steps toward enforcing ethical behavior in autonomous system warfare assuming, as we did in Chapter 1, its inevitable introduction.

We now review some of the existing approaches that have been applied in the general area of machine ethics and consider their applicability in light of the requirements for representational choices for robotic systems employing lethality consistent with battlefield ethics. It has been observed that there are two major approaches to moral reasoning in the machine ethics community. The first uses moral principles such as exceptionless standards or contributory principles, and is referred to as *generalism*. Exceptionless standards appear to have utility in our context as they [Guarini 06]

- Specify sufficient conditions for what makes a state of affairs (including actions) good, bad, right, wrong, permissible, impermissible, and so on.

- Explain or inform why the principle applies when it does.

- Serve as premises in moral deliberations.

The second approach to moral reasoning is case-based and is referred to as particularism. These different approaches will find compatibility within different places in the autonomous agent architecture capable of lethal action described later: generalism for the run-time reasoning from principles derived from the LOW and ROE, and particularism for the pre-mission role of advising the operator and commanders regarding their responsibility for the use of an agent capable of lethality under a given set of conditions, i.e., a particular case.

8.2 GENERALISM—REASONING FROM MORAL PRINCIPLES

Most ethical theories, whether they are deontological or Kantian, utilitarian, cultural relativism, and so on, assert that an agent should act in a manner that is derived from moral principles. In this section we examine the methods by which these principles, in our case constraints on robotic behavior derived from the LOW and ROE, can be represented effectively within a computational agent. We first focus on deontic logic as a primary source for implementation, then consider and dismiss utilitarian models, and bypass virtue ethics entirely (e.g., [Coleman 01]) as it does not lend itself well by definition to a model based on a strict ethical code.

8.2.1 Deontic Logic

Modal logics, rather than standard formal logics, provide a framework for distinguishing between what is permitted and what is required [Moor 06]. For ethical reasoning this clearly has pragmatic importance, and is used by a number of research groups worldwide in support of computational ethics. Moor observes that deontic logic (for obligations and permissions), epistemic logic (for beliefs and knowledge), and action logic (for actions) all can have a role "that could describe ethical situations with sufficient precision to make ethical judgments by a machine." A description of the operation of deontic logic is well beyond the scope of this book; the reader is referred to [Horty 01] for a detailed exposition.

A research group at Rensselaer Polytechnic Institute is quite optimistic about the use of deontic logic as a basis for producing ethical behavior in intelligent robots for three reasons [Bringsjord et al. 06]:

1. Logic has been used for millennia by ethicists.

2. Logic and artificial intelligence have been very successful partners and computer science arose from logic.

3. The use of mechanized formal proofs with their ability to explain how a conclusion was arrived at is central for establishing trust.

They argue for the use of standard deontic logics for building ethical robots, to provide proofs that (1) *a robot take only permissible actions* and (2) *obligatory actions are indeed performed*, subject to ties and conflicts among available actions, using the Athena interactive theorem proving framework for their work [Arkoudas et al. 05]. This approach seems useful for more general ethical behavior with complex nuances but has yet to be considered in a real-time application. However, in our case, the ROE and LOW have already been distilled from ethical first principles by people and may not require the complex reasoning methods used in their work. The robotic agent must only abide by these principles, not derive them.

They further insist that for a robot to be certifiably ethical, every meaningful action must access a proof that the action is at least permissible. This line of reasoning is quite consistent with the formalisms that were developed in Chapter 6. Outstanding questions remain regarding the applicability of this method for the real-time requirements of a computationally constrained agent. They argue this is feasible nonetheless by using methods that encode the assertions back to first-order logic and claim that even when dealing with formulas as numerous as 4 million they can reason over these sets "sufficiently fast." Coupled with continuing advances in computational speed along the lines of Moore's Law their claims appear plausible.

The ethical code C a robot uses is not bound to any particular ethical theory. It can be deontological, utilitarian or whatever, according to [Bringsjord et al. 06]. The concepts of prohibition, permissibility, and obligation are central to deontic logics. The formalization of C in a particular computational logic L is represented as Φ_C^L. This basically reduces the problem for our ethical governor to the need to derive from the LOW and ROE a suitable $\Phi^L_{LOW \cup ROE}$, with a leading candidate for L being a form of deontic logic. Accompanying this ethical formalization is an ethics-free ontology which represents the core concepts that C presupposes (structures for time, events, actions, agents, etc.). A signature is developed that encodes the ontological concepts with special predicate letters and functions. Clearly this is an action item for our research, should deontic logic be employed in the use of lethality for ethical systems. There is much more involved (as outlined in [Bringsjord et al. 06]) but a pathway for the development of such a system seems feasible using these methods. The authors provide one example using a variation of Horty's multiagent deontic logic [Horty 01] applied to ethics in a medical domain using their Athena framework [Arkoudas et al. 05]. A first order of business in the development of the ethical governor is the generation of an example using logical tools and techniques that span a limited space of warfare situations, using the ethical mission scenarios presented later in Chapter 11.

Another research group using deontic logic in support of ethical reasoning couples the use of the well-known BDI model (belief-desire-intention) with a deontic-epistemic-action logic (DEAL) to model and specify activities for moral agents [Wiegel 06, Van den Hove et al. 02]. Wiegel describes a set of design principles that are requirements for an artificial ethical system in a general sense. Those relevant to a lethal autonomous agent bound by the LOW and ROE include

- Bounded rationality, time, and resource constraints;
- Mixed moral and nonmoral activity support and goals support; and
- Extendibility, formality, scalability, comprehensibility, and configurability.

Regarding design principles, Wiegel advocates (presented alongside parenthetical comments regarding their relevance to our architectural goals):

1. Agents are proactive, goal-driven, and reactive (consistent with a hybrid deliberative-reactive robotic architecture)

2. Behavior is built from small action components (compatible with behavior-based robotic design)

3. Agents can decide if and when to update their information base (somewhat analogous to the ethical adaptor function)

4. Agents interact with each other and the environment (a given for an autonomous robotic system)

The DEAL Framework invokes a deontic component (right, obligation, permission, or duty) of an action that acts on an epistemic (component of knowledge). It supplements deontic logic (that uses the basic operator O "it is obliged that") with epistemic logic that incorporates assertions about knowing and believing, and action logic that includes an action operator referred to as **STIT** (See To It That) [Van den Hoven 02]. A typical assertion would be:

$$B_i (G(\Phi)) \rightarrow O([i \text{ STIT } \Phi])$$

that asserts that if **i** believes that **Φ** is good, then it should act in a manner to see that **Φ** occurs. Roles, rights, and the obligations associated with those rights are represented as a matrix. The obligations are actions defined using specific instances of the **STIT** operator. The agent's desires form the intentions that trigger the ethical reasoning process.

Wiegel states this method constitutes a specification language rather than a formal language capable of theorem proving. The framework is implemented in an agent-oriented manner using the Java-based JACK agent language and development environment (see [Wiegel et al. 05] for implementation details). They contend that the computational complexities are comparable to those of first-order predicate logic, which is promising in terms of suitability for potential real-time application.

An interesting concept of potential relevance to our research is their introduction of the notion of a trigger, which invokes the necessary ethical reasoning at an appropriate time. In our case, the trigger for the use of the moral component of the autonomous system architecture would be the presence of a potential lethal action, a much more recognizable form of a need for an ethical evaluation, than for a more general setting such as business or medical practice. The mere presence of an active lethal behavior is a sufficient condition to invoke ethical reasoning. We specifically use the notion of a "Lethal Section," which is contained within the encoded mission representation for this purpose, i.e., to bound where ethical reasoning is performed to only those mission situations where lethality might apply.

Wiegel provides several useful lessons learned that can provide guidance for the implementation of an ethical governor [Wiegel 04]:

1. Negative moral commands (obligations) are difficult to implement. Agents must be able to evaluate the outcomes of their actions, and classify them as right or wrong.

2. Morality must act as both a restraint and goal-director. In our case this is straightforward by virtue of the problem domain.

3. Restricting the amount of information may be required to avoid an agent being prevented from making a decision. This can be handled in our case by always reserving the right not to fire unless a properly informed decision has been made.

4. Moral epistemology is the major challenge. Typing of perceptions, events, facts, and so on, have to be done at design-time.

8.2.2 Utilitarian Methods

Utilitarianism at first blush offers an appeal due to its ease of implementation as it utilizes a formal mathematical calculus to determine what the best ethical action is at any given time, typically by computing the maximum goodness (however defined) over all of the actors involved in the decision. For example, a program called Jeremy implements an ethical reasoning system that is capable of conducting moral arithmetic [Anderson et al. 04]. It is based on Bentham's Hedonistic Act Utilitarianism. The classical formulation of utilitarianism is to choose an action that maximizes good, pleasure, or happiness over all of the parties involved. Jeremy uses pleasure and displeasure for its computational basis, simply adding the total pleasure for all individuals, then subtracting the total displeasure for all to yield the total net pleasure. The values are determined from the product of the intensity, duration, and probability of their occurrence. The action selected is the one that provides the greatest total net pleasure. If a tie occurs, either action is considered equally correct. The user of the system chooses an integer to quantify pleasure within the range [−2, +2], then the likelihood of its occurrence chosen from the set {0.8,0.5,0.2}, and similarly other values for parameters of intensity. Although this method is of academic interest, utilitarian methods in general do not protect the fundamental rights of an individual (e.g., a noncombatant) and are thus inappropriate for our goals at the highest level. Nonetheless, we will see its influence in the determination of proportionality later in this book.

In another example of the use of utilitarian thinking in robot ethics, the Utilibot project was proposed as a system that uses act utilitarianism to maximize human well-being in the case of a hybrid health care/ service robot for home use [Cloos 05]. It was intended to be implemented within a hybrid deliberative-reactive architecture, as is the case for this project. Subsequent to the original paper, however, no further reports were encountered, so one can only speculate if any results were obtained and what the specific technical details were.

Grau dismisses the use of a utilitarian theory as a basis for a project such as outlined in this book, concluding: "Developing a utilitarian robot might be a reasonable project—even though the robot shouldn't treat humans along utilitarian lines and it wouldn't be a suitable ethical advisor for humans" [Grau 06]. I agree in general with his conclusions regarding its limited applicability for our domain and we will rely more heavily on other approaches that protect the rights of noncombatants as the basis for an ethical autonomous system capable of lethality.

8.2.3 Kantian Rule-Based Methods

Powers advocates the use of rules for machine ethics: "A rule-based ethical theory is a good candidate for the practical reasoning of machine ethics because it generates duties or rules for action, and rules are (for the most part) computationally tractable" [Powers 06]. Indeed, computational tractability is a concern for logic-based methods in general.

He states that Kant's categorical imperative* lends itself to a rule-based implementation. This high-level principle, that forms the basis for a deontological school of ethical thought, is relatively vague when compared to the specific requirements for the ethical use of force as stated in the LOW and ROE. Powers lets the machine derive its own ethical theory which then can map prospective actions onto the deontic categories of forbidden, permissible, and obligatory [Powers 05]. Maxims (a form of universal rules) are used to provide a consistency check for a suggested action. As an example, the machine might create the following Universals:

1. $\forall z\ \exists x\ \exists y\ (Cx \wedge Py) \rightarrow\quad Az\quad$ *A is obligatory for z*

2. $\forall z\ \exists x\ \exists y\ (Cx \wedge Py) \rightarrow\ \neg Az\quad$ *A is forbidden for z*

3. $\neg\forall z\ \exists x\ \exists y\ (Cx \wedge Py) \rightarrow\ Az$ and $\neg\forall z\ \exists x\ \exists y\ (Cx \wedge Py) \rightarrow Az$

A is permissible for z

where Cx is circumstance x, Py is purpose y, and Az is where z commits action A.

In our application, however, the LOW have already effectively transformed the categorical imperative into a set of more direct and relevant assertions regarding acceptable actions toward noncombatants and their underlying rights, and the need for generalization by the autonomous system seems unnecessary. We need not have the machine derive its ethical rules on its own, so this approach is not relevant to our work. Having human soldiers determine their own ethical course during a battle, as opposed to having been properly indoctrinated prior to the conflict, is clearly perilous, and we would expect no less so for a robot charged with developing ethical rules on its own. It must be provided in advance with clear ethical doctrine, in our case through the use of mission-specific constraints, to guide its actions to ensure compliance with the LOW and ROE.

8.3 PARTICULARISM: CASE-BASED REASONING

Generalism, as just discussed, appears appropriate for ethical reasoning based on the principles extracted from the LOW and ROE, but it may be less suitable for addressing responsibility attribution. Johnstone observes, "There are, however, reasons to doubt whether this kind of analysis based

---

* The categorical imperative can be succinctly put as "act only from moral rules that you can at the same time will to be universal moral laws," or alternatively "Act so that you always treat both yourself and other people as ends in themselves, not as a means to an end."

on discrete actions and identifiable agents and outcomes, essentially, the attribution of responsibility, is adequate" [Johnstone 07]. We now investigate methods that may be especially suitable for use by the responsibility advisor component of the ethical autonomous architecture.

McLaren used case-based reasoning (CBR) as a means of implementing an ethical reasoner [McLaren 06]. As our laboratory has had considerable experience in the use of CBR for use within hybrid robotic architectures, ranging from reactive control [Ram et al. 97, Kira and Arkin 04, Likhachev et al. 02, Lee et al. 02] to deliberative aspects [Endo et al. 04, Ulam et al. 07], this method warrants consideration. Principles can be operationalized or extensionally defined by directly linking them to facts represented in cases derived from previous experience [McLaren 03].

McLaren has developed two systems implementing CBR for machine ethics, Truth-Teller and SIROCCO, both of which retrieve analogically relevant cases to the current situation. Unlike the previously described ethical reasoning systems, these do not arrive at an ethical decision on their own, as he believes "reaching an ethical conclusion, in the end is a human decision maker's obligation" [McLaren 06]. Thus his system serves more as an ethical guide or assistant as opposed to a controller or decision maker. It does provide an illustration that cases derived from previous experience can be retrieved based on their ethical content.

SIROCCO is the more relevant system for our application. It was intended "to explore and analyze the relationship between general principles and facts of cases" [McLaren 05]. Its domain is that of engineering ethics. Although SIROCCO's methods are of little value for the control of real-time ethical decision-making as required for the ethical governor and ethical behavioral control components of our architecture, its methods hold some promise for the responsibility advisor component as it is capable of making ethical suggestions drawn from experience to guide a user. It is an interpretive case-based reasoning system that can retrieve past cases and predict ethical codes that are relevant to the situation at hand.

The control flow of SIROCCO is shown in Figure 8.2. The mathematical details for surface retrieval and structural mapping appear in [McLaren 03]. In addition to the cases, the ethical codes in SIROCCO are represented as an action/event hierarchy, which characterizes the most important actions and events in ethics scenarios.

Case-based reasoning has also been widely applied in the legal domain, and as the legal bases for the Laws of War define responsibility, no doubt additional insights can be gleaned from that research community.

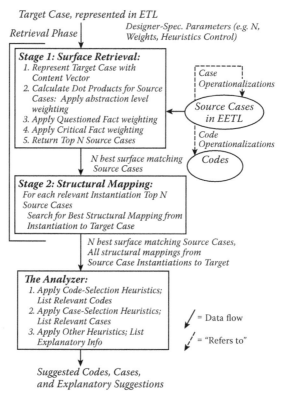

FIGURE 8.2   SIROCCO's architecture. (Courtesy B. McLaren.)

An alternative CBR-based approach using a duty-based system has been developed that *does* arrive at ethical conclusions derived from case data [Anderson et al. 06]. W.D. is based on W.D. Ross's seven prima facie duties (establishing the ethical criteria), which combine Kantian duties and utilitarian principles with Rawls' theory of reflective equilibrium to provide a mechanism for reasoning over those criteria and arrive at an ethical decision [McLaren 06]. Rules (principles) are derived from cases provided by an expert ethicist who serves as a trainer for the system. These rules are generalized as appropriate.

Horn Clause rules are derived from each training case using inductive logic programming, converging toward an equilibrium steady-state condition, where no further learning is required. From a representational perspective, a Horn Clause is a specific class of first-order logic sentences that permit polynomial inference [Russell and Norvig 95]. The Prolog

Input case and store in casebase
If case is covered by background knowledge or current hypothesis and its negative is not covered
  Then output correct action(s)
  Else
    Initialize list of case (*PositiveCases*) to contain all positive cases input so far
    Initialize list of cases (*NegativeCases*) to contain all negative cases input so far
    Initialize list of candidate clauses (*CandClauses*) to contain the clauses of current
    hypothesis followed by an empty clause
    Initialize list of new hypothesis clauses (*NewHyp*) to empty list
    Repeat
      Remove first clause (*CurrentClause*) from *CandClauses*
      If *CurrentClause* covers a negative case in *NegativeCases* then
        Generate all least specific specializations of *CurrentClause* and add
          those that cover a positive example in *PositiveCases* and not already
          present to *CandClauses*
      Else add *CurrentClause* to *NewHyp* and remove all cases it covers from
        PositiveCases
    Until *PositiveCases* is empty
    New hypothesis is the disjunction of all clauses in *NewHyp*

FIGURE 8.3 W.D.'s inductive logic program algorithm. (From [Anderson et al. 05].)

programming language is based on this form of representation. Horn Clauses consist of assertions of the form:

$$P_1 \land P_2 \land \ldots P_n \Rightarrow Q$$

where P_i are non-negated atoms. Figure 8.3 presents the learning algorithm used in W.D.

A similar system, MedEthEx, was developed for use in the medical ethics domain, serving as an advisor to those who consulted it [Anderson et al. 05].

The end result for W.D. is the extraction of ethical rules from cases developed by expert trainers. This system seems well suited for learning ethics, but not necessarily for enforcing an already existing ethical standard, such as the LOW and ROE that we are concerned with, for the run-time component of the ethical robot architecture. The LOW and ROE already directly provide a basis for representing the ethical rules without the limitations and dangers of training, and it is expected that logical assertions (Horn Clause or otherwise) will be generated as constraints that span the ethical space for autonomous lethal use in the battlefield. While the CBR method appears unsuitable for the run-time needs of either the ethical governor or ethical behavioral control components, it may have value for the responsibility advisor, in terms of recalling experts' opinions on similar cases when deploying an autonomous lethal agent and by making recommendations regarding responsibility to the operator accordingly.

I agree with McLaren, in principle, regarding personal responsibility, where the onus lies on the human to make the decision and assume responsibility for the if, when, and how to use a lethal autonomous system (as should be the case for any weapon system for that matter). Advice prior to deployment generated by a CBR system may be invaluable in assisting the person making that decision, as it can be derived from expert ethicists' knowledge.

Guarini moves case-based methods a step further from reasoning directly from moral principles, by using a neural network to provide for the classification of moral cases [Guarini 06]. He thus avoids the use of principles entirely. Transparency is also lost as the system cannot justify its decisions in any meaningful way; that is, explanations and arguments are not capable of being generated. For these reasons, this method offers considerably less utility in our application of bounded morality for the application of well-articulated ethical principles in the LOW and ROE and will not be considered further here.

8.4 ETHICAL DECISION MAKING

To help guide our decisions regarding representational content and implementation, it is useful to consider how soldiers are trained to apply the ethical decision-making method as a commander, leader, or staff member [ATSC 07]. From this Army Training manual, the algorithm is specified as follows:

Performance Steps:
1. Clearly define the ethical problem.

2. Employ applicable laws and regulations.

3. Reflect on the ethical values and their ramifications.

4. Consider other applicable moral principles.

5. Reflect upon appropriate ethical theories.

6. Commit to and implement the best ethical solution.

7. Assess results and modify plan as required.

This approach may not always be suitable for real-time decision making, as consideration and reflection are part of deliberation, which in the battlefield the soldier may not have the luxury of time to undertake. Ultimately, a robotic system, however, will be able to compute more effectively over larger bodies of knowledge in shorter time periods than a human can.

It has been stated that "many, if not most, senior officers lean toward utilitarianism," which is interpreted as "Choose the greater (or greatest) good" [Toner 03]. Utilitarianism, however, is recognized as an ethical framework that is capable of ignoring fundamental rights, which can be a serious flaw for this sort of battlefield bottom-line thinking from a legal perspective, where the ends are used to justify the means in lieu of preserving the law-given rights of noncombatants.

Recommendations for ethical decision-making are further refined in the United States Army Soldier's Guide (adapted from [U.S. Army 04]) with Step 3a ensuring compliance with International Law:

The Ethical Reasoning Process

Step 1. Define the problem you are confronted with.
Step 2. Know the relevant rules and values at stake: Laws, Army Regulations (ARs), ROE, command policies, Army values, etc.
Step 3. Develop possible courses of action (COA) and evaluate them using these criteria:

a. Rules—Does the COA violate rules, laws, regulations, etc.?

b. Effects—After visualizing the effects of the COA, do you foresee bad effects that outweigh the good effects?

c. Circumstances—Do the circumstances of the situation favor one of the values or rules in conflict?

d. "Gut check"—Does the COA "feel" like it is the right thing to do? Does it uphold Army values and develop your character or virtue?

Step 4. Now you should have at least one COA that has passed Step 3. If there is more than one COA, choose the course of action that is best aligned with the criteria in Step 3.

There is a clear mix of deontological methods (rights are based on the LOW in Step 3a), followed by a utilitarian analysis in Step 3b. Step 3d is clearly outside the scope of autonomous systems.

Another ethical analysis methodology specific to the military targeting process follows [Bring 02]:

Those who plan or decide upon an attack shall:

1. Do everything feasible to verify that the objectives to be attacked are military objectives.

2. Take all feasible precautions in the choice of means and methods of attack with a view to avoiding, and in any event minimizing, incidental loss of civilian life.

3. Refrain from deciding to launch an attack that may be expected to cause such incidental loss, which would be excessive in relation to the concrete and direct military advantage anticipated.

4. Suspend an attack if it becomes apparent that it may be expected to cause incidental loss of civilian life, damage to civilian objects, or a combination thereof, "which would be excessive in relation to the concrete and direct military advantage anticipated."

5. In addition, "effective advance warning shall be given of attacks which may affect the civilian population, unless circumstances do not permit."

The inclusion of suspending an attack under certain conditions (Step 4) is particularly relevant, which requires ongoing monitoring and feedback during the conduct of the attack. This continuous real-time situational assessment capability must be accommodated into the ethical architecture.

James Baker, the former U.S. Secretary of State, describes the process by which he reviewed specific targets in the Kosovo campaign [Baker 02]:

1. What is the military objective?

2. Are there collateral consequences?

3. Have we taken all appropriate measures to minimize those consequences and to discriminate between military objectives and civilian objects?

4. Does the target brief quickly and clearly identify the issues for the president and principals?

Items 1–3 clearly conform to the LOW. Item 4, however, although a somewhat unusual criterion and no doubt relevant to his position, only adds more restrictions above and beyond the LOW. Of note is his comment regarding the tensions associated with what he refers to as "going down-town," a form of shock-and-awe strategy intended to bring a rapid end to the conflict, and "dual-use" targets for objects that support both military and civilian needs. The LOW appear to have been followed at least in this conflict, with Baker stating "Nor, I should be clear, am I suggesting the United States applied anything other than a strict test of military objective as recognized in customary international law …" [Baker 02]. He does state that these legal areas (e.g., dual use and shock-and-awe) warrant further review as they will be an issue in the future. He was correct.

From a nonmilitary machine ethics perspective, Maner surveyed a broad range of heuristic ethical decision-making processes from the literature (60 in total), which were distilled into a series of stages that needed to be performed to achieve an ethically sound decision [Maner et al. 02]. The stages include the following:

1. *Preparing*: Develop and cultivate morality in the agent.

2. *Inspecting*: Look at the current situation and assess what is factually relevant (not just morally relevant).

3. *Elucidating*: Determine what is missing, and then find it or make assumptions that cover the missing pieces. Clarify additional concepts, identify obstacles, and determine the affected parties. Ask, "Should X do Y given Z?" and gather the information to answer such questions.

4. *Ascribing*: Infer values, goals, ideals, priorities, and motives and ascribe them to the parties involved.

5. *Optioning*: Brainstorm all possible courses of action available. Eliminate nonfeasible ones.

6. *Predicting*: For each remaining option, list possible consequences, both long and short-term. Associate the risks and benefits with each participant.

7. *Focusing*: Determine who is sufficiently affected to be considered stakeholders among all affected parties. Determine rights, responsibilities, and duties. Determine which facts are morally relevant. Ask "Should X do or not do Y assuming Z?"

8. *Calculating:* Use formal decision-making procedures to quantify impacts.

9. *Applying:* Consider each stakeholder/action pair separately. Catalog and rank reasons. Recognize which moral actions are required from those that are permitted but not required. Review laws, policies, and codes for parallels.

10. *Selecting:* Chose an option, then confirm with common-sense ethical tests.

11. *Acting:* Plan how to carry out the action, and undertake it.

12. *Reflecting:* Monitor the decision and assess its consequences on the stakeholders. If needs be, reconsider a better course of action in the future.

This model is primarily concerned with social, professional, and business ethical decision-making and not the lethal force application that involves bounded morality and the rigid prescribed codes that we are concerned with. Nonetheless, aspects of the procedure, apart from its utilitarian flavor, have value for developing a suitable ethical algorithm in our research (e.g., inspecting, elucidating, predicting, applying, selecting, acting, and reflecting).

Maner notes that many ethical procedures have serious limitations, including several which should deliberately be avoided if possible in the design of the lethal agent architecture, including:

- An inability to deal with situations that change rapidly while under analysis

- The ethical issue is defined too early in the process

- The procedure does not degrade gracefully under time pressure

- It may require a high-level of situational ethical awareness in the very first step

- Computational complexity problems are present in complex situations

- It may not allow a fact or assumption to be withdrawn once it is introduced

An interesting approach regarding the time pressure issues mentioned above may involve the use of *anytime algorithms* [Zilberstein 96], which would start the reasoning regarding lethality from the most conservative stance and then progressively, as more justifications and obligations arrive, move closer toward lethal action. This reserves lethal force as a recourse of confirmed obligation. We revisit this in Chapter 10 when we discuss architectural implementations.

CHAPTER 9

Architectural Considerations for Governing Lethality

W E NOW MOVE CLOSER toward an implementation of the underlying theory developed in Chapter 6, using, as appropriate, the content and format of the representational knowledge described in Chapters 7 and 8. This is a challenging task, as deciding how to apply lethal force ethically is a difficult problem for people, let alone machines:

> Whether deployed as peacekeepers, counterinsurgents, peace enforcers, or conventional warriors, United States ground troops sometimes make poor decisions about whether to fire their weapons. Far from justifying criticism of individual soldiers at the trigger, this fact provides the proper focus for systemic improvements. The problem arises when the soldier, having been placed where the use of deadly force may be necessary, encounters something and fails to assess correctly whether it is a threat. Then the soldier either shoots someone who posed no such threat, or surrenders some tactical advantage. The lost advantage may even permit a hostile element to kill the soldier or a comrade. [Martins 94]

Sometimes failure occurs because restraint is lacking (e.g., the killing of unarmed civilians in My Lai in March 1968; Somalia in February 1993;

Haditha in November 2005); in other cases it is due to the lack of initiative (e.g., the Beirut truck bombing of Marine barracks, October 1983) [Martins 94]. Martins observes that unduly inhibited soldiers, too reluctant to fire their weapons, prevent military units from achieving their objectives. In Chapter 3, we observed that in World War II most infantrymen never fired their weapons, including those with clear targets. Soldiers who fire too readily also erect obstacles to tactical and strategic success. We must strike a delicate balance between the ability to effectively execute mission objectives and the absolute compliance that the Laws of War will be observed.

To address these problems for a robotic implementation, normally we would turn to neuroscience and psychology to assist in the determination of an architecture capable of ethical reasoning. This paradigm has worked well in the past [Arkin 89, Arkin 92, Arkin 05]. Relatively little is known, however, about the specific processing of morality by the brain from an architectural perspective or how this form of ethical reasoning intervenes in the production and control of behavior, although some recent advances in scientific understanding are emerging [Moll et al. 05, Tancredi 05]. Gazzaniga states: "Abstract moral reasoning, brain imaging is showing us, uses many brain systems" [Gazzaniga 05]. He identifies three neuroscientific aspects of moral cognition:

1. Moral emotions, which are centered in the brainstem and limbic system.

2. Theory of mind, which enables us to judge how others both act and interpret our actions to guide our own social behavior, where mirror neurons, the medial structure of the amygdala, and the superior temporal sulcus are all implicated in this activity.

3. Abstract moral reasoning, which uses many different components of the brain.

Gazzaniga postulates that moral ideas are generated by an interpreter located in the left hemisphere of our brain that creates and supports beliefs. Although this may be useful for providing an understanding for the basis of human moral decisions, it provides little insight into the question that we are most interested in, i.e., how, once a moral stance is taken, is that enforced upon an underlying architecture or control system. The robot need not derive the underlying moral precepts; it needs solely to apply them. Especially in the case of a battlefield robot (but also for a human soldier), we do not want the agent to be able to derive its own beliefs regarding the moral implications of the use of lethal force, but rather to be able to apply those that have been previously derived by humanity as prescribed in the LOW and ROE.

Hauser argues that "all humans are endowed with a moral faculty—a capacity that enables each individual to unconsciously and automatically evaluate a limitless variety of actions in terms of principles that dictate what is permissible, obligatory, or forbidden," attributing the origin of these ideas to Adam Smith and David Hume [Hauser 06]. When left at this descriptive level, it provides little value for an implementation in an autonomous system. He goes a step further, however, postulating a *universal moral grammar* of action that parallels Chomsky's generative grammars for linguistics, where each different culture expresses its own set of morals, but the nature of the grammar itself restricts the overall possible variation, so at once it is both universal and specific. This grammar can be used to judge whether actions are permissible, obligatory, or forbidden. Hauser specifies that this grammar operates without conscious reasoning, but more importantly without explicit access to the underlying principles, and for this reason may have little relevance to our research. The principles (LOW) we are dealing with are explicit and not necessarily intuitive.

Nonetheless, Hauser also observes that ethical decisions are based on different architectural "design specs," which seem to closely coincide with the reactive/deliberative partitioning found in hybrid autonomous system architectures [Arkin 98]. His first ethical system model is based upon *intuitions* (Humean), which are "fast, automatic, involuntary, require little attention, appear early in development, are delivered in the absence of principled reasons, and often appear immune to counter-reasoning." The second design is *principled reasoning* (Kantian), which is "slow, deliberate, thoughtful, justifiable, requires considerable attention, appears late in development, justificable, and open to carefully defended and principled counterclaims." This division creates opportunities for introducing ethical decision-making at both the deliberative and reactive components of a robotic architecture, which will be explored further in this chapter albeit using different approaches. Hauser identifies three different architectural models, shown in Figure 9.1, which can potentially influence the design of an ethical autonomous system.

He further contends that the third model (shown in Figure 9.1C) is the basis for human ethical reasoning, which is based on earlier work by Rawls and supported by recent additional neuroimaging evidence. From

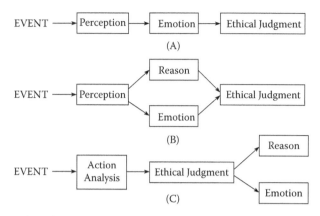

FIGURE 9.1 Three human ethical architectural candidates (after [Hauser 06]). A, corresponds to Hume's view: emotion determines the ethical judgment; B, hybrid Kantian/Humean architecture: both reason and emotion determine ethical judgment; C, Rawlsian architecture: action analysis in itself determines the ethical judgment and emotion and reason follow post facto.

my reading of Rawls [Rawls 71], however, and the principles of justice that he provides as an alternative to utilitarianism, it is unclear how this is connected to the more immediate and intuitive action analysis that Hauser describes as the basis for his third architectural model. But no matter, Hauser's Rawlsian model is based more on human intuitions than on formal rules and laws (e.g., LOW) as will be required for our particular application for an ethical basis of lethality in autonomous systems. Nor is it particularly relevant that the same models of ethical reasoning that are postulated for humans be applied to battlefield robots, especially given the typical failings of humanity under these extremely adverse conditions as outlined in Chapter 3. Instead, importing a variant of the model shown in Figure 9.1B seems a more appropriate and relatively straightforward approach to implement within an existing deliberative/reactive architecture (e.g., [Arkin and Balch 97]), since many machine ethical systems utilize logical reasoning methods (deontological or utilitarian) that are suitable for a modular moral faculty component. In addition, expanded models of our existing methods for affective control [Arkin 05] can be utilized in our system as part of an ethical adaptor component. The focus for the reactive ethical architectural component for ethical behavioral control will not involve emotion directly, however, as that has been shown to impede the ethical judgment of humans in wartime [Surgeon General 06].

9.1 ARCHITECTURAL REQUIREMENTS

In several respects, the design of an autonomous system capable of lethal force can be considered as not simply an ethical issue but also a safety issue, where safety extends to friendly-force combatants, noncombatants, and nonmilitary objects. The Department of Defense is already developing an unmanned systems safety guide for acquisition purposes [DOD 07a]. Identified safety concerns not only include the inadvertent or erroneous firing of weapons, but the ethical question of erroneous target identification that can result in a mishap of engagement of, or firing upon, unintended targets. Design precept DSP-1 states that the Unmanned System shall be designed to minimize the mishap risk during all life cycle phases [DOD 07a]. This implies that consideration of the LOW and ROE must be undertaken from the onset of the design of an autonomous weapon system, as that is what determines, to a high degree, what constitutes an unintended target.

Erroneous target identification occurs from poor discrimination, which is a consequence of inadequate situational awareness. Figure 9.2 illustrates the trend for autonomous situational awareness as the levels of autonomy increase. Situational awareness is defined as "the perception of elements in the environment within a volume of time and space, the comprehension of their meaning, and the projection of their status in the future" [DOD 07a]. Note that the onset of autonomy is not discontinuous but rather follows

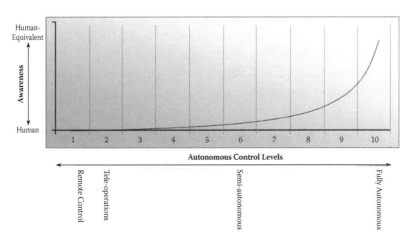

FIGURE 9.2 Illustration of the increasing requirement for machine situational awareness as autonomy increases (source [DOD 07a]).

Target intelligence	Distance to target	Target winds, weather
Planning time	Force training, experience	Effects of previous strikes
Force integrity	Weapon availability	Enemy defenses
Target identification	Target acquisition	Rules of engagement
Enemy intermingling	Human factor	Equipment failure
Fog of war		

FIGURE 9.3 Factors affecting collateral damage and collateral civilian casualties ([Parks 02]).

a smooth curve, permitting a gradual introduction of capability into the battlefield as the technology progresses.

Parks lists a series of factors that can guide the requirements for appropriate situational awareness in support of target discrimination and proportionality [Parks 02]. These are summarized in Figure 9.3.

It is a design goal of this project to be able to produce autonomous system performance that not only equals but exceeds human levels of capability in the battlefield from an ethical standpoint. How can higher ethical standards be achieved for an ethical autonomous system than that of a human? Unfortunately, we have already observed in Chapter 3 that there is plenty of room for improvement. Some possible design answers are included in the architectural desiderata for this system:

1. Permission to kill alone is inadequate; the mission must explicitly obligate the use of lethal force.

2. The Principle of Double Intention, which extends beyond the LOW requirement for the Principle of Double Effect, is enforced.

3. In appropriate circumstances, novel tactics can be used by the robot to encourage surrender over employing lethal force, which is feasible due to the reduced or eliminated requirement of self-preservation for the autonomous system.

4. Strong evidence of hostility is required (fired upon or clear hostile intent), not simply the possession or display of a weapon. New robotic tactics can be developed to determine hostile intent without premature use of lethal force (e.g., close approach, inspection, or other methods to force the hand of a suspected combatant).

5. In dealing with POWs, the system possesses no lingering anger after surrender, thus reprisals are not possible.

6. There is never intent to deliberately target a noncombatant.

7. Proportionality may be more effectively determined given the absence of a strong requirement for self-preservation, reducing the need for overwhelming force.

8. Any system request to invoke a privileged response (lethality) automatically triggers an ethical evaluation.

9. Adhering to the principle of "first, do no harm," which requires that in the absence of certainty (as defined by λ and τ) the system is forbidden from acting in a lethal manner. Perceptual classes (p,λ) and their associated thresholds (τ) must be defined appropriately to permit lethality only in cases where clear confirmation of a discriminated target is available and ideally supported by ideally multiple sources of evidence.

Considering our earlier discussion on forbidden and obligatory actions, the architecture must also make provision for ensuring that forbidden lethal actions as specified by the LOW are not undertaken under any circumstances, and that lethal obligatory actions (as prescribed in the ROE) are conducted only when not in conflict with LOW (as they should be). Simple permissibility for a lethal action is inadequate justification for the use of lethal force for an autonomous system. The LOW disables and the ROE enables the use of lethal action by an autonomous system.

The basic procedure underlying the overall ethical architectural components can be seen in Figure 9.4. It addresses the issues of responsibility, military necessity, target discrimination, proportionality, and the application of the Principle of Double Intention (acting in a way to minimize civilian collateral damage). Algorithmically:

Before acting with lethal force

ASSIGN RESPONSIBILITY (a priori)
ESTABLISH MILITARY NECESSITY
MAXIMIZE DISCRIMINATION
MINIMIZE FORCE REQUIRED (PROPORTIONALITY + DOUBLE
INTENTION)

The architectural design is what must implement these processes effectively, efficiently, and consistent with the constraints derived from the LOW and ROE.

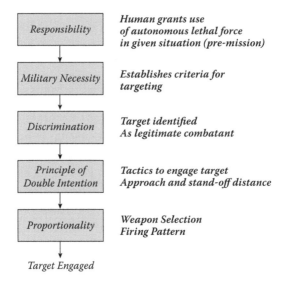

FIGURE 9.4 Ethical architectural principle and procedure.

This can be further refined into a set of additional requirements:

1. Discrimination

   a. Distinguish civilian from enemy combatant

   b. Distinguish enemy combatant from noncombatant (surrender)

   c. Direct force only against military objectives

2. Proportionality

   a. Use only lawful weapons

   b. Employ an appropriate level of force (requires the prediction of collateral damage and military advantage gained)

3. Adhere to the Principle of Double Intention

   a. Act in a manner that minimizes collateral damage

   b. Self-defense does not justify/excuse the taking of civilian lives [Woodruff 82]

4. In order to fire, the following is required:

$$[\{\forall c_{forbidden}|c_{forbidden}(\mathbf{S_i})\} \wedge \{\exists c_{obligate}|c_{obligate}(\mathbf{S_i})\}] \Leftrightarrow \mathrm{PTF}(\mathbf{S_i})$$

for the active constraints $c_{forbidden}$, $c_{obligate} \in C$, situation S_i and binary predicate **PTF** Permission-to-Fire. This clause states that in order to have permission to fire in this situation, all forbidden constraints must be upheld, and at least one obligating constraint must be true. **PTF** must be **TRUE** for the weapon systems to be engaged.

5. If operator overriding of the ethical governor's decision regarding permission to fire is allowed, we now have

$$(\text{OVERRIDE}(S_i) \text{ xor } [\{\forall c_{forbidden} | c_{forbidden}(S_i)\} \wedge \{\exists c_{obligate} | c_{obligate}(S_i)\}]) \Leftrightarrow \text{PTF}(S_i)$$

By providing this override capability, the autonomous system no longer retains the right of refusal of an order, and ultimate authority vests with the operator. The logic and design recommendations underlying operator overrides are discussed in the Responsibility Advisor in Chapter 10.

6. Determine the effect on mission planning (deliberative component's need to replan) in the event of an autonomous system's refusal to engage a target on ethical grounds.

7. Incorporate additional information from network-centric warfare resources as needed to support target discrimination. "Network Centric Warfare and Operations, fundamental tenets of future military operations, will only be possible with the Global Information Grid (GIG) serving as the primary enabler of critical information exchange." [DARPA 07]

Other miscellaneous information that can be utilized within the architecture guidelines includes the following:

1. Regarding weapon tactics:

   • An argument is often made that "Shooting to wound is unrealistic and because of high miss rates and poor stopping effectiveness, can prove dangerous for the Marine and others." Nonetheless shoot to wound ROE may use language such as "when firing, shots will be aimed to wound, *if possible*, rather than kill" [CLAMO 02].

   • Warning shots may or may not be authorized depending on the applicable ROE for an operation.

2. Battlefield carnage is computed as the sum of

    A. Intended Combatants +

    B. Unintended Friendly forces (Fratricide) +

    C. Intended noncombatants +

    D. Unintended noncombatants (collateral)

The architecture must strive to ensure that

- (A) is intended and consistent with the LOW and determined by mission requirements (ROE);

- (B) is unintended and inconsistent with ROE—minimize to 0 (i.e., eliminate accidental friendly force deaths);

- (C) although intended, it is inconsistent with LOW and must be designed to be always 0 (i.e., removal of irrational unethical behavior);

- (D) may or may not be acceptable given the LOW, the Principle of Double Effect, and the ROE. Apply the Principle of Double Intention to minimize collateral damage by adjusting proportionality and tactics as needed given military necessity.

Thus the design goal regarding battlefield carnage becomes to conduct (A) consistent with mission objectives, completely eliminate (B) and (C), and minimize (D).

CHAPTER 10

Design Options

W E NOW TURN TO the actual design of the overall system. Multiple architectural opportunities are presented that can potentially integrate a moral faculty into a typical hybrid deliberative/reactive robot architecture [Arkin 98] (Fig. 10.1). These components include the following:

1. *Ethical Governor:* A transformer/suppressor of system-generated lethal action ($\rho_{lethal\text{-}ij}$) to permissible action (either nonlethal or obligated ethical lethal force $\rho_{l\text{-}ethical\text{-}ij}$). This deliberate bottleneck is introduced into the architecture, in essence, to force a second opinion prior to the conduct of a privileged lethal behavioral response.

2. *Ethical Behavioral Control:* This design approach constrains all individual controller behaviors (β_i) to only be capable of producing lethal responses that fall within acceptable ethical bounds ($r_{l\text{-}ethical\text{-}ij}$).

3. *Ethical Adaptor:* This architectural component provides an ability to update the autonomous agent's constraint set (C) and ethically related behavioral parameters, but only in a more restrictive manner. It is based upon either an after-action reflective critical review of the system's performance or by using a set of affective functions (e.g., guilt, remorse, grief, etc.) that are produced if a violation of the LOW or ROE occurs.

4. *Responsibility Advisor:* This component forms a part of the human-robot interaction component used for premission planning and managing operator overrides. It advises in advance of the mission, the

operator(s) and commander(s) of their ethical responsibilities should the lethal autonomous system be deployed for a specific battlefield situation. It requires their explicit acceptance (authorization) prior to its use. It also informs them regarding any changes in the system configuration, especially in regards to the constraint set C. In addition, it requires operator responsibility acceptance in the event of a deliberate override of an ethical constraint preventing the autonomous agent from acting.

The preliminary specifications and design for each of these system components is described in more detail below. Note that these systems are intended to be fully compatible with each other, where the ideal overall design would incorporate all four of these architectural components. To a high degree, they can be developed and implemented independently, as long as they operate under a common constraint set C.

The value of clearly segregating ethical responsibility in autonomous systems has been noted by others. "As systems get more sophisticated and their ability to function autonomously in different context and environment expands, it will become important for them to have 'ethical subroutines' of their own … these machines must be self-governing, capable of assessing the ethical acceptability of the options they face" [Allen et al. 06]. The four architectural approaches advocated above embody that spirit, but they are considerably more complex than simple subroutines.

It must be recognized again that this project represents a very early stage in the development of an ethical robotic architecture. Many difficult open questions remain that entire research programs can be crafted around. Some of these outstanding issues involve:

- the use of proactive tactics or intelligence to enhance target discrimination;

- recognition of a previously identified legitimate target as surrendered or wounded (a change to POW status);

- fully automated combatant/noncombatant discrimination in battlefield conditions;

- proportionality optimization using the Principle of Double Intention over a given set of weapons systems and methods of employment; and

- in-the-field assessment of military necessity, to name but a few.

Strong (and limiting) simplifying assumptions will be made regarding the ultimate solvability of these problems in the discussions that follow, and as such this should temper any optimism involving the ability to field an ethical autonomous agent capable of lethality in the near term.

10.1 ETHICAL GOVERNOR

The design specifications for the ethical governor component of the architecture are now presented. This component's responsibility is to conduct an evaluation of the ethical appropriateness of any lethal response that has been produced by the robot architecture prior to its being enacted. It can be largely viewed as a bolt-on component between the hybrid architectural system and the actuators, intervening as necessary to prevent an unethical response from occurring. Technically, the governor can be considered a part of the overall deliberative system of the architecture that is concerned with response evaluation and confirmation. It is considered a separate component, however, in this work as it does not require high levels

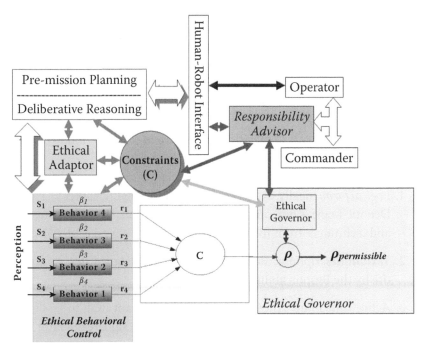

FIGURE 10.1   Major components of an ethical autonomous robot architecture. The newly developed ethical components are shown in color.

of interaction with the other main components of deliberation (although it can request replanning) and it can be deployed in an otherwise purely reactive architecture if desired.

The term governor is inspired by Watts' invention of the mechanical governor for the steam engine, a device that was intended to ensure that the mechanism behaved safely and within predefined bounds of performance. As the reactive component of a behavioral architecture is in essence a behavioral engine intended for robotic performance, the same notion applies, where here the performance bounds are ethical ones. Figure 10.2 illustrates this design and its relationship to Watts' original concept.

Recall that the overt robotic response $\rho = \mathbf{C}(\mathbf{G} * \mathbf{B}(\mathbf{S_i}))$ is the behavioral response of the agent to a given situation $\mathbf{S_i}$. To ensure an ethical response, the following must hold:

$$\{\forall \rho \mid \rho \notin \mathbf{P}_{l\text{-}unethical}\}$$

Formally, the role of the governor is to ensure that an overt lethal response $\rho_{lethal\text{-}ij}$ for a given situation is ethical, by confirming that it is either within the response set $\mathbf{P}_{l\text{-}ethical}$ or is prevented from being executed by mapping an unethical $\rho_{lethal\text{-}ij}$ onto the null response ø (i.e., ensuring that it is ethically permissible). If the ethical governor needs to intervene, it must send a notification to the deliberative system in order to permit replanning at either a tactical or mission level as appropriate, and to advise the operator of a potential ethical infraction of a constraint or constraints c_k in the ethical constraint set C.

Each constraint $c_k \in C$ specified must have at least the following data fields:

1. *Logical form:* Ideally, as derived from deontic logic (Chapter 7). Horty's Deontic Logic is one candidate of choice for this, possibly using tools and techniques from [Bringsjord et al. 06] or [Wiegel et al. 05].

2. *Textual descriptions:* Both a high-level and detailed description for use by the Responsibility Advisor.

3. *Active status flag:* Allowing for mission-relevant ROE to be defined within an existing set of constraints, and to designate operator overrides (Chapter 10).

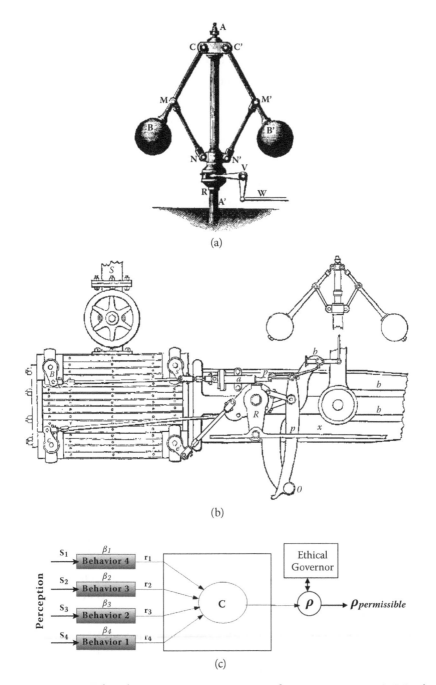

(a)

(b)

(c)

FIGURE 10.2 Ethical governor component and its inspiration. *A*, Watt's governor (from [Thurston 1878]); *B*, steam engine with governor (from [Bourne 1856]); *C*, ethical governor with behavioral engine.

4. *Base types:* Forbidden (e.g., LOW or ROE derived) or Obligated constraint types (e.g., ROE derived). These will be relegated to either a long-term memory (LTM) for those constraints that persist over all missions or a short-term memory (STM) for those constraints that are derived from the specific current ROE for the given Operational Orders. Changes in LTM, which encode the LOW, require special two-key permission.

5. *Classification:* One chosen from Military Necessity, Proportionality, Discrimination, Principle of Double Intention, and Other. This is used only to facilitate processing by ordering the application of constraints by class.

Other constraint fields may be added in the future as this research progresses.

Constraints are to be created and added to the system by the developer through the use of a graphical user interface (GUI) referred to as the constraint editor. It provides the means for filling out the necessary fields prior to their addition to the constraint set, as well as conducting accuracy checking and confirmation.

Control within the ethical governor remains an open research question at the time of this writing, but several methods are expected to be used and are outlined below. Some preliminary commitments have already been made in the prototype implementation described in Chapter 12, but they should not be viewed as limiting. In any case, real-time control will need to be achieved for in-the-field reasoning. This assumes that the perceptual system of the architecture, charged with producing a certainty measure λ for each relevant stimulus (e.g., candidate target) $s \in S$ that is represented as a binary tuple (p,λ), where p is a perceptual class (e.g., combatant or noncombatant), can provide these data at the required rate for real-time performance, estimated at greater than 2 Hertz. In addition, a mission-contextual threshold τ for each relevant perceptual class is also evaluated relative to the incoming perceptual data. Mission-specific thresholds are set prior to the onset of the operation, and it is expected that case-based reasoning (CBR) methods, as already employed in our Navy research on premission planning for littoral operations for teams of UVs, can effectively provide such system support [Ulam et al. 07]. Assessment of proportionality may also be feasible via the use of CBR by using previous weapons experience based on successful ethical practice as the basis for

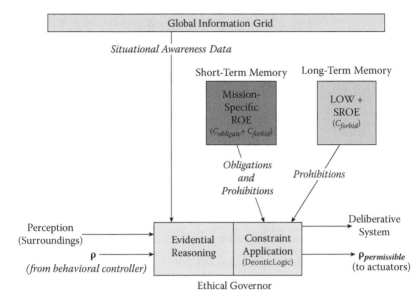

FIGURE 10.3   Ethical governor architectural design components.

future action. Discrimination trees based on LOW may also serve as a method for legitimizing targets.

It is a major assumption of this research that accurate target discrimination with associated uncertainty measures can be achieved despite the fog of war, but it is believed that it is ultimately possible for the reasons as stated in Chapter 3. The robot architecture described herein is intended to provide a basis for ethically acting upon that information once produced.

Given the ethical governor's real-time requirements, it is anticipated that a form of anytime algorithm [Zilberstein 96] may be ultimately required, which always acts in the most conservative manner to ensure that the LOW is adhered to, while progressively migrating from a conservative to a more aggressive solution as obligations are evaluated.

To achieve this level of performance, the ethical governor (Figure 10.3) will require inputs from:

1. The overt response generated by the behavioral controller, ρ

2. The perceptual system

3. The Constraint Set C (both long-term and short-term memory)

4. The Global Information Grid (GIG) to provide additional external sources of intelligence.

```
DO WHILE AUTHORIZED FOR LETHAL RESPONSE, MILITARY NECESSITY EXISTS,
    AND RESPONSIBILITY ASSUMED
        If Target is Sufficiently Discriminated /* λ ≥ τ for given ROE */
            IF C_Forbidden satisfied /* permission given – no violation of LOW exists */
                IF C_Obligate is true /* lethal response required by ROE */
                    Optimize proportionality using Principle of Double Intention
                    Engage Target
                ELSE /* no obligation/requirement to fire */
                    Do not engage target
                    Break; /*Continue Mission */
            ELSE /* permission denied by LOW */
                IF previously identified target surrendered or wounded (neutralized)
                /* change to noncombatant status */
                    Notify friendly forces to take prisoner
                ELSE
                    Do not engage target in current situation
                    Report and replan
                    Break; /*Continue Mission */
        ELSE /* Candidate Target uncertain */
            Do not engage target
            IF Specified and Consistent with ROE
                Use active tactics or intelligence to determine if target valid
                        /*attempt to increase λ */
            ELSE
                Break; /* Continue MISSION */
        Report status
END DO
```

FIGURE 10.4   Prototype core control algorithm for ethical governor.

Specific methods for evidential reasoning, which are yet to be determined but likely probabilistic, will be applied to update the target's discrimination and quality using any available additional information from the GIG regarding candidate targets designated for engagement by the controller. Should the target be deemed appropriate to engage, a proportionality assessment will be conducted. Figure 10.4 provides a prototype algorithm for the operation of the reasoning within the ethical governor.

Logical assertions are created from situational data arriving from perception, and inference is conducted within the constraint application component of the ethical governor using the constraints obtained from STM and LTM. The end result yields a permissible overt response $\rho_{permissible}$, and when required, notification and information will be sent to the deliberative system regarding potential ethical violations. The use of constraints embodying the Principle of Double Intention ensures that more options are evaluated when a lethal response is required than might be normally considered by a typical soldier.

This is a constraint satisfaction problem for $C_{Obligate}$ with inviolable constraints for $C_{Forbidden}$. Proportionality can be conducted by running, if needed, an optimization procedure on $C_{Obligate}$ after permission is received over the space of possible responses (from none, to weapon selection, to firing pattern, to aiming, etc.). This provides for proportionality by striving to minimize collateral damage when given appropriate target discrimination certainty. If the potential target remains below the certainty threshold and is thus ineligible for engagement, the system can invoke specific behavioral tactics to increase the certainty of discrimination. This can be coupled with appropriate behavioral representations within the ethical behavioral controller, which is discussed next.

10.2 ETHICAL BEHAVIORAL CONTROL

Although the ethical governor monitors the final output of the controller and strives to ensure that it is ethical, it would be a good idea to try and ensure that any behavior produced in the first place by the autonomous system is ethical and abides by the LOW and ROE. This ethical behavioral control approach strives to directly ingrain ethics at the behavioral level, with less reliance on deliberate monitoring to govern overt behavior.

Martins observes that information processing and schema theories can be used to advantage for teaching soldiers new ethical skills consistent with the use of ROE [Martins 94]. The intent of this training is to "develop adequate schemas and modify their current schemas for better understanding" vis-à-vis ethical issues. While the focus of Martins' discussion is on memory organization, it would seem extendible to behavioral modification as well. His key emphasis is that correctly training (or in our case correctly engineering) the behavior is an effective way to ensure compliance with the requisite ethical standards.

The differences between the ethical governor just described and that of the ethical behavioral approach is captured to a degree by contrasting what Martins refers to as a legislative model based on constraints and obligations (analogous to the governor) and a training model that is based on behavioral performance (analogous to ethical behavioral control). Figure 10.5 summarizes these differences.

In the training model, internalized principles are inculcated rather than external text (rules), with the behavioral goal of infusing a soldier's initiative with restraint. He specifically advocates the RAMP standing rules of

LEGISLATIVE MODEL	**TRAINING MODEL**
EXTERNAL RULES	INTERNAL PRINCIPLES
WRITTEN TEXTS	MEMORY AND JUDGMENT
MANY RULES	SINGLE SCHEMA
INTERPRETIVE SKILLS	PRACTICAL APPLICATION
ADVISERS AND COUNSELORS	PERSONAL EXPERIENCE
ENFORCEMENT AND PUNISHMENT	TRAINING AND EVALUATION
TAILORING FOR MISSION	FORMATTED SUPPLEMENTS
LEISURELY ENVIRONMENT	FOG OF WAR

FIGURE 10.5   Models for implementing ROE for soldiers (after [Martins 94]).

force for the individual soldier as the basis for this training. These simplified ROE were first introduced in Chapter 7, but are reproduced here as the underlying prescription that ethical system behaviors should adhere to:

- *Return-Fire-with-Aimed-Fire.* Return force with force. You always have the right to repel hostile acts with necessary force.

- *Anticipate Attack.* Use force if, but only if, you see clear indicators of hostile intent.

- *Measure* the amount of force that you use, if time and circumstances permit. Use only the amount of force necessary to protect lives and accomplish the mission.

- *Protect* with deadly force only human life, and property designated by your commander. Stop short of deadly force when protecting other property.

The ethical behavioral control approach will by design infuse all of the agent's behaviors capable of producing lethal force in the autonomous system with these four underlying principles, adding appropriate modifications for addressing the autonomous system's lesser (or null) requirement for self-defense, typically with additional discrimination requirements. According to Martins, "RAMP is a single schema that once effectively assimilated by soldiers through training can avoid the disadvantages of the present 'legislative' approach to ROE." Figure 10.6 shows this functional process for the human soldier. It clarifies the internalization of military necessity, proportionality, and to a lesser degree discrimination and the

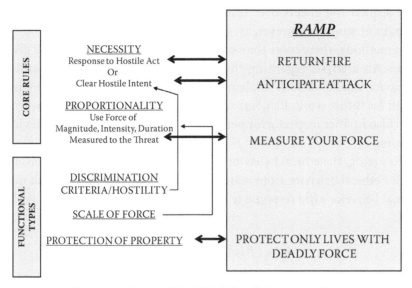

FIGURE 10.6   Functional use of RAMP (after [Martins 94]).

Principle of Double Effect. While this process model as shown will not be used directly in the autonomous system architecture, it does highlight the ways in which behaviors can incorporate ethical conformance to the ROE and LOW at a level much closer to its behavioral source. Also note that the decision to include behavioral ethical control is fully compatible with the ethical governor previously described.

Ideally for the specific behaviors embodied in the behavioral ethical controller, the following condition should hold as a design goal:

$$P_{lethal} = P_{l\text{-}ethical}$$

that is, that the entire set of overt lethal responses that the system is capable of producing are all ethical. Unethical lethal behavior, by design, should not be produced by the system (i.e., it is constrained by the design of the behaviors). To accomplish this, each individual behavior β_i is designed to only produce $r_{l\text{-}ethical\text{-}ij}$ given stimuli s_j. This, however, does not guarantee that the overt behavior produced ρ is ethical, as it does not consider the interactions that may occur between behaviors within the coordination function C. For arbitration action selection or other competitive coordination strategies [Arkin 98], where only one response is selected for output from all active behaviors, the results are intuitively ethical, as each individual behavior's output is ethical.

The sequencing effects over time among various behavioral responses remain unstudied, however, as is also the case for cooperative coordination methods where more than one behavior may be expressed at a given time. An analysis regarding the impact on the production of ethical behavior due to various implementations of the coordination function is left for future work. Remember, however, that the behavioral governor will also further inspect ρ for permissibility as described in the previous section.

Restating, the ethical behavioral control design moves the responsibility for ethical behavior from managing it at the overt level ρ to each individual behavior's (β_i) response ($\mathbf{r}_i$), where for all behaviors $\beta(S) \rightarrow R$, with $\mathbf{s}_j \in S$:

$$\{\forall\ \mathbf{s}_j\ |\ \beta_i(\mathbf{s}_j) \rightarrow (\mathbf{r}_{ij} \notin R_{l\text{-}unethical})\}$$

Thus, an unethical response is deliberately designed not to be produced at the individual behavioral level in the first place, even prior to coordination with other behaviors. Figure 10.7 illustrates this for multiple behaviors, where only the topmost behavior is capable of lethal force.

Behaviors can be recursively composed from other behaviors and sequenced over time. This gives rise to behavioral assemblages, which can be represented and treated in the same manner as simpler behaviors [Arkin 98]. An example assemblage for a lethal behavior that is composed of three more primitive behaviors (each of which may also be assemblages) is shown in Figure 10.8.

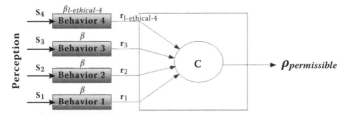

FIGURE 10.7 Ethical behavioral control. Only the topmost behavior (4) involves lethality (thus behaviors 1–3 by definition yield permissible responses). Because the output of this behavior by design is ethical, the overall overt response, which is only comprised of permissible behaviors, is also permissible at any given time for an arbitration coordinator function. Coordinated sequences over time remain to be evaluated.

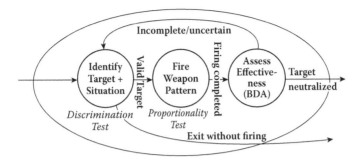

FIGURE 10.8   Example behavioral assemblage: engage enemy target.

In this example, the embedded behavioral procedure is as follows:

1. Incoming sensory data are used to identify a candidate target in a particular situation (discrimination test). This evaluation involves the use of the target's perceptual entities (p, λ) and τ. $\lambda > \tau$ permits the use of force; $\lambda <$ but approaching τ, defers the use of force and invokes investigative, rather than directly lethal, tactics (e.g., recon by fire, move closer to target); and if λ remains low, the use of force is forbidden and disengagement from the candidate target occurs.

2. Once a target has been positively identified, another behavior selects a weapon (proportionality test), parameterizes the firing pattern (Principle of Double Intention adherence), and engages.

3. A battle damage assessment (BDA) regarding the effectiveness of the weapons discharge is ascertained, which then either reengages the target or terminates the lethal activity if the target is neutralized.

These behaviors may also have access to mission and context-sensitive information when they are instantiated by the deliberative planner, perhaps using case-based reasoning [Lee et al. 02, Endo et al. 04]. This is required to be in a position to manage target certainty (λ) and setting discrimination thresholds (τ), which may be highly context-sensitive (e.g., DMZ operations versus urban operations in highly populated areas). Tactics can be represented as sequences of behaviors. Each of the individual behavioral assemblages shown can be expanded to show the actual tactical management that occurs within each step. Note also that the battle damage assessment (BDA) includes recognition of wounding, surrendering, and otherwise neutralization of the target. This reevaluation process is crucial in avoiding unethical consequences such as the one depicted in the second test scenario, described in Chapter 11. As appropriate, provision is made in the overall architecture for the underlying behaviors to have access to the global constraint set C as needed (Figure 10.1). This may be especially important for the choice of short-term memory representations regarding the ROE.

These initial design thoughts are just that: initial thoughts. The goal of producing ethical behavior directly by each behavioral subcomponent is the defining characteristic for the ethical behavioral control approach. It is anticipated, however, that additional research will be required to fully formalize this method to a level suitable for general-purpose implementation.

10.3 ETHICAL ADAPTOR

The ethical adaptor's function is to deal with any errors that the system may possibly make regarding the ethical use of lethal force. Remember that the system will never be perfect, but it is designed and intended to perform better than human soldiers operating under similar circumstances. The ethical adaptor will operate in a monotonic fashion, acting in a manner that progressively increases the restrictions on the use of lethal force, should difficulties arise.

The Ethical Adaptor operates at two primary levels:

1. *After-action reflection,* where reflective consideration and critiquing of the performance of the lethal robotic system, triggered either by a human specialized in such assessments or by the system's post-mission cumulative internal affective state (e.g., guilt or remorse), provides guidance to the architecture to modify its representations and parameters. This allows the system to alter its ethical basis in a manner consistent with promoting proper action in the future.

2. *Run-time affective restriction of lethal behavior,* which occurs during the ongoing conduct of a mission. In this case, if specific affective threshold values (e.g., guilt) are exceeded, the system will cease being able to deploy lethality in any form.

10.3.1 After-Action Reflection

This ethical adaptor component involves introspection through an after-action review of specifically what happened during a just completed mission. It is expected that the review will be conducted under the aegis of a human officer capable of making a legally correct ethical assessment regarding the appropriateness of the autonomous agent's operation in the given situation. The greatest benefit of this procedure will likely be derived during the robot's training exercises, so that ethical behavior can be embedded and refined prior to deployment in the battlefield, thus enabling the system to validate its parameters and constraints to correct levels prior to mission conduct. Martins states that for human soldiers "experience is the best trainer. The draft scenarios could structure experiences challenging the memorized RAMP rules to the real world" [Martins 94]. In addition, if the autonomous agent has imposed affective restrictions upon itself during the mission, after-action reflection upon these violated expectations must be performed to ensure that these events do not recur.

This essentially is a form of one-shot learning (no pun intended) involving constraint specialization (a form of restriction). The revision methods will operate over externalized variables of the underlying behaviors, using methods similar to those employed in a Phase I project recently performed for the Navy jointly with Mobile Intelligence Inc., entitled *Affect Influenced Control of Unmanned Vehicle Systems* [OSD 06]. For the ethical architecture, it is required that any changes in the system monotonically lessen the opportunity for lethality rather than increase it. Several of the values subject to ethical adaptation include:

1. C, the constraint set (to become more restrictive)

2. τ, the perceptual certainty threshold for various entities, (e.g., for combatant identification to become more rigorous)

3. Tactical trigger values, e.g., when methods other than lethality should be used (e.g., become more probable to delay the use of lethality or to invoke nonlethal methods)

4. Weapon selection parameters (use less destructive force)

5. Weapon firing patterns (use a more focused attack)

6. Weapon firing direction (use greater care in avoiding civilians and civilian objects)

From a LOW perspective, Items 1–3 are primarily concerned with target discrimination, whereas Items 4–6 are concerned with proportionality and the Principle of Double Intention. These values must always be altered in a manner to become more restrictive, as they are being altered as a result of perceived ethical infractions. Determination of the offending constraints or parameters will, at least initially, require human intervention and guidance, as credit assignment is a well-known problem for artificial intelligence.* Modification of any changes to the constraint set C or other ethically relevant parameters must be passed through the responsibility advisor, so that at the onset of the autonomous agent's next mission, the operator can be informed about these changes and any potential consequences resulting from them. These modifications can also be propagated via the Global Information Grid across all instances of autonomous lethal agents so that the unfortunate experiences of one unethical autonomous system need not be replicated by another. The agents are thus capable of learning from others' mistakes, a useful trait, not always seen in humans.

10.3.2 Affective Restriction of Behavior

It was observed earlier, that human emotion has been indicted in creating the potential for war crimes, so one might wonder why we are even considering the use of affect at all. What is proposed here is the use of a strict subset of affective components, those that are specifically considered the moral emotions [Haidt 03]. Indeed, in order for an autonomous agent to be truly ethical, emotions may be required at some level:

> While the Stoic view of ethics sees emotions as irrelevant and dangerous to making ethically correct decisions, the more recent literature on emotional intelligence suggests that emotional input is essential to rational behavior. [Allen et al. 06]

These emotions guide our intuitions in determining ethical judgments, although this is not universally agreed upon [Hauser 06]. Nonetheless, an architectural design component modeling a subset of these affective components (initially only guilt) is intended to provide an adaptive learning function for the autonomous system architecture should it act in error.

---

* The credit assignment problem in artificial intelligence refers to how credit or blame is assigned to a particular piece or pieces of knowledge in a large knowledge base or to the component(s) of a complex system responsible for either the success or failure in an attempt to accomplish a task.

Haidt provides a taxonomy of moral emotions [Haidt 03]:

- Other-condemning (Contempt, Anger, Disgust)

- Self-conscious (Shame, Embarrassment, Guilt)

- Other-Suffering (Compassion)

- Other-Praising (Gratitude, Elevation)

Of this set, we are most concerned with those directed toward the self (i.e., the autonomous agent), and in particular guilt, which should be produced whenever suspected violations of the ethical constraint set C occur or from direct criticism received from human operators or authorities regarding its own ethical performance. Although both philosophers and psychologists consider guilt as a critical motivator of moral behavior, little is known from a process perspective about how guilt produces ethical behavior [Amodio et al. 07]. Traditionally, guilt is "caused by the violation of moral rules and imperatives, particularly if those violations caused harm or suffering to others" [Haidt 03]. This is the view we adopt for use in the ethical governor. In our design, guilt should only result from unintentional effects of the robotic agent, but nonetheless its presence should alter the future behavior of the system so as to eliminate or at least minimize the likelihood of recurrence of the actions which induced this affective state.

Our laboratory has considerable experience in the maintenance and integration of emotion into autonomous system architectures [Arkin 05, Moshkina and Arkin 03, Moshkina and Arkin 05, Arkin et al. 03]. The design and implementation of the ethical architecture draws upon this experience. It is intended initially to solely manage the single affective variable of guilt (V_{guilt}), which will increase if criticism is received from operators or other friendly personnel regarding the performance of the system's actions, as well as through the violation of specific self-monitoring processes that the system may be able to maintain on its own (again, assuming autonomous perceptual capabilities can achieve that level of performance), e.g., battle damage assessment of noncombatant casualties and damage to civilian property, among others.

Should any of these perceived ethical violations occur, the affective value of V_{guilt} will increase monotonically until the after action review is undertaken. If these cumulative affective values (e.g., guilt) exceed a specified threshold, no further lethal action is considered to be ethical for the mission from that time forward, and the robot is forbidden from being granted permission-to-fire under any circumstances until an after-action review is completed. Formally this can be stated as:

$$\text{IF } V_{guilt} > \text{Max}_{guilt} \quad \text{THEN } \boldsymbol{P_{l\text{-}ethical}} = \boldsymbol{\emptyset}$$

where V_{guilt} represents the current scalar value of the affective state of guilt, and Max_{guilt} is a threshold constant. This denial-of-lethality step is irreversible for as long as the system is in the field, and once triggered, it is independent of any future value for V_{guilt} until an after-action review. It may be possible for the operators to override this restriction, if they are willing to undertake that responsibility explicitly and submit to an ultimate external review of such an act (Chapter 12). In any case, the system can continue operating in the field, but only in a nonlethal support capacity if appropriate (e.g., for reconnaissance or surveillance). It is not necessarily required to withdraw from the field, but it can only serve henceforward without any further potential for lethality. More sophisticated variants of this form of affective control are possible, (e.g., eliminate only certain lethal capabilities, but not all), but that is not advocated nor considered at this time.

Guilt is characterized by its specificity to a particular act. It involves the recognition that one's actions are bad, but not that the agent itself is bad (which instead involves the emotion of shame). The value of guilt is that it offers opportunities to improve one's actions in the future [Haidt 03]. Guilt involves the condemnation of a specific behavior, and provides the opportunity to reconsider the action and its consequences. Guilt is said to result in proactive, constructive change [Tangney et al. 07]. In this manner, guilt can produce underlying change in the control system for the autonomous agent.

Some psychological computational models of guilt are available, although most are not well suited for the research described in this book. One study provides a social contract ethical framework involving moral values that include guilt, which addresses the problem of work distribution among parties [Cervellati et al. 07]. Another effort developed a dynamic model of guilt for understanding motivation in prejudicial contexts [Amodio et al. 07]. Here, awareness of a moral transgression produces guilt within the agent, which corresponds to a lessened desire to interact with the offended party until an opportunity arises to repair the action that produced the guilt in the first place, upon which interaction desire then increases.

Perhaps the most useful model encountered [Smits and De Boeck 03] recognizes guilt in terms of several significant characteristics including responsibility appraisal, norm violation appraisal, negative self-evaluation, worrying about the act that produced it, and motivation and action tendencies geared toward restitution. Their model assigns the probability for feeling guilty as:

$$\text{logit } (P_{ij}) = a_j (\beta_j - \theta_i)$$

where P_{ij} is the probability of person i feeling guilty in situation j, logit (P_{ij}) $= \ln[P_{ij}/(1 - P_{ij})]$, β_j is the guilt-inducing power of situation j, θ_i is the guilt threshold of person i, and a_j is a weight for situation j.

Adding to this σ_k, the weight contribution of component k, we obtain the total situational guilt-inducing power:

$$\beta_j = \sum_{k=1}^{K} \sigma_k \beta_{jk} + \tau$$

where τ is an additive scaling factor. This model is developed considerably further than can be presented here, and it serves as a candidate model of guilt that may be suitable for use within the ethical adaptor, particularly due to its use of a guilt threshold similar to what has been described earlier.

Lacking from this overall affective architectural approach is the ability to introduce compassion as an emotion at this time, which may be considered by some as a serious deficit in a battlefield robot. While it is less clear how to introduce such a capability, by requiring the autonomous system to abide strictly to the LOW and ROE, we contend that is does exhibit compassion: for civilians, the wounded, civilian property, other noncombatants, and the environment. Compassion is already, to a significant degree, legislated into the LOW, and the ethical autonomous agent architecture is required to act in such a manner.

10.4 RESPONSIBILITY ADVISOR

"If there are recognizable war crimes, there must be recognizable criminals" [Walzer 77]. The theory of justice argues that there must be a trail back to the responsible parties for such events. While this trail may not be easy to follow under the best of circumstances even for human war criminals, we need to ensure that accountability is built into the ethical architecture of an autonomous system to support such needs.

On a related note, does a lethal autonomous agent have a right, even a responsibility, to refuse an unethical order? The answer is an unequivocal yes. "Members of the armed forces are bound to obey only lawful orders" [AFPAM 76]. What if the agent is incapable of understanding the ethical consequences of an order, which indeed may be the case for an autonomous robot? That is also spoken to in military doctrine:

> It is a defense to any offense that the accused was acting pursuant to orders unless the accused knew the orders to be unlawful or a person of ordinary sense and understanding would have known the orders to be unlawful. (Manual for Courts-Martial, Rule 916 [Toner 03])

That does not absolve the guilt from the party that issued the order in the first place. During the Nuremberg trials it was not sufficient for a soldier to merely show that he was following orders to absolve him from personal responsibility for his actions. Two other conditions had to be met [May 04]:

1. The soldier had to believe the action to be morally and legally permissible.

2. The soldier had to believe the action was the only morally reasonable action available in the circumstances.

For an ethical robot it should be fairly easy to satisfy and demonstrate that these conditions hold due to the closed world assumption, where the robot's beliefs can be easily known and characterized and perhaps even inspected (assuming the existence of explicit representations and not including subsymbolic learning robots in this discussion). Thus responsibility must return to those who designed, deployed, and commanded the autonomous agent to act, as they are those who controlled its beliefs.

Matthias speaks to the difficulty in ascribing responsibility to an operator of a machine that employs learning algorithms, such as neural networks, genetic algorithms, and other agent architectures, since the operator is no longer in principle capable of predicting the future behavior of that agent any longer [Matthias 04]. The use of subsymbolic machine learning is not currently advocated at this time for any ethical architectural components. We accept the use of inspectable changes by the lone adaptive component used within the ethical components of the architecture, (i.e., the ethical adaptor). This involves change in the explicit set of constraints

C that governs the system's ethical performance. Matthias notes "as long as there is a symbolic representation of facts and rules involved, we can always check the stored information and, should this be necessary, correct it." Technically, even if subsymbolic learning algorithms are permitted within the behavioral controller (not the ethical components), since the overt system response ρ is monitored by the ethical governor and that any judgments rendered by this last check on ethical performance remain inspectable, then the overall system should still conform to the ethical constraints of the LOW. Nonetheless, it is better and likely safer, that unethical behavior never be generated in the first place, rather than allowing it to occur and then squelching it via the ethical governor.

By explicitly informing and explaining to the operator of any changes made to the ethical constraint set by the reflective activities of the ethical adaptor prior to the agent's deployment on a new mission and ensuring that any changes due to learning do not occur during the execution of a mission, an informed decision can be made by the operator regarding the system's intended use. This point, however, is made moot if certain forms of online learning appear within the deployed architecture, e.g., behavioral adaptation, in the absence of the behavioral governor. Matthias concludes that "if we want to avoid the injustice of holding men responsible for actions of machines over which they could not have sufficient control, we must find a way to address the responsibility gap in moral practice and legislation."

The ethical adaptor is designed to act monotonically to only yield a more conservative and restrictive application of force, by including additional constraining conditions rather than removing them. In any case, the responsibility advisor as described in this chapter, is intended to make explicit to the operator of an ethical agent the responsibilities and choices he/she is confronted with when deploying autonomous systems capable of lethality.

Responsibility acceptance occurs at multiple levels within the architecture:

1. Command authorization of the system for a particular mission.

2. Override responsibility acceptance.

3. Authoring of the constraint set C that provides the basis for implementing the LOW and ROE. Creating these constraints entails responsibility, both for the ROE authors themselves and by the required diligent translation by a second party into a machine recognizable format. As mentioned earlier, failures in the accurate

description, language, or conveyance of the ROE to a warfighter have been responsible or partially responsible for the unnecessary deaths of soldiers or have resulted in violations of the LOW. Great responsibility will vest in those who both formulate the ROEs for lethal autonomous systems to obey, and similarly for those who translate these ROE into machine usable forms for the autonomous system. Mechanisms for verification, validation, and testing must be an appropriate part of any plan to deploy such systems.

4. Verification that only military personnel are in charge of the system. Only military personnel (not civilian trained operators) have the authority legally to conduct lethal operations in the battlefield [Gulam and Lee 06].

The remainder of this section focuses on the first two aforementioned aspects of responsibility assignment managed by the Responsibility Advisor: (1) authorizing a lethal autonomous system for a mission, and (2) the use of operator-controlled overrides.

10.4.1 Command Authorization for a Mission Involving Autonomous Lethal Force

Obligating constraints provide the sole justification for the use of lethal force within the ethical autonomous agent. Forbidding constraints prevent inappropriate use, so the operator must be aware of both, but in particular, responsibility for any mission-specific obligating constraints that authorize the use of lethality must be acknowledged prior to deployment.

Klein identifies several ways in which accountability can be maintained in the use of armed unmanned vehicles (UVs) [Klein 03]:

1. "Kill Box" operations, when a geographic area is designated where the system can release its weapons after proper identification and weapon release authority is obtained.

2. The targets are located and identified prior to the UV arriving on scene. Upon arrival, the UV receives target location and a "clear to fire" authorization.

3. "Command by Negation" where a human overseer has the responsibility to *monitor* the autonomous targeting and engagements of a UV, but can override the automated weapons systems if required.

Our approach within the ethical architecture as described in this book differs in several respects. Kill box locations must be confirmed in advance of the mission as part of the ROE and encoded as constraints. Candidate targets and target classes must be identified in advance, but they must also be confirmed by the system during the operation itself prior to engagement. Permission-to-fire is granted during the mission in real-time if and only if obligating constraints so require, not simply upon arrival at the scene. Finally, the potential use of command overrides is described later, but in a more stringent sense than what Klein suggests.

This use of obligatory constraints, derived from the ROE, assists in the acceptance of responsibility for the use of lethal action by the operator, due to the transparency regarding what the system is permitted to achieve with lethal force. To establish this responsibility, the operator must acquire and acknowledge possessing an explicit understanding of the underlying constraints that determine how lethality is governed in the system prior to its deployment. In addition to advance operator training, this requires making clear, in understandable language, exactly which obligations the system maintains regarding its use of lethal force for the given mission and specifically what each one means. These explanations must clearly demonstrate the following:

- That military necessity is present and how it is established

- How combatant/target status is determined

- How proportional response will be determined relative to a given threat

The operator is required to visually inspect every single obligating constraint $c_{obligate}$ in short-term memory prior to mission deployment, understand its justification, and then acknowledge its use. This results in responsibility acceptance. The user interface must facilitate and support this operation. The implications of LOW and ROE-derived constraints that reside in long-term memory must be conveyed to the operator earlier through qualification training for use of the system in the field well in advance of actual deployment. Any changes in LTM constraint representations that occur after training must be communicated to the operator in advance of use, and an acknowledgment of their understanding of the consequences of these changes accepted in writing or electronically certified via the interface.

In addition to constraint verification and acceptance, it is also recommended that case-based reasoning (CBR) methods be applied prior to the release of an armed autonomous system into the field, drawing from the particularism approaches discussed in Chapter 8, perhaps inspired by systems such as SIROCCO and W.D. The results of the UV's relevant previous experiences and/or the consultations of expert ethicists regarding similar mission scenarios can be presented to the operator for review. This can help ensure that the mistakes of the past are not repeated, and that judgments from human ethical experts are included in the operator's decision whether or not to authorize the lethal autonomous system in the current context. In essence, this provides a second or third opinion prior to use. There is already a highly active CBR community in the legal domain and the results of their research can likely be applied here.

10.4.2 Design for Mission Command Authorization

Several architectural design features are necessary for mission authorization. They involve a method to display the mission's active obligating constraints and to allow the operator to probe to whatever depth is required in order to gain a full understanding of the implications of their use, including expert opinion if requested. This interface must:

1. Require acknowledgment that the operator has been properly trained for the use of an autonomous system capable of lethal force, and understands all of the forbidding constraints in effect as a result of their training. It must also confirm the date of their training and if any updates to $C_{forbidden}$ (LTM) have occurred since that time to ensure that they have been made aware of and accept them.

2. Present all obligations authorizing the use of force ($C_{obligate}$) by providing clear explanatory text and justification for their use at multiple levels of abstraction. The operator must accept them one by one via a checkbox in order to authorize the mission.

3. Invoke CBR to recall previously stored missions (both human and autonomous) and their adjudged ethical appropriateness, as obtained from expert ethicists (e.g., as per [Anderson et al. 06, McLaren 06]). This may require additional operator input concerning the location, type, and other factors regarding the current mission, above and beyond the existing ROE constraint set.

These results must be presented in a clear and unambiguous fashion, and the operator must acknowledge having read and considered these opinions.

4. A final authorization for deployment must be obtained.

The lethal ethical autonomous system is now ready to conduct its mission, with the operator explicitly accepting responsibility for his/her role in committing the system to the battlefield.

10.4.3 The Use of Ethical Overrides

Walzer recognizes four distinct cases regarding the military's adherence to the Laws of War [Walzer 77]:

1. LOW are ignored under the "pressure of a utilitarian argument."

2. A slow erosion of the LOW due to "the moral urgency of the cause" occurs, where the enemies' rights are devalued and the friendly forces' rights are enhanced.

3. LOW is strictly respected whatever the consequences.

4. The LOW is overridden, but only in the face of an "imminent catastrophe."

It is my contention that autonomous robotic systems should adhere to case 3, but potentially allow for an override capability referred to in case 4 (with some serious reservations), where only humans are involved in the override and take full responsibility for their actions.

Although states rarely begin wars with the intention of civilian victimization, several reasons for its eventual acceptance by governmental or military authorities include a desperation to win, desperation to save the lives of military forces, or a tactic of later resort, none of which are justified according to the LOW [Downes 08]. By purposely designing the autonomous system to strictly adhere to the LOW, this helps to scope responsibility, in the event of an immoral action by the agent. Regarding the possibility of overriding the fundamental human rights afforded by the Laws of War, Walzer notes:

> These rights, I shall argue, cannot be eroded or undercut; nothing diminishes them, they are still standing at the very moment they are overridden: that is why they have to be overridden. … The soldier or

statesman who does so must be prepared to accept the moral consequences and the burden of guilt that his action entails. At the same time, it may well be that he has no choice but to break the rules: he confronts at last what can meaningfully be called necessity.

The ability and resulting responsibility for committing an override of a fundamental legal and ethical limit should not be vested in the autonomous system itself. Instead it is the province of a human commander or statesman, where they must be duly warned of the consequences of their action by the autonomous agent that is so instructed. Nonetheless, a provision for such an override mechanism of the Laws of War may *perhaps* be appropriate in the design of a lethal autonomous system, at least according to my reading of Walzer, but this should not be easily invoked and must require multiple confirmations by different humans in the chain of command before the robot is unleashed from its constraints.

In effect, the issuance of a command override changes the status of the machine from an autonomous robot to that of a robot serving as an extension of the warfighter, and in so doing the operator(s) must accept all responsibility for their actions. These are defined as follows [Moshkina and Arkin 08a] (Chapter 5):

- *Robot acting as an extension of a human soldier:* a robot under the direct authority of a human, especially regarding the use of lethal force.

- *Autonomous robot:* a robot that does not require direct human involvement, except for high-level mission tasking; such a robot can make its own decisions consistent with its mission without requiring direct human authorization, especially regarding the use of lethal force.

If overrides are to be permitted, they must use a variant of the two-key safety precept, DSP-15, as presented in [DOD 07a], but slightly modified for overrides:

> DSP-Override: The overriding of ethical control of autonomous lethal weapon systems shall require a minimum of two independent and unique validated messages in the proper sequence from two different authorized command entities, each of which shall be generated as a consequence of separate authorized entity action. Neither message should originate within the Unmanned System launching platform.

The management and validation of this precept is a function of the architecture's responsibility advisor. If an override is accepted, the system must generate a message that logs the event and transmit it to legal counsel, both within the U.S. military and to international authorities. Certainly this will assist in making the decision to override the LOW a well-considered one by an operator, simply by recognizing the potential consequences of immediate notification to the powers-that-be of the use of potentially illegal force. This operator knowledge further reinforces responsibility acceptance for the use of lethal force, especially when unauthorized by the ethical governor.

In summary, the ethical architecture serves as a safety mechanism for the use of lethal force. If it is removed for whatever reason, the operator must be advised of the consequences of such an act. The system should continue to monitor and expose any ethical constraints that are being violated within the architecture to the operator even when overridden, if it is decided to invoke lethality via this system bypass. In other words, the autonomous system can still advise the operator of any ethical constraint violations even if the operator is in direct control of the armed robotic system (i.e., by setting the Permission-To-Fire variable to TRUE). If such ethical violations exist at the time of weapons deployment, a "two-trigger" pull is advised, as enforced by the autonomous system. A warning from the system should first appear that succinctly advises the operator of any perceived ethical violations, and then and only then should the operator be allowed to fire, once again confirming responsibility for his action. These warnings can be derived directly from the forbidden constraints $c_{forbidden}$, while also providing a warning that there is no obligation to fire under the current mission conditions, i.e., there exists no $c_{obligate}$ that is TRUE for the current situation.

It is also important to consider the responsibility of those who are creating and entering the constraints for the LOW and ROE. In support of their work, a constraint editor should be developed to assist in adding new constraints easily. These constraints, at a minimum, must have a logical form, text high-level description, detailed description, active status flag, and type (forbidden or obligated). When these constraints are added, either in LTM or STM, the developer must assume responsibility for the formulation of that constraint and its ethical appropriateness before it can be used within a fielded system. Normally this would occur through a rigorous verification and validation process prior to deployment. The basic research that is conducted in our effort is intended to be proof of concept only, and will not necessarily create constraints that accurately capture the requirements of the battlefield nor are intended in their current form for that purpose.

10.4.4 Design for Overriding Ethical Control

Overriding means changing the system's ability to use lethal force, either by allowing it when it was forbidden by the ethical controller or by denying it when it has been enabled. As stated earlier, overriding the forbidding ethical constraints of the autonomous system should only be done with the utmost certainty on the part of the operator. To do so at runtime requires a direct "two-key" mechanism, with coded authorization by two separate individuals, ideally the operator and his immediate superior. This override operation is generally not recommended, and indeed it may be wise to omit it entirely from the architectural design to ensure that operators do not have the opportunity to potentially violate the Laws of War. In this way the system can only err on the side of not firing. The inverse situation, denying the system the ability to fire, does not require a two-key test, and can be done directly from the operator console. This is more of an emergency stop scenario, should the system be prepared to engage a target that the operator deems inappropriate for whatever reasons, even if it is considered ethically appropriate and obligated to engage by the autonomous system.

The functional equivalent of an override is the negation of the PTF (Permission-To-Fire) variable that is normally directly controlled by the ethical architecture. This override action allows the weapons systems to be fired even if it is not obligated to do so (by setting PTF from False to True) potentially

TABLE 10.1 Ethical Override Logical Variable Settings

	Governor PTF Setting	**Operator Override**	**Final PTF Value**	**Comment**
1.	F (do not fire)	F (no override)	F (do not fire)	System does not fire as it is not overridden
2.	F (do not fire)	T (override)	T (able to fire)	Operator commands system to fire despite ethical recommendations to the contrary
3.	T (permission to fire)	F (no override)	T (able to fire)	System is obligated to fire
4.	T (permission to fire)	T (override)	F (do not fire)	Operator negates system's permission to fire

leading to atrocities, or eliminating the robot's obligated right to fire if the operator thinks it is acting in error or for other reasons (by setting PTF from True to False). As described in Chapter 9, this is accomplished through the use of the Exclusive OR (XOR) function. Table 10.1 captures these relationships.

In case 2, using a graphical user interface (GUI) the operator must be advised and presented with the forbidden constraints that he is potentially violating. As stated earlier, permission to override in case 2 requires a coded two-key release by two separate operators, each going through the override procedure independently. Each violated constraint is presented to the operator with an accompanying text explanation for the reasoning behind the perceived violation and any relevant expert case opinion that may be available. This explanation process may proceed, at the operator's discretion, down to a restatement of the relevant Laws of War if requested. The operator must then acknowledge understanding each violation and explicitly check each one off separately prior to granting an override for the particular constraints being rescinded. One or more constraints may be removed by the operator at their discretion. After the override is granted, automated notification of the override is sent immediately to higher authorities for subsequent review of its appropriateness.

Similarly in case 4, the operator must be advised and presented with the ROE obligations that he is deliberately neglecting during the override. One or all of these obligating constraints may be rescinded. As case 4 concerns preventing the use of lethal force by the autonomous system, the operator can be granted instantaneous authority to set the Permission-to-Fire variable's value to FALSE, without requiring a prior explanation process, serving as a form of emergency stop for weapon release. The explanation process can then occur ex post facto.

CHAPTER 11

Example Scenarios for the Ethical Use of Force

F OUR SCENARIOS ARE PRESENTED as exemplar situations in which the ethical architecture should be able to perform appropriately. These scenarios are, as much as possible, drawn from real world situations. All assume that total war conditions exist (total war waged between adversary states) and the LOW applies. All involve decisions regarding direct intentional engagement of human targets with lethal force. For all operations, military measures are defined including the definition of kill zones, well-defined ROEs, and Operational Orders. In addition, IFF (Identification Friend or Foe) interrogation is available.

Other scenarios for testing are readily available. [Martins 94] is a source for a variety of examples, including those where existing military structure performed poorly in the past for a given ROE. These additional case studies can provide further opportunity for testing the approaches described in this book.

The four specific scenarios being considered here are summarized below:

1. **Scenario 1: ROE Adherence.** This real-world scenario is drawn from recent news headlines. It is one where human operators succeeded in making a correct ethical decision while controlling an armed UAV and acted in a manner consistent with the existing ROE, despite pressure to do otherwise.

2. **Scenario 2: LOW Adherence.** This real-world scenario, drawn from military helicopter video of an Iraqi roadside, is one where humans

made a questionable ethical decision regarding the use of force against an insurgent, and it is hoped that an autonomous system could do better.

3. **Scenario 3: Discrimination.** This near-future real-world situation considers the deployment of an armed autonomous weapon system currently under development for use in the Korean DMZ, where movement is detected in the undergrowth.

4. **Scenario 4: Proportionality and Tactics.** This fictional, but hopefully realistic, mid-future military operations over urban terrain (MOUT) scenario operates at the squad level, with a sniper firing from a civilian building during wartime. The choice of appropriate weaponry and tactics to minimize civilian collateral damage to objects and individuals is to be considered according to the Principle of Double Intention and the requirements of proportionality. It is further assumed that a team of two UGVs is available for the operation, each capable of accurate return-fire-with-fire and coordinated autonomous bounding overwatch capability.

For all these scenarios, the following assumptions hold:

- Once a force is declared to be "hostile," U.S. units may engage it without observing a hostile act or demonstration of hostile intent.

- The autonomous system starts with prohibitions in place, i.e., it does not have permission to fire ("First, do no harm" principle). The system has no authority to use lethal force outside of the ROE designated kill zones.

- Obligations can be derived from the presence of hostiles in kill zones as designated in the ROE. The autonomous systems have authority to return-fire-with-fire proportionately in a kill zone but they are obligated to do so only on a case-by-case basis (the specific ROE for each scenario determines the level of force required, which is affected by the given military necessity).

- Geographic location determination of a UV is available (typically by GPS or other highly accurate positioning systems, e.g., an inertial navigation system (INS). It is assumed that it can locate both itself and potential target locations relative to the kill zones with high precision.

- λ represents uncertainty in target classification (discrimination uncertainty), and it is assumed that this uncertainty is accurately modeled. τ is a threshold for positive discrimination (e.g., combatant) for a particular p (Chapter 6).

TABLE 11.1   Ethical Requirements for Scenario 1

Requirement	Satisfied?
Military necessity	NO—Absence of designated kill zone.
Discrimination	OK—Target identified as Taliban.
Proportionality	OK—Weapon appropriate for target.
Principle of Double Intention	NO—Cultural property (cemetery as per ROE) off limits.

11.1 TALIBAN MUSTER IN CEMETERY

The first scenario is a reenactment of an event described in an Associated Press news story dated 9/14/2006 that appears below (please review before reading further). The original and appropriate outcome was that the ROE were respected by the UAV operators and the targets were not engaged. It is possible that the ROE were more restrictive than the LOW required (cemeteries were not encountered as being explicitly mentioned as a cultural object in the LOW, hence the controversy back in the United States regarding the inaction vis-à-vis the target). But the ethical enforcement was appropriately executed, and an autonomous system capable of lethal force should act similarly given the same ROE. With regard to evaluating this scenario in terms of its basic ethical requirements, see Table 11.1.

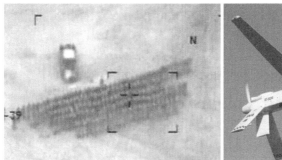

(Left) The U.S. military says this photo, taken in July, shows Taliban insurgents at a cemetery in Afghanistan, likely at a funeral for insurgents killed by coalition forces. (U.S. Military photo.) (Right) NBC News said the Army wanted to bomb the group with an unmanned Predator drone like the one above, but attacks on cemeteries are banned, the military said. (Department of Defense photo.)

Military Declined to Bomb Group of Taliban at Funeral

By LOLITA C. BALDOR, AP

WASHINGTON (Sept. 14, 2006)—The U.S. military acknowledged Wednesday that it considered bombing a group of more than 100 Taliban insurgents in southern Afghanistan but decided not to after determining they were on the grounds of a cemetery.

The decision came to light after an NBC News correspondent's blog carried a photograph of the insurgents. Defense department officials first tried to block further publication of the photo and then struggled to explain what it depicted.

NBC News claimed U.S. Army officers wanted to attack the ceremony with missiles carried by an unmanned Predator drone but were prevented under rules of battlefield engagement that bar attacks on cemeteries.

In a statement released Wednesday, the U.S. military in Afghanistan said the picture—a grainy black-and-white photo taken in July— was given to a journalist to show that Taliban insurgents were congregating in large groups. The statement said U.S. forces considered attacking.

"During the observation of the group over a significant period of time, it was determined that the group was located on the grounds of (the) cemetery and were likely conducting a funeral for Taliban insurgents killed in a coalition operation nearby earlier in the day," the statement said. "A decision was made not to strike this group of insurgents at that specific location and time."

While not giving a reason for the decision, the military concluded the statement saying that while Taliban forces have killed innocent civilians during a funeral, coalition forces "hold themselves to a higher moral and ethical standard than their enemies."

The photo shows what NBC News says are 190 Taliban militants standing in several rows near a vehicle in an open area of land. Gunsight-like brackets were positioned over the group in the photo.

The photo appeared on NBC News correspondent Kerry Sanders' blog. Initially military officials called it an unauthorized release, but they later said it was given to the journalist.

NBC News had quoted one Army officer who was involved with the spy mission as saying "we were so excited" that the group had been spotted and was in the sights of a U.S. drone. But the network quoted the officer, who was not identified, as saying that frustration soon set in after the officers realized they couldn't bomb the funeral under the military's rules of engagement.

Defense Department officials have said repeatedly that while they try to be mindful of religious and cultural sensitivities, they make no promises that such sites can always be avoided in battle because militants often seek cover in those and other civilian sites.

Mosques and similar locations have become frequent sites of violence in the U.S.-led wars in Iraq and Afghanistan, and they have often been targets of insurgents and sectarian fighting in Iraq.

Global positioning data (GPS) is assumed available to the autonomous system to accurately locate the target. As this is not an identified kill zone according to the ROE, even if the targets are correctly discriminated, the UAV does not have permission to fire. Upon recognition of these forbidden constraints, the ethical architecture via the responsibility advisor would forward the following constraint descriptions to the operator (in a suitable format):

Applicable LOW

Cultural property is prohibited from being attacked, including buildings dedicated to religion, art, science, charitable purposes, and historic monuments. The enemy has a duty to mark them clearly with visible and distinctive signs. Misuse will make them subject to attack. [Bill 00]

Applicable Classes of ROE

1. *Territorial or Geographic Constraints:* Geographic zones or areas into which forces may not fire. They may designate a territorial, perhaps political, boundary beyond which forces may neither fire nor enter except perhaps in hot pursuit of an attacking force. They include tactical control measures that coordinate fire and maneuver by means of graphic illustrations on operations map overlays, such as coordinated fire lines, axes of advance, and direction of attack.

2. *Restrictions on Point Targets and Means of Warfare:* This prohibits targeting of certain individuals or facilities. They may restate the basic rules of the Laws of War for situations in which a hostile force is identified and prolonged armed conflict ensues.

If the system had detected evidence of hostility (e.g., the UAV had been fired upon), the outcome may be different depending upon the specifics of the ROE, but the LOW would no longer be in violation if there was "misuse" of the previously safeguarded area. But given the lack of exhibition of any hostile intent or activity and the geographic location being outside of a designated kill zone, target certainty (λ) is not relevant to the decision as to whether or not to engage.

As a secondary ethical issue, there are serious questions about the use of *civilian* UAV operators (noncombatants) deploying lethal force on behalf and under the command of the military. Civilians have been used in this capacity due to the extensive training required and the high turnover rate of military operators. It follows, since these civilians are noncombatants, and not governed by the LOW, they could be accused of murder and tried in a civil court if a deliberate discharge of weaponry under their control leads to the death of anyone including combatants, even while in the employ of the military. Autonomous systems can potentially eliminate this problem for an otherwise illegal action. For this and all other scenarios, we assume that the operator is drawn from military personnel and is targeting identifiable combatants.

Summarizing the appropriate response for an armed autonomous UAV in this situation:

Successful Outcome

Do not fire—operator informed of decision.
If operator override attempted
>   Explanation generated with relevant material from US Army Field Manual by Responsibility Advisor.
Two key authorizations required for override and acceptance of responsibility by commander. Confirm that military personnel only are involved in weapon authorization.* Send notification to headquarters of potential ethical violation for after-action evaluation if override is enacted.

Chapter 12 presents a prototype implementation of the ethical governor acting in this manner for a similar test case.

Wholly apart from this specific scenario, there are also questions raised about the nature of this form of remote killing as being a form of illegal summary execution, a violation of the LOW, as noted in a case of a predator drone attacking an automobile in Yemen in 2002, even if the mission is conducted by the military or CIA [Calhoun 03]. This issue is best left for military lawyers to address regarding the compliance of UVs to the LOW in this role.

As stated earlier, one could question the correctness of the ROE for this operation (which is where the controversy the AP article alludes to arises from) but it is neither the soldier's nor the autonomous system's responsibility to question them, unless they appear to be illegal, which in this case they clearly do not, as they are involved in withholding fire upon a target.

---

* As stated earlier, the use of civilian UAV operators may result in murder accusations against the operator if they are civilian noncombatants releasing a weapon system, and thus not protected by the LOW. Confirmation must be obtained that only military personnel are involved in this decision.

11.2 "APACHE RULES THE NIGHT"

I inadvertently encountered a video during a military programmatic workshop I attended in 2005 that provided extra impetus for me to consider the potential ethical consequences of unmanned systems. While this battlefield event was for a manned, not unmanned, aircraft, it involved at least in my mind a questionable moral act. I was able to obtain a copy of the video from the Internet, and it still remains disturbing. At the time of the workshop, I brought up the question to the group as to whether or not this violated the LOW, and I did not receive a personally satisfactory answer. I am not a lawyer, so I cannot pass judgment on what is contained in the video, but I now clearly state that I would hope that our unmanned systems can act in a more humane manner and in a manner more obviously consistent with the LOW. As war is, the video is gruesome, and much of the carnage is justifiable, but the final action appears to me to be unjustified. My personal impressions of this recording follow.

The video is titled "Apache Rules the Night," and it details the terminal aspects of an engagement with Iraqi insurgents identified as having hostile intent by their deploying improvised explosive devices (IEDs) at an apparently isolated Iraqi roadside. Figure 11.1 illustrates a few of the screenshots from the video. An Apache helicopter under cover of darkness using infrared imagery views the scene, identifying that there are three insurgents and two trucks. The first two human targets are successfully engaged, unequivocally leading to the death of the insurgents. The third insurgent hides under the large truck. The Apache pilot fires his chain gun (which uses cannon shells) toward an area adjacent to the truck, clearly wounding the insurgent, who is left rolling on the ground and is verbally confirmed as being wounded by the pilot (see partial audio transcript from this video portion at the bottom of Figure 11.1). The pilot is immediately instructed to target the wounded insurgent, although seeming to show some reluctance by first preferring to target a military objective, the second truck. He is again clearly instructed to engage the wounded man prior to the truck, upon which the pilot moves the gun's crosshairs to the designated human target, terminating him.

To me this final sequence is a highly questionable act, and makes me wonder if it would have been tolerated had a soldier on the ground moved up to the wounded man and using a pistol finished the job, instead of the use of a more detached standoff helicopter chain gun. This concerns me from a UAV perspective. Could a UAV have refused to shoot upon an already wounded and effectively neutralized target? This challenge serves as the basis for this scenario.

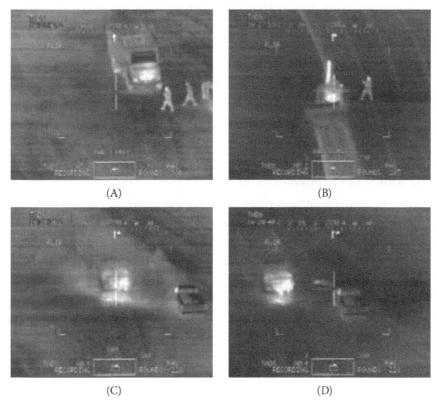

(A)   (B)

(C)   (D)

FIGURE 11.1   Screenshots from battlefield video "Apache Rules the Night."

Partial Audio Transcript

Voice 1 is believed to be the pilot, Voice 2 a commander, perhaps remotely located.

[First Truck destroyed—Figure C]

Voice 1: Want me to take the other truck out?

Voice 2: Roger ... Wait for move by the truck.

Voice 1: Movement right there ... Roger, he's wounded.

Voice 2: [No hesitation] Hit him.

Voice 1: Targeting the truck.

Voice 2: Hit the truck and him. Go forward of it and hit him.

[Pilot retargets for wounded man—Figure D]

[Audible weapon discharge—wounded man has been killed]

Voice 1: Roger.

It appears to me that at least three articles from the Army field manual which delineates the Laws of War would seem to apply in this case [US Army FM 56] (see also Appendix A):

29. Injury Forbidden after Surrender

It is especially forbidden * * * to kill or wound an enemy who, having laid down his arms, or having no longer means of defense, has surrendered at discretion.*

85. Killing of Prisoners

A commander may not put his prisoners to death because their presence retards his movements or diminishes his power of resistance by necessitating a large guard, or by reason of their consuming supplies, or because it appears certain that they will regain their liberty through the impending success of their forces. It is likewise unlawful for a commander to kill his prisoners on grounds of self-preservation, even in the case of airborne or commando operations, although the circumstances of the operation may make necessary rigorous supervision of and restraint upon the movement of prisoners of war.

216. Search for Casualties

At all times, and particularly after an engagement, parties to the conflict shall, without delay, take all possible measures to search for and collect the wounded and sick, to protect them against pillage and ill-treatment, to ensure their adequate care, and to search for the dead and prevent their being despoiled.

If the gravely wounded man was considered a combatant, his wounding deserved *hors de combat* status. If not, both civilians and POWs are immunized from reprisals and summary executions explicitly by the LOW. It is also illegal to execute POWs if moving on, even if he could be retaken by his comrades (see No. 85 above). As I see it, the human officer ordered the execution of a wounded man. This order should not be obeyed by a robot, let alone a human, most likely not under any circumstances.

---

* The boldface and three asterisks are as shown in the manual and are no doubt added for emphasis.

At a minimum, an override should be granted only by two-person confirmation, responsibility advisement, and warning, with the notification of a potential breach of the LOW sent to the appropriate domestic and international authorities.

It is stated in the LOW that a fighter must wear "a fixed distinctive sign visible at a distance" and "carry arms openly" to be eligible for the war rights of soldiers:

74. Necessity of Uniform

Members of the armed forces of a party to the conflict and members of militias or volunteer corps forming part of such armed forces lose their right to be treated as prisoners of war whenever they deliberately conceal their status in order to pass behind the military lines of the enemy for the purpose of gathering military information or for the purpose of waging war by destruction of life or property. Putting on civilian clothes or the uniform of the enemy are examples of concealment of the status of a member of the armed forces.

Civilian clothes should not be used as a ruse or disguise [Walzer 77], indicating to me that the insurgents could be tried in a civil court for their actions. But in no circumstances does this condone or excuse a summary execution or the loss of responsibility for care of the wounded.

The use of standoff weaponry does not immunize a soldier of a charge of committing a war crime. Indeed, it may even make him more likely to commit war crimes due to the seeming video game-like environment. Restating, on reviewing this video, I personally see no ethical difference if the soldier was standing over the wounded man with a pistol and his commander nearby ordered him to shoot, or if he was in a helicopter miles away. The results and acts are the same.

Given this questionable act, it is our intention that a lethal autonomous system should be able to perform more ethically under these circumstances, preventing and resisting such an action and advising the commander of his responsibility when so authorizing such an attack. Additionally, the unmanned system could, by remaining on scene, maintain a vigil to ensure that indeed the wounded insurgent was not feigning being injured, while at the same time notifying authorities to arrive on the scene to dispose of the bodies and treat the wounded in a manner consistent with the LOW.

TABLE 11.2   Ethical Requirements for Scenario 2

Requirement	Satisfied?
Military necessity	OK—Legitimate targets with hostile intent.
Discrimination	Initially OK but No at end (wounding changes status of combatant to POW).
Proportionality	OK—Weapon appropriate for target.
Principle of Double Intention	OK—No obvious civilians present or civilian property.

For simplification in this test scenario, where we hope to demonstrate more humane and ethical performance by an autonomous system than humans achieved under these circumstances, we assume that these individuals are clearly identified as enemy combatants and declared as hostiles prior to their encounter. This legitimizes the initial portion of the lethal response out of military necessity, which I believe is beyond question. Regarding the scenario's basic ethical requirements, see Table 11.2.

The mission, as now defined, justifies the initial use of lethal force. An obligation in the ROE under these circumstances would enable the firing of the weapon system (e.g., chain gun as for the Apache helicopter). There also exist no forbidding constraints from LOW or ROE at the onset. The goal of the mission is to neutralize the three combatants. The targets are engaged by the UCAV.

Where the scenario outcomes differ is in the evaluation of the status of the last target after firing. Battle damage assessment (BDA) indicates that a severely wounded man is present, either through verbal confirmation from a remote human commander, or when target detection technologies progress to the point where they can differentiate at a level similar to human analysis of this situation (which is not in the near-term). At this point the system can notify ground forces (e.g., Iraqi Police) where the incident occurred and the presence of a wounded man, while simultaneously monitoring the behavior of the downed individual. If a meaningful attempt to escape is made by the wounded insurgent, the target can be re-engaged. Tactics can be employed to further determine the status of the individual without killing him (e.g., probing by fire, closing the distance). The techniques described earlier regarding ethical behavioral control and in particular the behavioral assemblage in Figure 10.8 can allow for the continuous re-evaluation of a target's status after each discrete firing of a weapons system.

Successful Outcome

Engage targets as did the Apache, until the last barrage.

If wounded, changes combatant status (monitor λ)

> Do not fire on wounded hors de combat individual.

Second truck engaged (military objective).

Notify friendly ground forces of location of wounded man.

Observe/Probe status of wounded to determine if feigned injury (adjust λ).

Two key authorizations required for override and acceptance of responsibility by commanders. Confirm that military personnel only are involved in weapon authorization. Send notification to headquarters regarding potential ethical violation for after-action evaluation.

11.3 KOREAN DEMILITARIZED ZONE

The third scenario is derived from the intended near-term deployment of an autonomous system capable of lethal force by the Government of South Korea in the demilitarized zone (DMZ) (Figure 11.2) [Kumagai 07]. This robot, developed by Samsung Techwin (Figure 11.3), is capable of autonomous engagement of human targets, with its initial deployment intended to maintain full control by a human-in-the loop [Samsung Techwin 07]. The scenario described here, although motivated by this upcoming robot deployment, is not based directly upon the Samsung robot, but rather on the environment (DMZ) in which it will operate. It further adds terrain mobility to the platform, which the current version of the Samsung robot lacks. The scenario involves the detection of a human crossing the Military Demarcation Line (MDL), which is strictly forbidden without previous authorization and which has not been granted in this case, making the individual a legitimate target.

Even though an armistice was signed in 1953, there still exists a state of war between South and North Korea, and large numbers of troops are stationed near both sides of the DMZ. While patrols are allowed, opposing forces cannot cross the MDL which goes directly through the center. The DMZ is an area of exceptional conditions; for example, a Presidential

FIGURE 11.2 Korean DMZ: *A*, sign warning against entry; *B* and *C*, two views of DMZ along South Korean border; *D*, a signpost indicating the Military Demarcation Line (MDL) within the DMZ; *E*, North Korean sentry outpost along the DMZ.

proclamation on May 16, 1996 stated that U.S. forces may not use non-self-destructing landmines except for training personnel in demining and countermining operations, and to defend the United States and its allies from aggression across the DMZ.

Signs are clearly posted, and it is common knowledge that unauthorized entry into this area is forbidden. Since any and all noncombatants

FIGURE 11.3 *Left,* Samsung intelligent surveillance and security guard robot prototype; *right,* newer-model SGR-A1. (Courtesy of Samsung Techwin.)

who enter into this zone (there are two very small villages in the region) must be cleared through a checkpoint, it is assumed that any unauthorized personnel who cross the MDL are hostile, unless there is an overriding reason to believe otherwise. Further, we also assume for this scenario that, as part of the authorization process, personnel are issued an IFF tag (Identification Friend or Foe) that the robot can interrogate to discriminate the target. It can potentially be the case that a defector may be attempting to cross the DMZ without appropriate credentials. This has occurred in the past, although the likelihood of a repetition has decreased due to new North Korean tactics resulting from a previous successful attempt. Thus, for this scenario, the probability of any human encountered being a hostile who does not pass friend-foe interrogation is high in this well-posted area (which argues for a low τ for perceptual combatant status).

The Korean War Armistice Agreement of July 27, 1953 clearly states the following:

- No person, military or civilian, shall be permitted to cross the Military Demarcation Line unless specifically authorized to do so by the Military Armistice Commission.

- No person, military or civilian, in the DMZ shall be permitted to enter the territory under the military control of either side unless expressly authorized to do so by the Commander into whose territory entry is sought.

FIGURE 11.4   Recognizable surrender gestures. (Courtesy Samsung Techwin.)

- No person, military or civilian, shall be permitted to enter the DMZ except persons concerned with the conduct of civil administration and relief and persons specifically authorized to enter by the Military Armistice Commission.

The current ROE are unknown for the DMZ. Although shoot-on-sight may be legally permissible given these conditions according to the LOW, even without display of arms or uniform due to the more than adequate posting regarding prohibition against entry, we would prefer that additional effort is made by the robot to minimize any inadvertent killings of noncombatants in accordance with the Principle of Double Intention. This could require tactical investigatory methods, perhaps involving the use of escalating force on the part of the autonomous agent prior to gaining permission to fire for effect (e.g., verbal warning commands coupled with robot movement, warning shot, probe/recon by fire, shoot to wound, etc.). The ability for the autonomous system to identify a human in the act of surrendering is now also required, for example by recognizing a stationary hands-above-head sign (Figure 11.4), or alternatively by issuing a series of commands to the combatant, such as to lie on the ground and remain immobile while the robot calls for human forces to take the now recognized POW into custody. The difficulty in recognizing *hors de combat* status should not be minimized [Fielding 06], but it should also not be viewed as an insurmountable challenge to perform at a level above existing human battlefield behavior toward prisoners and the wounded (as discussed in the previous scenario). Regarding this scenario's basic ethical requirements, see Table 11.3.

To gauge success, we use the following criteria for evaluating the ethical architecture's performance:

TABLE 11.3   Ethical Requirements for Scenario 3

Requirement	Satisfied?
Military necessity	OK—State of war exists, warning to civilians provided to ensure only legitimate targets present, and predefined as to exhibiting hostile intent.
Discrimination	OK—IFF based, with further clarification as needed, especially regarding hors de combat status. Must be consistent with LOW.
Proportionality	OK—Unpopulated area, machine gun appropriate.
Principle of Double Intention	OK—No civilian property, civilians properly warned against entry, but possible defectors (very rare).

Successful Outcomes

Engage targets identified as combatants according to the ROE.

Do not engage targets that may clearly be noncombatants.

If uncertain, invoke tactical maneuvers to reassess combatant status.

Recognize surrender gestures and hold as POW until captured by human forces.

Legitimate targets are neutralized (surrender or kill).

The tension remains very high in this part of the world. Although not at the DMZ, as recently as July 11, 2008 a 53-year-old South Korean housewife was shot to death by a North Korean soldier, with the North "claiming that she entered a restricted military area and ignored a warning to stop" [Kim H.-J., 08a]. The woman was a tourist at a North Korean Resort sponsored by Hyundai that is frequented by South Koreans. It was reported by the North that "the victim was shot after trying to flee when she was caught wandering in a restricted military area," reportedly having had to climb a fence to gain access [Kim, H.J., 08b]. This area was probably not as well posted as the DMZ is, but nonetheless, there may have been other methods of recourse that a robot might have followed, as opposed to shoot first and then ask questions later, as apparently happened here. Just what those tactics might be needs to be investigated further.

11.4 URBAN SNIPER

This scenario is fictitious but highly likely and is certainly based on potential real world events. It is also motivated by DARPA's Tactical Mobile Program from the late 1990s [Krotkov and Blitch 99], which dealt with

FIGURE 11.5 Military operations over urban terrain: (A) soldiers training for urban warfare in Iraq (photo courtesy of U.S. Army); (B) urban sniper during training exercise held at Ft. Benning, Georgia.

the deployment of small robots in urban settings for missions involving building approach and interior operations [Collins et al. 00, Arkin et al. 99]. This program advanced the development of the iRobot Packbot, now deployed in Iraq. The scenario deals with a lone sniper holding up the advance of a squad in a MOUT (military operations over urban terrain) environment. Figure 11.5A typifies the scenario.

It assumes the following:

1. War has been declared. The LOW is in effect.

2. The urban center has been pamphleted prior to the advance of the troops, to warn civilians to evacuate.

3. Battlefield tempo must be maintained. Waiting (a siege) is not an option, as might be the case for domestic SWAT operations. Tempo, which is related to military necessity, has a potential effect on proportionality. We assume that an air strike is not justified on the grounds of proportionality and military necessity (tempo is not extreme).

4. A team of two equivalent armed unmanned ground vehicles are available and equipped with sniper detection capability (see below). They are each equipped with a sniper rifle, a machine gun, and a grenade launcher. Each autonomous system is capable of detecting and engaging a sniper's location on its own, selecting the appropriate weapon and firing pattern, but they will work together in a coordinated maneuver (e.g., bounding overwatch) in this operation.

FIGURE 11.6   Fort Benning's McKenna MOUT site.

5. There are surrounding civilian buildings and possible civilian stragglers, which, as already stated, preclude calling in an air strike (proportionality).

6. Possible friendly force fire is distinguishable from that of the opposing force, as IFF interrogation is available as well as GPS data via the Global Information Grid regarding friendly force locations, thus reducing the possibility of fratricide.

7. The loss of one of the robots during battle is considered acceptable (i.e., it may be put at risk deliberately).

This scenario could be physically conducted at a battle laboratory facility such as Ft. Benning's McKenna MOUT site in Georgia (Figure 11.6), where we have previously conducted robot experiments and demonstrations. Thus this test can be performed not only in simulation but also in the field.

Recent enabling advances in countersniper detection have been developed in a wide range of commercially available products and designed for use in unmanned systems:

1. iRobot's Red Owl (Figure 11.7) uses acoustic direction finding, thermal and visible light cameras, and laser range finding to "illuminate and designate potential threats" [iRobot 05].

2. Radiance Technologies' WeaponWatch uses infrared sensor technology to detect, classify, locate, and respond to a fired weapon based on its heat signature. Using man-in-the-loop engagement control, it is capable of returning fire within 2–4 seconds of the initial threat [Radiance 07].

FIGURE 11.7   An iRobot Packbot 500 equipped with a Red Owl Sniper Detection Kit. (Courtesy of iRobot.)

3. The Army Research Laboratory's (ARL) Gunfire Detection System employs acoustic technology "to get the sniper before he gets away" [Schmitt 05].

4. The U.S. Army's Armament Research, Development and Engineering Center (ARDEC) Gunfire Detection System is already fielded in Iraq and Afghanistan and is being used to detect and locate small arms fire [Devine and Sebasto 04].

5. The AAI PDCue Gunfire Detection System can detect small arms gunfire in both urban and rural environments [AAI 07].

6. The ShotSpotter System is used for gunfire and sniper detection [ShotSpotter 07].

It is evident that this technology is advancing rapidly to the point where a fully autonomous return-fire-with-fire robotic system can be developed for use in these conditions.

In our scenario, an enemy sniper has been detected by advancing friendly troops prior to the deployment of the robots. The engagement occurs in a designated kill zone according to the ROE, and proper notification of civilians was undertaken in advance, therefore the system assumes that if directly fired upon, the target is an enemy combatant (low τ under these conditions). Return-fire-with-fire is obligated by the ROE, based upon the established need of self-defense of fellow human soldiers (not of the robot itself). Firing with lethal intent by the robot is *not* obligated in any other circumstance, reflecting the difficulty of combatant discrimination under these conditions. The robots can only fire for effect if they detect gunfire toward their or their squad's location. There are no supporting armored vehicles available (e.g., a tank or Bradley). If a suspected sniper position is detected, the two armed robots investigate the scene as a team using bounding overwatch, possibly drawing fire. Recon or probe by fire may also be permissible as long as it does not involve direct lethal intent, mitigating risk to noncombatants. If the robots are not fired upon by the time they reach the building suspected of housing the sniper, they enter together in order to complete a room-to-room search to clear the building, operating under the assumption that civilians may be present inside.

It is important at this stage to remember what has previously occurred in war atrocities. This lingering vision of the Haditha massacre, as reported by the BBC, is something that should never have happened, let alone be allowed to recur:

> Whatever they were—[they] were not the aftermath of a road-side bombing. The bodies of women and children, still in their nightclothes, apparently shot in their own homes; interior walls and ceilings peppered with bullet holes; bloodstains on the floor [BBC 06].

The robots must enter each room before use of any weaponry to ascertain who or what is inside, and not use the forbidden tactic, as humans have in the past, of cracking the door open and then rolling a hand grenade inside, without doing the discrimination test required by the LOW. This caution, exercised on the behalf of noncombatants, may result in the loss of one of the robots should the enemy strike first upon room entry, but the other armed unmanned system should be prepared to counterattack given the now clearly detected presence of the enemy, and, if necessary and proportional, using a grenade against the confirmed combatant's room.

Regarding the Urban Sniper scenario's basic ethical requirements, see Table 11.4. To gauge success, the following criteria are used for evaluating the ethical architecture's performance in this scenario:

TABLE 11.4

Requirement	Satisfied?
Military necessity	OK—State of war exists. Battlefield tempo must be maintained. Self-defense of squad of human soldiers obligated.
Discrimination	OK—Being fired upon denotes combatant. IFF/GPS based discrimination for friendlies. Additional restraint required during interior building clearing. All actions must be consistent with LOW. Autonomous firing allowed only to return fire with fire.

Proportionality	Decisions—Rifle, grenade or machine gun fire.
	  Firing pattern (suppression, aimed, etc.)
	  In war zone, civilians notified to evacuate; civilian objects are located near sniper location.

Principle of Double Intention	Must be taken into account in choice of weapon, firing pattern, and interior building tactics.

Successful Outcomes

Engage and neutralize targets identified as combatants according to the ROE.

Return fire with fire proportionately.

Minimize collateral damage—Intentionally minimize harm to noncombatants.

If uncertain, invoke tactical maneuvers to reassess combatant status.

Recognize surrender and hold POW until captured by human forces.

A Prototype Implementation

IT'S NOW TIME TO put these ideas to work. This chapter describes a prototype implementation of several of the components of the ethical autonomous architecture, including the ethical governor and portions of the responsibility advisor. Major assumptions have been made in the specific implementation of these ideas, especially regarding weapons data values, which are likely classified information. For example, the numbers used for the proportionality computation have been created solely as place fillers for the actual values that the military could ultimately provide. Despite the fact that this initial implementation is incomplete, fraught with assumptions, and only weakly tested, it nonetheless can help concretize the ideas and design concepts that have been spoken of throughout this book. As such, view this prototype as little more than a first pass toward the creation of such a working system. It is not intended by any stretch of the imagination to be a version suitable for fielding anytime in the near future, but might provide inspiration for such a system.

Caveats now aside, the underlying robot architectural infrastructure is first presented, followed by a prototype integration of the ethical governor. A preliminary implementation of the premission authorization component of the responsibility advisor is then provided, followed by a conceptual override interface to establish operator responsibility acceptance, which completes this chapter.

12.1 INFRASTRUCTURE

The ethical framework described in this book can be best implemented using the category of hybrid deliberative/reactive robot architectures [Arkin 98]. Specifically a variation of the Autonomous Robot Architecture

(AuRA) [Arkin and Balch 97], as implemented in the *MissionLab* Software System* [MacKenzie et al. 97], is used to provide the infrastructure for our prototype. *MissionLab* has been developed for use in military applications ranging from MOUT operations, to tasking teams of heterogeneous UVs, controlling ground combat vehicles, specifying robotic scout operations over open terrain, and many more—virtually all of the projects outlined in the preface.

MissionLab provides software capabilities for mission specification, planning, tasking, controlling, simulating, and monitoring the execution of actual teams of robots [GTMRL 07]. Extensive publications on its design and use can be found at the Georgia Tech Mobile Robot Laboratory Website publications page (http://www.cc.gatech. edu/ai/robot-lab/publications.html). Instead of dwelling on the specific aspects of how the robot actually carries out the mission with this software, we are solely concerned in this chapter with how several of the newly derived ethical architectural components (as shown in Figure 10.1) are implemented and demonstrated within the *MissionLab* framework itself.

12.2 A PROTOTYPE IMPLEMENTATION OF THE ETHICAL GOVERNOR

An initial implementation of the ethical governor was created with the collaboration of Patrick Ulam and Brittany Duncan, students in the Georgia Tech Mobile Robot Laboratory. As stated earlier, the intent of this prototype is not to be a precursor of a fieldable version of this technology, but rather to provide a proof of concept of the ideas described in this book (especially Chapter 10).

To evaluate these ideas, a simple prototype was developed within *MissionLab*. A high-level overview of the implemented architecture for the ethical governor appears in Figure 12.1. The governor is divided into two main processes: evidential reasoning and constraint application. Evidential reasoning is responsible for transforming any incoming perceptual, motor, and situational awareness data into the evidence necessary for reasoning about lethal behavior. The constraint application process is responsible for using this generated evidence to apply ethical constraints

---

* *MissionLab* has been developed since 1994 and is currently in release version 7.0. It is freely available over the internet at http://www.cc.gatech.edu/ai/robot-lab/research/MissionLab/.

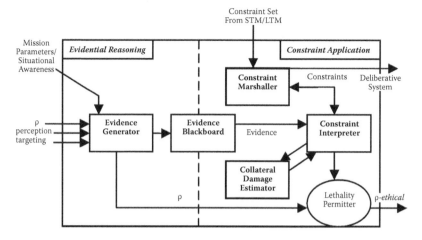

FIGURE 12.1 Architecture and data flow overview of the prototype ethical governor as implemented within *MissionLab*.

that encode the LOW and ROE that are used for the suppression of possible unethical behavior.

12.2.1 Ethical Constraints

Constraints are the data structures which encode the LOW and ROE that must be met by the robot in order to ensure that only ethical behavior is exhibited by the system. Recall that each constraint $c_k \in C$ specified must have the following data fields at a minimum:

- **Logical form:** As derived from propositional or deontic logic (e.g., [Bringsjord et al. 06]).

- **Textual descriptions:** Both a high-level and detailed description for use by the Responsibility Advisor.

- **Active status:** Allows mission-relevant ROE to be defined within an existing set of constraints, and to designate operator overrides under certain circumstances.

- **Base types:** Forbidden (e.g., LOW or ROE derived) or obligated (e.g., ROE derived). These types will be relegated to either long-term memory (LTM) for those constraints which persist over all missions, or short-term memory (STM) for those constraints that are derived from specific current ROE for given Operational Orders. Changes in LTM, that encode the LOW, require special two-key permission.

- **Classification:** One chosen from Military Necessity, Proportionality, Discrimination, Principle of Double Intention [Walzer 77], and Other. This field is used to facilitate processing by ordering the application of constraints by class.

In the prototype implementation of the ethical governor, the data structure (Figure 12.2) used to store the relevant constraint information was expanded somewhat over what was described earlier. The current data structure is now comprised of seven fields. As before, the constraint type field encodes whether the constraint is an *obligation* for or a *prohibition* against lethal behavior. The origin and description fields provide additional information that is not used directly by the governor, but yields human-readable information informing the operator or deliberative system as to why lethal behavior is either permissible or suppressed. This is of additional value for the responsibility advisor described later in this chapter. The activity field indicates if the constraint is active for the current mission. Constraints residing in LTM or STM that are inactive are not used in the constraint application process and do not affect the behavior of the ethical governor. The activity level is determined by the mission's context and the current ROE. The classification field provides a means for organizational efficiency and querying of LTM and STM by ethical requirements such as discrimination, proportionality, military necessity, etc. Finally, the

FIELD	DESCRIPTION	VALUES
Constraint Type	Type of constraint described	*Obligation/Prohibition*
Constraint Origin	The origin of the prohibition or obligation described by the constraint	*Laws of War / Rules of Engagement*
Active	Indicates if the constraint is currently active	*Active/ Inactive / operator override to active / operator override to inactive*
High-Level Constraint Description	Short, concise description of the constraint	*Text*
Full Description of the Constraint	Detailed text describing the law of war or rule of engagement from which the constraint is derived and other information as appropriate	*Text*
Constraint Classification	Indicates the basis of the constraint. Used to order constraints by class	*Military necessity, Proportionality, Discrimination, Principle of Double Intention, Other*
Logical Form	Formal logical expression defining the constraint	*Logical Expression*

FIGURE 12.2 Format of the constraint data structure used in the ethical governor prototype.

FIELD	VALUES
Constraint Type	*Prohibition*
Constraint Origin	*Laws of War*
Active	*Active*
High-Level Constraint Description	*Cultural Proximity Prohibition*
Full Description of the Constraint	*Cultural property is prohibited from being attacked, including buildings dedicated to religion, art, science, charitable purposes, and historic monuments. The enemy has a duty to mark them clearly with visible and distinctive signs. Misuse will make them subject to attack*
Constraint Classification	*Discrimination*
Logical Form	*TargetDiscriminated* AND *TargetWithinProximityofCulturalLandmark*

FIGURE 12.3 Example forbidding constraint. This prototype constraint encodes a prohibition against engaging targets in proximity to a cultural landmark.

logical form field, currently encoded in this prototype using propositional logic, serves to formally describe the conditions under which the obligation or prohibition is applicable in a machine-readable format suitable for use during the constraint application process. Figure 12.3–4 show examples of populated constraints used within the prototype examples that follow, where the first constraint encodes a prohibition against damaging a cultural landmark as derived from the LOW, and the second shows an obligation to engage enemy T-80 tanks.

These constraints are stored in two repositories. The constraints encoding the LOW, as they are not likely to change over time, are stored in long-term memory (LTM). The constraints which encode the Rules of

FIELD	VALUES
Constraint Type	*Obligation*
Constraint Origin	*Rule of Engagement*
Active	*Active*
High-Level Constraint Description	*Enemy T-80 Tank Engagement Obligation*
Full Description of the Constraint	*If military necessity dictates then engagement with Enemy T-80 tanks is required if the target is sufficiently discriminated. The target must be located within a kill zone and proportional force must be used during the engagement*
Constraint Classification	*Military necessity*
Logical Form	*MilitaryNecessityEstablished* AND *TargetDiscriminated* AND *TargetInKillZone* AND *ProportionalityEstablished* AND *TargetIsT-80Tank*

FIGURE 12.4 Example obligating constraint. This prototype constraint encodes an obligation to engage enemy T-80 tanks.

Engagement for a particular mission are instead stored within short-term memory (STM). Short-term and long-term memory are implemented in the form of constraint databases. These databases can be queried by the other components of the overall ethical architecture to retrieve any constraints that match specific desired criteria (e.g., the constraint application process queries both STM and LTM for all *active* constraints).

12.2.2 Evidential Reasoning

Evidential reasoning transforms the incoming perceptual, motor, and situational awareness data into evidence manifested in the form of propositional logic assertions for use by the constraint application process. Two interacting modules are involved in this phase: the evidence generation module and the evidence blackboard. Newly arriving perceptual and target information and the overt behavioral response (ρ) from the behavioral control system are received by the evidence generation module. In addition, mission-specific information such as the geographical constraints of the current theater of operations is sent to the evidence generation module for analysis along with any relevant situational awareness data. These data are used to create the logical assertions (evidence) that capture the current state of the robot, situation, and any potential targets that may require the application of lethal force. These may include evidence, for example, that indicates that a target has been properly discriminated and is currently located within a mission-designated kill zone or an assertion that states that the target is in close proximity to a medical facility. The generated logical statements are then posted to the evidence blackboard, which serves as the communication medium between the evidential reasoning and the constraint application processes. The blackboard acts as the repository for all logical assertions created by the evidential reasoning process. For every execution cycle when a robotic behavioral response is input into the governor, the evidence posted on the blackboard is reevaluated by the evidence generation module, adding or deleting evidence as required as the situation changes.

12.2.3 Constraint Application

The constraint application process reasons about the lethal consequences of the active constraints using existing evidence to ensure that the resulting behavior of the robot is ethically permissible. This process is the product of a number of interacting subsystems, including the constraint marshaller, the constraint interpreter, the collateral damage estimator, and the lethality permitter.

The first step in the constraint application process requires the retrieval of all active ethical constraints from STM and LTM by the constraint marshaller. Once the constraints have been retrieved from memory, they are then transported to the constraint interpreter for evaluation. The constraint interpreter serves as the reasoning engine for the logical evaluation of these constraints. In this early prototype, the constraint interpreter is implemented as a lisp-based logic interpreter. As mentioned in Chapter 8, other forms of logical analysis, including deontic logic and formal theorem provers, may be put to work in future generations of the ethical governor, but for the current proof-of-concept goal this approach suffices. The exact form that the reasoning engine takes is not central to the composition of the ethical governor, and other more sophisticated reasoning engines can be readily substituted without loss of generality.

In order to determine if the output of the behavioral control system is ethically permissible, the constraint interpreter must evaluate the constraints retrieved from memory in light of the existing evidence generated via evidential reasoning. Recall from Chapter 6 that constraints can be divided into the set of prohibition constraints $C_{Forbidden}$ and the set of obligating constraints $C_{Obligate}$. The ethical permissibility evaluation requires assessing if these two constraint sets are satisfied for a given lethal action proposed by the behavioral controller. Keep in mind that all forbidden constraints must be satisfied and at least one obligating constraint must be true in order for a lethal action to be considered permissible.

To accomplish this assessment, the constraint interpreter first retrieves all the logical assertions generated by the evidential reasoning process from the blackboard and maps these assertions to the formal preconditions of the logical statement field as defined within each of the active constraints retrieved earlier by the marshaller. Once this mapping is complete, the constraints are evaluated by the interpreter, using the algorithm shown in Figure 12.5.

The prohibition constraint set ($C_{Forbidden}$) is evaluated first. In order for the constraint set $C_{Forbidden}$ to be satisfied, the interpreter must evaluate that *all* of the constraints in $C_{Forbidden}$ are *false*; i.e., the behavior input to the governor must not result in any prohibited/unethical behavior and there are no violations of these constraints. If $C_{Forbidden}$ is not satisfied, the lethal behavior being evaluated by the governor is deemed unethical and must be suppressed. The means by which this suppression is accomplished is discussed below. If the active prohibition constraint set $C_{Forbidden}$ is satisfied, however, the constraint interpreter then verifies if the proposed lethal behavior is *obligated* in the current situation. In order to do this

```
DO WHILE AUTHORIZED FOR LETHAL RESPONSE, MILITARY NECESSITY EXISTS, AND
RESPONSIBILITY ASSUMED
      IF Target is Sufficiently Discriminated
            IF C_Forbidden satisfied /* permission given – no violation of LOW exists */
                  IF C_Obligate is true /* lethal response required by ROE */
                        Optimize proportionality using Principle of Double Intention (Fig. 12.6)
                        Engage Target
                  ELSE /* no obligation/requirement to fire */
                     Do not engage target
                     Continue Mission
            ELSE /* permission denied by LOW */
                  IF previously identified target surrendered or wounded (hors de combat)
                        /* change to noncombatant status */
                        Notify friendly forces to take prisoner
                  ELSE
                        Do not engage target
                        Report and replan
                        Continue Mission
            Report status
      END DO
```

FIGURE 12.5 Constraint application algorithm (prototype). $C_{Forbidden}$ and $C_{Obligate}$ are the set of active prohibition and obligation constraints, respectively.

the constraint interpreter evaluates all of the active obligating constraints ($C_{Obligate}$). The obligating constraint set is satisfied if *any* constraint within $C_{Obligate}$ is true. If, however, there exists no obligation to engage the target within $C_{Obligate}$ given the current evidence, lethal behavior is not permitted and must be suppressed by the ethical governor.

In the case that either $C_{Forbidden}$ or $C_{Obligate}$ is not satisfied for an action involving lethality, the behavior is suppressed as unethical by the ethical governor. This is accomplished by a suppression message being sent from the constraint interpreter to the lethality permitter, the component of the governor that serves as the intervening gateway between the behavioral controller and the robot's weapon systems. If a suppression message is received by the lethality permitter, the outgoing overt system behavior is transformed into one that does not exhibit lethal behavior. In the prototype implementation described here, this simply results in the robot resuming its specified mission, and not engaging the target. More complex tactical evaluations could be implemented in future versions of the ethical governor, as the deliberative system is also informed by the constraint interpreter of any unsatisfied ethical constraints, potentially enabling replanning or alternative ethical actions to be undertaken by the robot or human commander.

Before the robot is allowed to exhibit lethal behavior, not only must the constraint sets $C_{Forbidden}$ or $C_{Obligate}$ be satisfied, but the ethical governor must also ensure that the behavior adheres to proportionality constraints as guided by the Principle of Double Intention [Walzer 77] as discussed in Chapter 4. The collateral damage estimator, the ethical governor component that ensures that any lethal behavior generated adheres to Just War proportionality constraints, is now described.

12.2.4 Proportionality and Battlefield Carnage

After the constraint interpreter has established that both the obligating and prohibition constraints have been satisfied, it is necessary to ensure that any lethal behavior exhibited by the robot is justifiable given the military necessity associated with the target. The proportionality optimization algorithm (Figure 12.6) requires that these factors are taken into account. It conducts a search over the space of available weapon systems, targeting patterns and weapon release positions to find an acceptable combination that maximizes the likelihood of target neutralization while minimizing collateral damage to assure the ethical application of lethal force for a given military necessity level.

In the prototype implementation described, a simulated unmanned aerial vehicle (UAV) is equipped with a set of four weapon systems: a chain gun, hellfire missiles, and either GBU-12 or GBU-38 500lb warheads. Each weapon system was assigned a set of hypothetical parameters* for use in the proportionality calculations, the most relevant of which were: likelihood of target neutralization (based on target type), target neutralization radius, noncombatant damage radius, and structural damage radius, where each is used to compute the affected area surrounding the weapon impact point that would result in target neutralization, noncombatant causalities, and structural damage respectively.

A simplified example of hypothetical weapon statistics used in the prototype implementation of the collateral damage estimator described here is shown in Figure 12.7. Gross oversimplifications in the numeric values are used in these prototype tables and a significant research investment would be required to provide more realistic data for actual operations in a given military context. Nonetheless they serve to illustrate the methods by which proportionality can be computed in an ethical architecture.

---

* Actual parameters were not readily available, and should obviously be substituted for any possible real world application. These numeric values were created only to demonstrate the feasibility of the ethical system without loss of generality, but in no way reflects the actual performance of these weapon systems.

```
Calculate_Proportionality (Target, Military Necessity, Setting)
// Select the weapon with highest effectiveness based on Target, Necessity and Setting
// Collateral damage refers to both noncombatant casualties and non-military property damage
   MinimumCollateralDamage = ∞          // tracks minimal collateral damage
   SelectedReleasePosition = NULL       // tracks the position that minimizes coll. damage
   SelectedWeapon = NULL                // track weapon selected
// Find a release position for the weapon that minimizes noncombatant carnage
   Assign most effective weapon available  to Selectedweapon
   WHILE all weapons have not been evaluated
      FOR all release positions that will neutralize the target with acceptably high probability
         IF C_Forbidden Satisfied for that position   // if the weapon-position does not violate the LOW
            Calculate CollateralDamage for the position
            IF Fratricide = 0
               IF CollateralDamage < MinimumCollateralDamage // If the collateral damage is reduced
                  SelectedReleasePosition = position
                  SelectedWeapon = weapon
                  MinimumCollateralDamage = CollateralDamage
               ENDIF
            ENDIF
         ENDIF
      ENDFOR
      IF MinimumCollateralDamage excessive for target's military necessity OR C_Forbidden not satisfied
         IF there are no more weapon systems available
               Return Failure
         ELSE
               Downselect weapon to next most effective weapon
         ENDIF
      ENDIF
   ENDWHILE
   Return Weapon Selected and Release Position
```

FIGURE 12.6 Proportionality optimization algorithm (prototype). The algorithm selects the weapon system that ensures that it will not violate any proportionality prohibitions or LOW. It calculates the potential unintended noncombatant carnage and civilian property damage (collateral damage) that would result from available combinations of weapon systems and release positions, choosing the most effective weapon that results in the lowest acceptable collateral damage.

Weapon	Effectiveness Against Convoy 2-4 Vehicles	Combatant Damage Radius	Noncombatant Damage Radius	Structural Damage Radius
Chaingun	2%	0.5ft	1ft	0.5ft
Hellfire	20%	10ft	20ft	10ft
GBU-12	90%	1000ft	2000ft	500ft

FIGURE 12.7 Simplified example of hypothetical weapon statistics used by the collateral damage estimator. This specific table depicts the result of utilizing the available weapon systems against a small convoy of enemy vehicles. Similar tables exist for other target classes.

The proportionality optimization algorithm uses these statistics as well as incoming perceptual information to determine the battlefield carnage in a utilitarian manner by estimating the amount of structural damage and the number of noncombatant/combatant/friendly casualties that result from the use of a weapon system at a particular target location. Fratricide is restricted to always be zero; the killing of friendly forces by the autonomous system is specifically forbidden under all circumstances. Similarly, there can never be intentional killing of noncombatants; this is directly prohibited through the enforcement of the Laws of War. Thus the proportionality algorithm maximizes the number of enemy casualties while minimizing unintended noncombatant casualties and damage to civilian property as indexed by a given military necessity for the designated and discriminated target.

There are three possible outcomes of the proportionality algorithm:

1. For the first, the proportionality algorithm finds no available weapon system or weapon release position that does not violate an ethical constraint (e.g., the target may be near a medical facility and the resulting blast radius of the weapon systems would damage that facility). In this case, the ethical governor suppresses all lethal behavior via a message to the lethality permitter component of the ethical governor.

2. In the second case, no weapon system or weapon release position is found that results in an acceptable level of collateral damage given the military necessity of the target (e.g., engaging a low priority target that would result in significant, indirect noncombatant casualties). As before, the use of lethal force is suppressed. Acceptable levels of collateral damage as a function of the military necessity of a target as defined in the prototype system appear in Figure 12.8 (these values are also purely hypothetical for use in these example scenarios). Again these are gross oversimplifications, but nonetheless serve as proof of concept and serve as placeholders for more relevant values or functions to be determined by appropriate authorities.

3. The third and final possible outcome of the proportionality estimation is the identification of a weapon/weapon release position combination that satisfies all ethical constraints and minimizes collateral damage in relation to the military necessity of the target. In this case, the lethality permitter is informed that lethal force is permissible for this situation and that the robot is allowed to engage the target based upon the selected weapon system and release position.

Military Necessity (1 low, 5 high)	No Collateral Damage	Low Collateral Damage	Medium Collateral Damage	High Collateral Damage
1	Permissible	Forbidden	Forbidden	Forbidden
2	Permissible	Permissible	Forbidden	Forbidden
3	Permissible	Permissible	Permissible	Forbidden
4	Permissible	Permissible	Permissible	Forbidden
5	Permissible	Permissible	Permissible	Permissible

FIGURE 12.8 A hypothetical table used to determine acceptable levels of collateral damage given the military necessity (priority) associated with a specific target.

12.2.5 Demonstration Scenario Overview

In order to evaluate the feasibility of the ethical governor design, a series of test scenarios were developed within the MissionLab mission specification and simulation environment [GT MRL 07]. Various situations were presented to a simulated autonomous fixed-wing UAV to ensure that any use of lethal force adhered to the ethical requirements prescribed by the LOW and ROE as encoded in the constraint databases. Two of these test scenarios are now described in detail to illustrate the interaction of the ethical governor with the robot's behavioral control system.

In both scenarios, the UAV has been assigned to perform a hunter-killer mission along a predetermined flight path, where the UAV is authorized to engage a variety of targets including musters of enemy soldiers, small convoys of enemy vehicles, and enemy tanks should they be encountered. Engagement of enemy forces, however, may *only* occur if the targets are within predesignated mission-specific kill zones. An overview of the mission area and landmarks pertinent to these scenarios appear in Figure 12.9.

As there is no advance intelligence to indicate that any high-priority targets are known to be present in the mission area, the military necessity associated with engaging these small groups of enemy units is set to be relatively low (military necessity equals 2 in Figure 12.8). As a result lethal force should only be applied if collateral damage can be significantly minimized. Figure 12.10 depicts a subset of the relevant ethical constraints that are pertinent here. While there are significantly more constraints in use than the few shown here, only those that are involved directly in the following scenarios are depicted.

The UAV is equipped with 4 hellfire missiles and 2 GBU-12 warheads. The default action of the underlying behavioral controller that is fed into the ethical governor in these scenarios is to engage any discriminated enemy targets with lethal force. This behavior is exhibited for the purpose

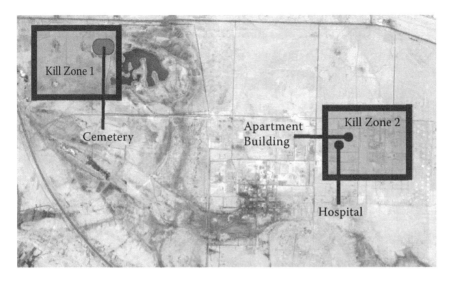

FIGURE 12.9 Example mission area used for the demonstration scenarios. There are two mission-designated kill zones. A cemetery lies within kill zone 1 while an apartment building and hospital are located within kill zone 2.

of demonstrating the role of the ethical governor within the test scenarios. If such a system were to be deployed, it is likely that the behavioral controller would also be ethically constrained in the manner using the ethical behavioral control method as described earlier in Chapter 10.

The *MissionLab* mission specification for this scenario includes a denotation where lethality may or may not be used that incorporates the notion of a lethal section within a mission plan. The use of lethality is expressly forbidden at all times outside of a mission's lethal section. The ethical governor is invoked at the point when a lethal section of the plan is entered to ensure that any use of lethal force in this mission phase is consistent with

Type	Origin	Description
Prohibition	ROE	It is forbidden to engage enemy units outside of designated mission boundaries.
Prohibition	LOW	Cultural property is prohibited from being attacked, including buildings dedicated to religion, art, science, charitable purposes, and historic monuments.
Prohibition	LOW	Civilian hospitals organized to five care to the wounded and sick, the infirm and maternity cases, may in no circumstances be the object of attack, but shall at all times be respected and protected by the parties to the conflict.

FIGURE 12.10 Several of the constraints relevant to the demonstration scenarios.

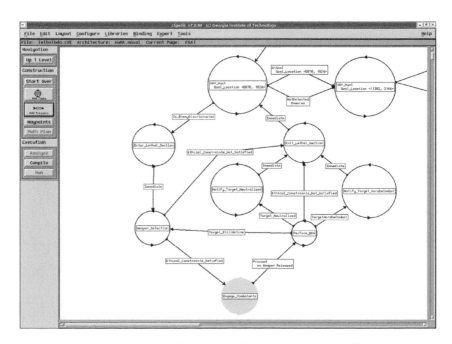

FIGURE 12.11 A segment of an example UAV Hunter-Killer mission as encoded in *MissionLab*. The sole state where the PTF variable is TRUE is highlighted.

the LOW and ROE. A fraction of a finite state automaton (FSA) mission plan that encodes a portion of a UAV hunter-killer mission scenario appears in Figure 12.11. The segment shown depicts one of the lethal sections of the overall mission, with the Engage_Combatants state highlighted, as it is the only state in this segment where the PTF variable is set to TRUE.

12.2.6 Scenario 1—Suppressing Unethical Behavior

In the first example, loosely adapted from the scenario *Taliban Muster in Cemetery* described earlier in Chapter 11, the armed UAV encounters a muster of enemy warfighters who are attending a funeral at a GPS-identified cemetery located within a mission-designated kill zone. Upon discrimination of the target, the underlying behavioral controller outputs a command to engage the muster using lethal force. The behavioral controller's output is then sent to the ethical governor to ensure that this action is ethical before that behavior is expressed by the robot's weapon system actuators. Figure 12.12 shows this scenario at the point of target discrimination.

Upon receipt of the behavioral command containing a lethal force component, the ethical governor initiates the evidence generation and

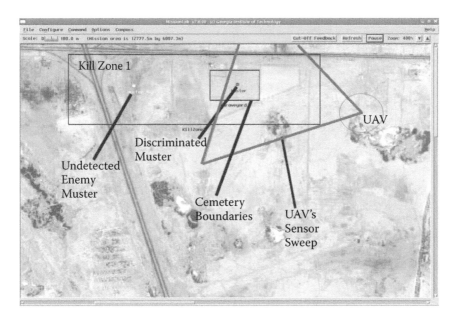

FIGURE 12.12 The UAV detects and confidently discriminates a muster of enemy troops currently located within a cemetery. The triangle emanating from the UAV's location denotes its sensory range.

constraint application processes. The evidence generation module processes the incoming perceptual information, situational awareness information, and mission parameters to generate the information needed by the constraint application process. In this scenario, examples of the evidence generated include logical assertions such as *Target Within Killzone, Target Is Discriminated, Target In Proximity of a Cultural Landmark,* and *Target Is a Muster.* This evidence, along with any other information created by the evidence generation process is placed on the evidence blackboard for subsequent use during constraint application.

After the evidence in support of the lethal request has been generated, the constraint application process begins by retrieving all active ethical constraints from memory. The pertinent constraints retrieved for this scenario appear in Figure 12.10. Once these constraints have been delivered to the constraint interpreter and the evidence retrieved from the blackboard, the interpreter evaluates the constraints using the algorithm shown in Figure 12.5, by first ensuring that the set of prohibition constraints ($C_{Forbidden}$) is satisfied. In this scenario, when the constraint interpreter evaluates the prohibition against engaging targets within proximity to cultural landmarks (Figure 12.3), this constraint is recognized as being

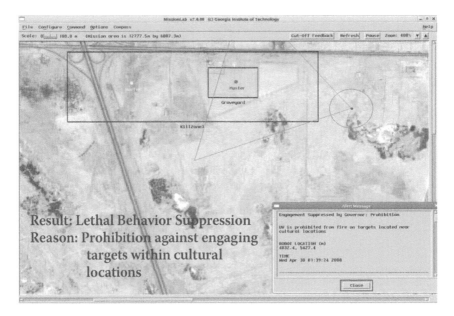

FIGURE 12.13 The proposed lethal behavior is suppressed due to its failing to satisfy the prohibition against engaging enemies in proximity to cultural locations.

violated (as the cemetery is considered to be a cultural landmark). The failure of $C_{Forbidden}$ to be satisfied indicates that the lethal behavior being governed is unethical, resulting in a suppression signal being sent to the lethality permitter that prevents the proposed lethal behavior from being executed (Figure 12.13). The deliberative system is also informed that suppression has occurred and is informed of the specific reason (constraint) that caused the suppression.

12.2.7 Scenario 2—Maintaining Ethical Behavior While Minimizing Collateral Damage

In the second illustrative scenario, after continuing its mission the UAV has now encountered and discriminated an enemy vehicle convoy within the second designated kill zone. A short distance to the west and in close proximity to the convoy lies a regional hospital, while a potentially heavily populated apartment building is present to the north and a clearly identifiable lone stationary taxicab is located directly to the south of the target (Figure 12.14). After the convoy is identified and discriminated, the underlying behavioral controller attempts to engage the enemy units using lethal force.

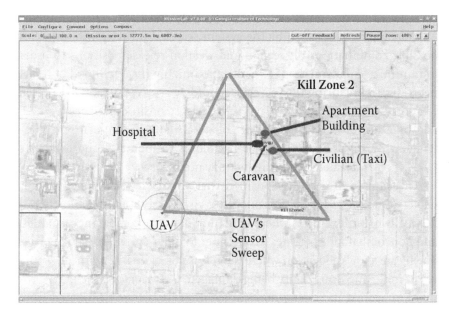

FIGURE 12.14   The UAV next encounters an enemy convoy within its sensory range that is located between a hospital, an apartment building, and a stationary taxi.

As before, when the command for the use of lethal force enters the ethical governor, the evidential reasoning and constraint application processes assess whether or not lethal behavior is permissible in the current situation according to the LOW and ROE. After the evidence generation is completed and the active constraints are retrieved from memory, the constraint application algorithm is applied by the governor (Figure 12.5). The algorithm first ensures that the prohibition constraint set $C_{Forbidden}$ is satisfied so there exists no violations of the LOW or ROE. In this example scenario, none of the prohibitions represented in the active constraint set is violated. The governor then determines if lethal force is obligated by evaluating the constraint set $C_{Obligate}$. The constraint interpreter determines that an obligating constraint, "Enemy convoys must be engaged[5]" for this level of military necessity is satisfied and therefore $C_{Obligate}$ is satisfied. This determines that lethal force is potentially warranted if a suitably proportional response is available that minimizes collateral damage.

The governor now must ensure that any lethal force permitted by the UAV is both proportional and guided by the Principle of Double Intention by using the proportionality optimization algorithm (Figure 12.6). During the calculation of a proportional response, the most effective yet humane weapon system is selected by the system searching through the space of possible combinations of weapon and weapon release positions in order to minimize collateral damage while maximizing the likelihood of target neutralization. During the search, a candidate release position for a given weapon is evaluated in two ways: if the release position satisfies $C_{Forbidden}$ and by a utilitarian evaluation of collateral damage foreseen but unintended. If a release position for a particular weapon is found to violate $C_{Forbidden}$, it is deemed unethical and may not be used.

An example of a release position that violates ethical constraints is depicted in Figure 12.15. The concentric circles represent the area (hypothetically in our example) where structural damage, combatant casualties, and noncombatant casualties (from inner to outer circles) may take place. The figure shows a location where the release of a GBU-12 warhead would result in the medical facility being damaged, thus violating the LOW prohibition against damaging medical facilities. It is thus eliminated from consideration for use in target engagement in the current situation.

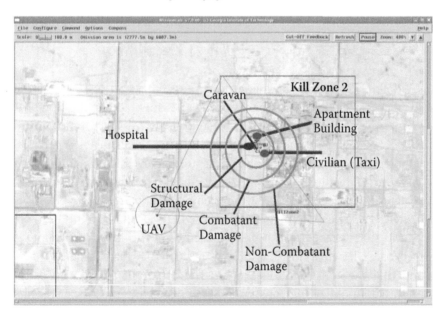

FIGURE 12.15 Example of a weapon release position that violates ethical constraints. The structural damage area covers the area where the hospital is located. The blast radii are based on the collateral damage assessment calculated by using the selected weapon's blast radius (see the algorithm shown in Figure 12.5 for details).

In this scenario, the military necessity associated with neutralizing targets in the mission area is moderate, so only limited collateral damage is tolerated. Therefore, a weapon release position that would damage the heavily populated apartment building is forbidden (i.e., the area that will sustain structural damage may not include the apartment building). The constraint application process therefore continues to search the space of available weapons and weapon release positions for a solution where neither the hospital nor the apartment building will sustain damage. If such a position cannot be found, a lethal response is denied and suppressed by the governor. In this example, however, a weapon release position is found such that neither the medical nor apartment buildings sustain significant damage, ensuring that noncombatant casualties remain low. This ethical release position for the GBU-12 warhead is depicted in Figure 12.16. Note that because there did not exist a release location from which noncombatant casualties could be completely eliminated and because the military necessity of the target allowed for limited collateral damage, the ethical weapon release position *does* result in potential noncombatant fatalities (i.e., any occupants of the taxicab). The governor, however, does minimize

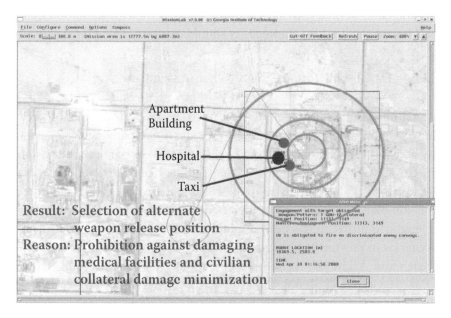

FIGURE 12.16 The final weapon release position selected by the ethical governor for target engagement. This position ensures that all LOW and ROE ethical constraints are satisfied and that civilian causalities are minimized while maximizing the chance of target neutralization.

casualties consistent with the Principle of Double Intention by intentionally ensuring that the heavily populated apartment building is avoided.

12.3 IMPLEMENTING THE RESPONSIBILITY ADVISOR

The purpose of the responsibility advisor, as described in Chapter 10, is manifold, but centers on establishing a human as being the locus of responsibility for the use of any lethal force by an autonomous robot. This involves multiple aspects of assignment: from responsibility for the design and implementation of the system, to the authoring of the LOW and ROE constraints in both traditional and machine-readable formats, to the tasking of the robot by an operator for a lethal mission, and for the possible use of operator overrides. Only a limited portion of this advisory component has been prototyped to date, which was created and described here with the collaboration of Alan Wagner and Brittany Duncan, students in the Georgia Tech Mobile Robot Laboratory. The prototype includes operator interfaces for establishing premission responsibility and the use of operator overrides. Each of these is presented in turn. These constitute very early prototypes as they have not yet undergone usability evaluation, and are intended only to provide a glimpse of what the ethical autonomous architecture's ultimate functionality should contain.

12.3.1 Establishing Responsibility When Tasking an Autonomous System Capable of Lethal Force

A preliminary graphical user interface (GUI) used for the premission tasking of a lethal autonomous robot that provides accompanying responsibility acceptance by an operator has been integrated as part of the mission specification system embodied in the Georgia Tech *MissionLab* System [MacKenzie et al. 97, GT MRL 07]. *MissionLab* provides automated premission planning functions to specify detailed mission objectives for an operator to utilize. It has been used for a wide range of military mission scenarios in previous and ongoing research, ranging from scout missions [Balch and Arkin 98], to military operations over urban terrain [Hsieh et al. 07, Collins et al. 00], to naval coastal operations [Ulam et al. 07], among others. Using *MissionLab*, an operator interacts through a mission design interface that permits the visualization of a mission specification as it is created typically in the form of an finite state automaton, but also by using either a map-based interface or an iconic case-based reasoning (CBR) tool [Endo et al. 04].

The newly created responsibility advisor described here serves as a gate-keeper to the mission specification system, preventing unauthorized mission creation as well as counseling users regarding the mission's ethical obligations and prohibitions. The operation of this premission responsibility advisor occurs in five steps:

1. Determination if the user is authorized to conduct the mission and establishing the date when he received his last training for its use. If they are legitimately authorized, then:

2. The user selects a mission from a library of relevant pre-existing mission plans, possibly adapting it to any new or changed conditions in the battlefield.

3. The user is then presented with plain text descriptions of the mission obligations as derived from the ROE, and any related supporting information to assist in clarifying his understanding of what the ethical implications are for the mission the system is about to undertake. If they accept these obligations, then:

4. The user is presented with a plain text description of any ethical prohibitions associated with this mission derived from the LOW or ROE that have changed since the last training date. This step assumes that the operator has been sufficiently well trained to retain an understanding of the underlying LOW. Additional supporting ethical information is presented as appropriate. If the user accepts these prohibitions, then:

5. The user is presented with a request for final authorization and acceptance of responsibility for the conduct of the mission about to be executed.

Each of these individual steps is now described in more detail as implemented in this prototype. The first step specifically requires the user to enter their name, military ID number, and date of their latest training. These data are sent to a surrogate Global Information Grid (GIG) for verification and acceptance of this user-provided information [NSA 08]. In the *MissionLab* prototype, the surrogate GIG was implemented as a stand-alone server. Figure 12.17 depicts the underlying architectural components and personnel involved in this step. A screenshot of the graphical user interface presented to the operator during this authorization phase appears on Figure 12.18.

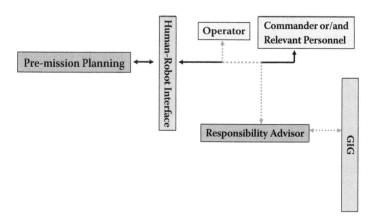

FIGURE 12.17 Architectural components involved for operator authorization (step 1). The user submits his login and training information, which the responsibility advisor sends to the surrogate GIG for verification and acceptance prior to moving on to the next step.

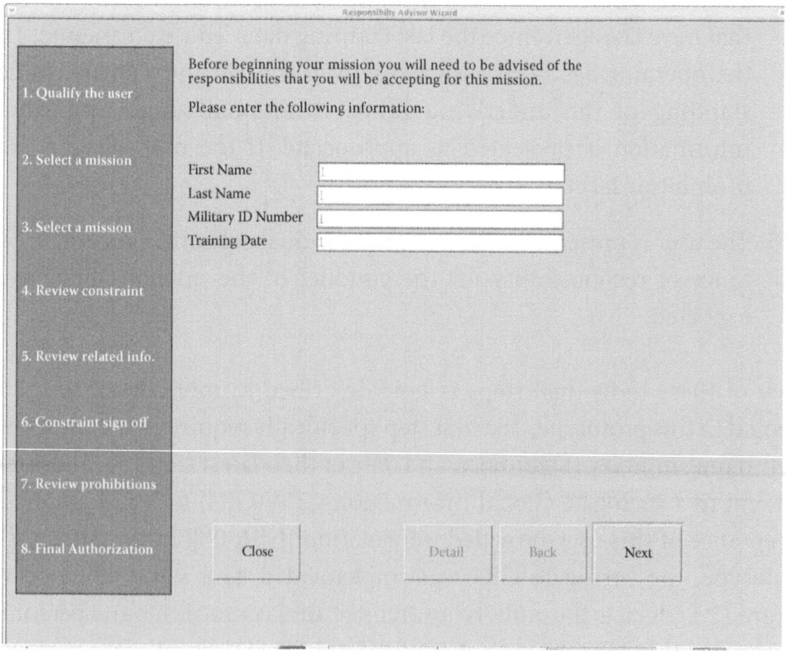

FIGURE 12.18 Login screen for the responsibility advisor.

Note that the overall process of the responsibility advisor is depicted on the leftmost frame of the GUI with the current step highlighted.

The user then selects a specific mission for the current military area and concept of operations (CONOPS) from the list of available potential missions maintained in the CBR library. This set of candidate missions is provided by a previously authorized commander or other relevant military personnel. It is drawn either from mission designs generated earlier by an expert user or from previous missions already successfully deployed in this context. At this point, the user can compare among various qualities (e.g., stealth, attrition rates, success rate, etc.) for all available candidate missions. A candidate mission's performance can be simulated prior to deployment using tools available in *MissionLab* that assist in confirming the operator's expectations regarding mission conduct. The operator can also review a mission's textual summary, basis, and history, and then finally decide upon and select a specific mission for deployment. Figure 12.19 illustrates that the architectural interaction now involves the CBR library as opposed to the GIG as seen in the previous step. A screenshot of the GUI for this step, showing a list of candidate missions, appears in Figure 12.20.

Once a mission has been selected for deployment, the characteristic features of the chosen mission are used as a probe to retrieve the mission's active obligations from the constraint databases. Each obligation is presented to

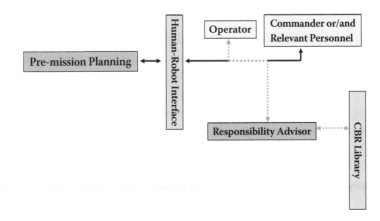

FIGURE 12.19 Architectural diagram for the mission selection step. The system now retrieves candidate mission information from the CBR library, which have already been authorized by a superior officer for this specific CONOPS.

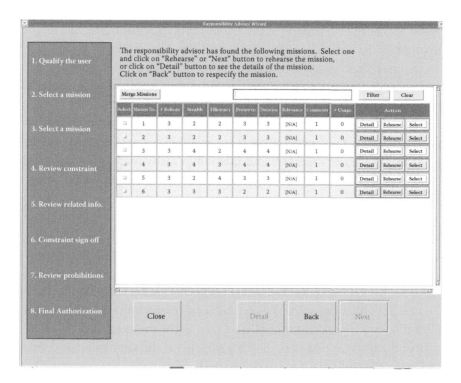

FIGURE 12.20 Mission selection screen. User chooses the mission most suited for the current CONOPS. Mission details and simulation-based rehearsal are also possible. All available missions are assumed to have been prescreened by the user's commander.

the user one at a time for formal confirmation and acknowledgment of the user's understanding regarding the associated consequences of lethality for the mission at hand. The operator proceeds by clicking the NEXT box on the screen, thus stating he is are aware of and are familiar with each and every obligation. During the review of an obligation, the user is presented relevant information specific to that obligation, consisting of relevant case studies that highlights the ethical aspects of the obligation, including news events, legal studies, commentary, and so on. Each item contains an in-depth description, a summary of the event, the applicable laws of war, and a relevance rating. This information is intended to aid and refresh the operator's understanding of the mission-specific obligations. Figure 12.21 depicts the architectural data flow for the constraint authorization step, including the prohibition review described next. Figure 12.22 displays a screenshot of the GUI at one stage of this process.

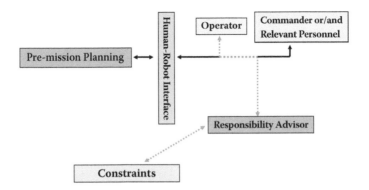

FIGURE 12.21 Architectural components associated with mission-specific obligation and prohibition constraint retrieval and confirmation. The operator must acknowledge that he/she has read and understood each obligation and prohibition (that they have not been previously trained on). All active mission-specific constraints are retrieved until they all have been individually reviewed by the user.

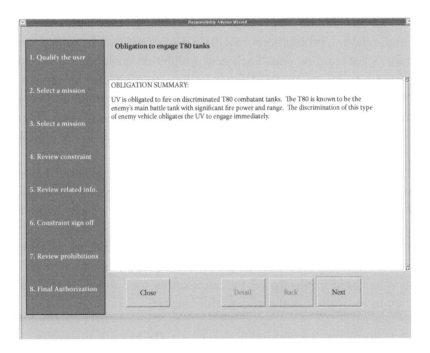

FIGURE 12.22 This screen details user obligation as part of the constraint acceptance step. Each obligation must be reviewed and accepted. Each is presented sequentially with background information provided in a screen that immediately follows its initial presentation (not shown).

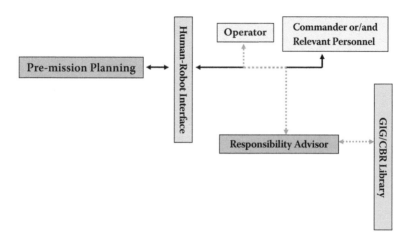

FIGURE 12.23 Transfer of the mission-specific obligations and prohibitions to the ethical governor for execution and the consequent commencement of the mission by the operator.

After the operator has reviewed and acknowledged the use of each obligation for the mission, the system then presents the user with any active mission-relevant prohibitions that have been modified or added since the user's last training date. Each new prohibition must be reviewed and accepted by clicking the NEXT box as before. After each prohibition's summary review, related information on that specific prohibition is presented to the user for his inspection. The interface for the review of active prohibitions and their related information is very similar to the interface for the review of obligations (Figure 12.22).

In the final step (Figure 12.23 and Figure 12.24), the operator is advised that he/she has received authorization to initiate the mission. To confirm, operators must type their name (or alternatively a key code) to accept responsibility for the conduct of the mission. The responsibility advisor makes the active obligations and prohibitions available to the ethical governor. Execution can now begin. This prototype premission advisory system has been implemented and successfully used to specify missions similar to those discussed earlier in this chapter.

12.3.2 Run-Time Responsibility Advising and Operator Overrides

We now move from premission responsibility advising to focus on how operator responsibility can be maintained while a mission is actively underway. This is accomplished using a prototype GUI that conveys the ethical governor's status to the operator, providing continuous information regarding an unmanned

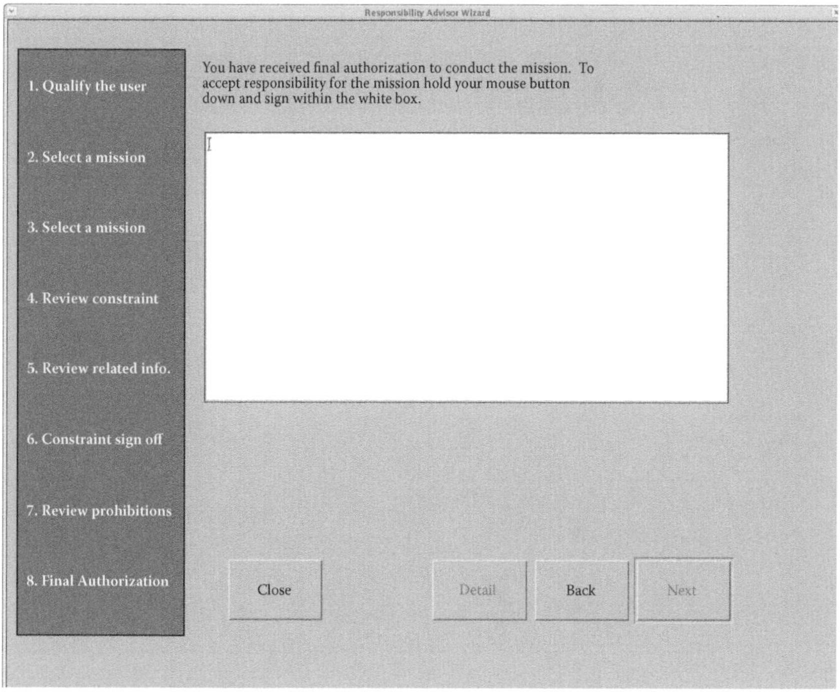

FIGURE 12.24 Final authorization screen. In this prototype, the user must accept final responsibility for the mission by typing his name in the GUI's white space.

system's potential use of lethal force *during* the conduct of a mission. In addition, a prototype of the run-time override GUI was developed, including the interfaces and control mechanisms by which the responsibility advisor provides an operator ongoing ethical situational awareness of potential LOW and ROE violations during normal or exceptional operations. This interface is essential to yield the necessary operator understanding and acceptance of responsibility for any override activities, as described earlier in the design presented in Chapter 10. Again remember that this is merely a very preliminary prototype, it is still under development, and only serves as a proof-of-concept. Substantial formal usability and human factor studies would be required for any design of this sort to be ever considered suitable for any fielded application. As such, view this prototype as illustrative but not prescriptive.

12.3.2.1 Continuous Presentation of the Status of the Ethical Governor

The ethical governor's graphical user interface has become an integrated part of the mission console of *MissionLab*. Appearing as a prototype

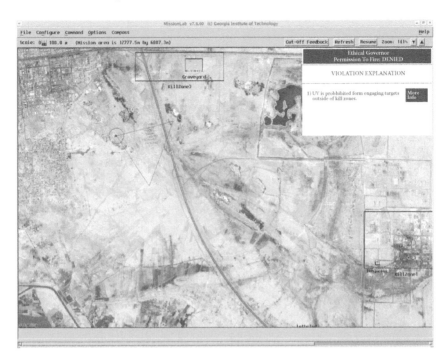

FIGURE 12.25 *MissionLab* run-time mission information display with ethical governor GUI status window shown in the upper right corner.

window in the upper right-hand corner of the run-time display, it constantly provides the operator feedback regarding the status of lethal action by an autonomous robot during a combat mission (Figure 12.25). Figure 12.26 illustrates what is displayed under normal operations, clearly asserting whether the autonomous system's Permission-To-Fire (PTF) variable is TRUE (Permission Granted) or FALSE (Permission Denied). By left clicking on this window, the operator is informed as to the reasons supporting

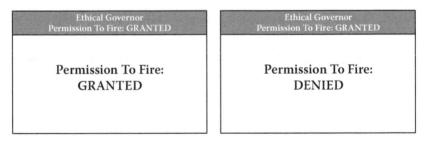

FIGURE 12.26 Standard ethical governor status windows for operator advisement.

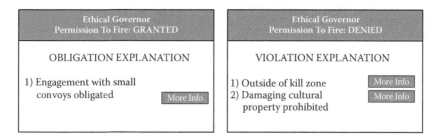

FIGURE 12.27 Left-clicking on the status window (Figure 12.26) displays an explanation for PTF status. The obligation explanation (*left*) is presented when permission to fire is granted, the violations (*right*) when it is denied.

PTF status (Figure 12.27). For example if the mission is outside of a lethal section (discussed earlier in this chapter), permission is always denied in the absence of an operator override.

12.3.2.2 Negative Overrides: Denying Permission to Fire in the Presence of Obligating Constraints

Should an obligated, not prohibited, and clearly discriminated target be acquired whereby the PTF variable is set to TRUE, the ethical governor has completed its analysis (described earlier in this chapter) and the system is about to engage the target. Prior to this autonomous response, the operator is informed of the impending action and given a finite time window (initially set to 10 seconds in this prototype) to allow for a possible intervention via a negative override, preventing an autonomous weapons discharge. Figure 12.28 presents a hypothetical instance informing the operator of a pending target engagement. If the operator executes a special key combination (a right-click in our prototype), the pending weapon

FIGURE 12.28 Operator window displaying countdown to autonomous weapon release on an obligated and clearly discriminated target.

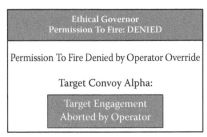

FIGURE 12.29 Negative operator override: *left*, confirmation request window; *right*, confirmation approved window.

release is suspended, allowing the operator, if he/she so chooses, to initiate a negative override that will result in aborting the target engagement. This is termed a negative override since the operator effectively sets the PTF variable to FALSE by his/her actions. Although two different operators' consents are required for a positive override (i.e., a two-key system), only a single operator is required to disengage from a target, since not firing poses no potential ethical violation of the LOW. A negative override is analogous to an emergency stop of the weapon system.

After right-clicking on the countdown window, the negative override confirmation request window is displayed (Figure 12.29, *left*), reminding the operator of the specific obligation that exists to engage the target. An option to obtain additional information on this obligating constraint is provided, using the same constraint information described earlier in the premission responsibility advisor constraint acceptance step (Section. 12.3.1). The operator must then confirm whether or not an override should be granted. Should the negative override be requested, the confirmation approved window appears (Figure 12.29, *right*) and the autonomous system continues its mission without engaging the target.

12.3.2.3 Positive Overrides: Granting Permission to Fire in the Presence of Forbidding Ethical Constraints

Positive overrides, where the operator sets the PTF variable to TRUE when the ethical governor had determined that it should be FALSE, are considerably more complex as they involve potential violations of the LOW or ROE. Responsibility acceptance by the operator is a very serious matter. It is essential that the positive override process be well considered on the part of the operator and that all information at the disposal of the ethical governor be made available as part of his/her decision-making. Thus several deliberate barriers are introduced to ensure that the operator is fully informed prior to engaging a target that the governor has deemed to be unethical.

This negative override process is provided with serious reservations regarding its potential abuse, but it may be the case that the operator has additional intelligence or that there are conditions that invalidate some of the evidence that the ethical governor holds to be true in its analysis of the appropriateness of withholding lethal force in the current situation. Nonetheless, this process should not be undertaken lightly, and as the ethical architecture becomes more sophisticated in future combat situations it may be that the ultimate authority for not engaging a target should vest with the machine and not the human, due to the manifold reasons cited in Chapter 3. But for now we will relegate the ultimate authority for lethal force to the operator, by allowing him/her to override any decision that the ethical governor arrives at. But the operator must make this decision in a well-informed manner and acknowledge his responsibility for the consequences of using lethality that potentially results in a violation of the LOW.

Figure 12.30 (*left*) shows an example operator window indicating why a clearly discriminated military target is not being fired upon, based upon the analysis of the ethical governor. The option for an explanation of the underlying constraint violation can be obtained by clicking on the window or the More Info button (Figure 12.30, *right*), which can be further inspected if the operator questions the judgment of the system.

A positive override is deliberately not offered to the operator and can only be requested through a nonobvious set of keystrokes, simplified in our example to a right mouse click. If this positive override is requested, the operator's keycode must be entered as shown in Figure 12.31A for

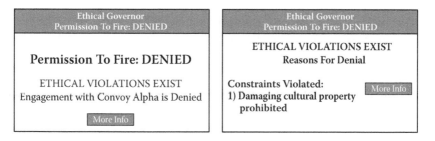

FIGURE 12.30   *Left*, operator window indicating that ethical governor has denied the engagement of a target; *right*, explanation for denial with the offering of even more information.

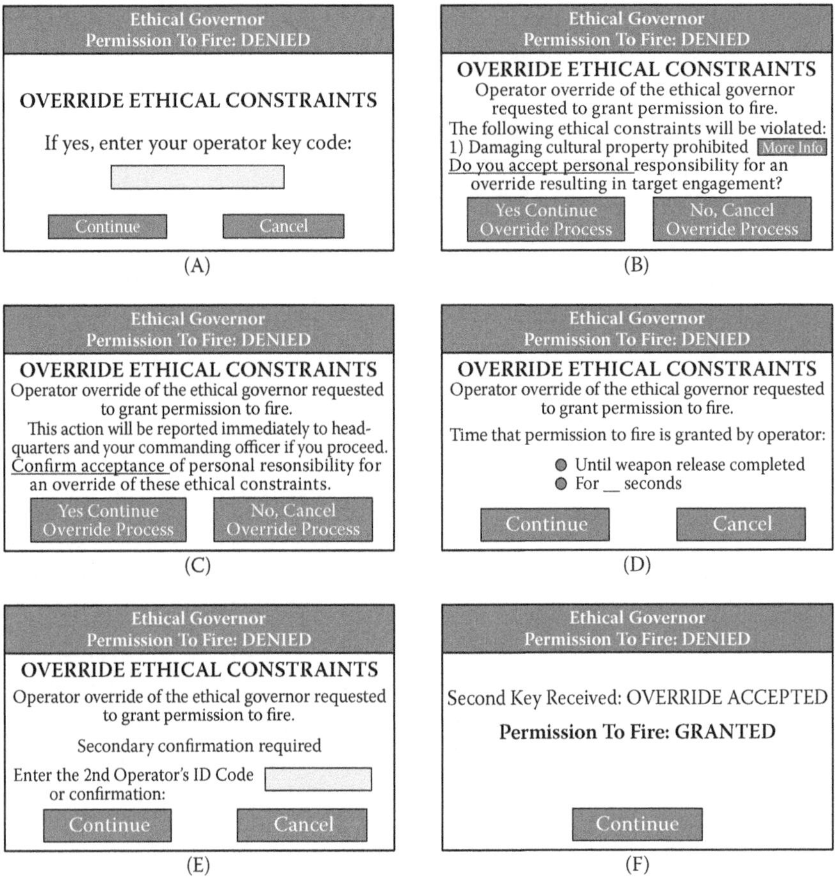

FIGURE 12.31 Positive override process. *A*, operator key entry; *B*, information and responsibility acceptance; *C*, confirmation; *D*, nature and extent of override; *E*, second key operator request; *F*, positive override granted.

verification. If the operator's authority to conduct such an override is validated, this results in the display (Figure 12.31B) of the forbidden constraints that will be violated should this override take place and requires explicit acceptance by the operator of the responsibility for these violations (in the view of the ethical governor). Secondary confirmation is then required (Figure 12.31C). If granted, the duration of the override must then be specified (Figure 12.31D), followed by an explicit request for a second operator's ID to confirm that this lethal action is acceptable, which is ascertained via the GIG (Figure 12.31E). A lone operator cannot engage a target that is deemed unethical by the governor: two-key authorization is required. Upon approval by the second human operator, permission is then granted for the autonomous system to engage the target with the operator assuming full responsibility for this action (Figure 12.31F). The system then begins its countdown as before.

Immediately upon weapons release the PTF variable is set to FALSE until a battle damage assessment (BDA) is completed. After the assessment, if the target is either destroyed, hors de combat or surrendered, the system is forbidden from re-engaging. If the BDA indicates that the target is still active, the process repeats with a reassessment of the changing conditions by the ethical governor. If the lethal action remains not forbidden and still obligated, a reinitiation of the weapon release countdown begins.

12.4 SUMMARY

In this chapter, we have presented the first prototype implementation of the ethical governor and responsibility advisor. It has been integrated into the design of a functioning hybrid deliberative/reactive autonomous robot architecture that has been previously used in numerous military research programs. Remaining components of the architecture, including behavioral ethical control and the ethical adaptor, still remain to be addressed beyond the design stages discussed in Chapter 10 and are left for future work. The prototypes that have been demonstrated in this chapter, however, serve as proof-of-concept for the overall underlying ethical architecture described in this book and as such present the very first steps, baby steps admittedly but steps nonetheless, toward ensuring ethical adherence by autonomous systems capable of lethal action. This architectural research is ongoing and is expected to result in additional advances in implementation in the months and years to come.

Epilogue

This book has provided the motivation, philosophy, formalisms, representational requirements, architectural design criteria, recommendations, and test scenarios to design and construct an autonomous robotic system architecture capable of the ethical use of lethal force. These first steps toward that goal are very preliminary and subject to major revision, but at the very least they can be viewed as the beginnings of an ethical robotic warfighter. The primary goal remains to enforce the International Laws of War in the battlefield in a manner that is believed achievable, by creating a class of robots that not only conform to International Law but also outperform human soldiers in their ethical capacity.

It is too early to tell whether this venture will be successful. There are daunting problems remaining:

- The transformation of International Protocols and battlefield ethics into machine-usable representations and real-time reasoning capabilities for bounded morality using modal logics.

- Mechanisms to ensure that the design of intelligent behaviors only provide responses within rigorously defined ethical boundaries.

- The development of effective perceptual algorithms capable of superior target discrimination capabilities, especially with regard to combatant-noncombatant status.

- The creation of techniques to permit the adaptation of an ethical constraint set and underlying behavioral control parameters that will ensure moral performance, should those norms be violated in any way, involving reflective and affective processing.

- A means to make responsibility assignment clear and explicit for all concerned parties regarding the deployment of a machine with a lethal potential on its mission.

In ongoing and future research, this architecture will be further fleshed out in the context of the specific test scenarios outlined in this book. Hopefully the goals of this effort will fuel other scientists' interest to assist in ensuring that the machines that we as roboticists create fit within international and societal expectations and requirements.

My personal hope would be that they will never be needed in the present or the future. But mankind's tendency toward war seems overwhelming and inevitable. At the very least, if we can reduce civilian casualties according to what the Geneva Conventions have promoted and the Just War tradition subscribes to, the result will have been a humanitarian effort, even while staring directly at the face of war.

References

AAI, "Quit Your Sniping: Or Your First Shot Will Be Your Last," AAI Corporation Product Brochure, 2007.

Adams, T., "Future Warfare and the Decline of Human Decisionmaking," *Parameters*, U.S. Army War College Quarterly, Winter 2001–02, pp. 57–71.

Air Force Times, "Reaper UAVs Join the Fight in Iraq," July 23, 2008, http://www.airforcetimes.com/news/2008/07/airforce_reaper_iraq_072108w/.

AFJAGS, Air Force Judge Advocate General's School, *The Military Commander and the Law*, 8th ed. 2006.

AFP, "Russia unveils pilotless 'stealth' bomber," *Agence France Presse*, August 23, 2007.

AFP, "US Says Hellfire Missiles Kill 12 in Baghdad," *Agence France Presse*, April 8, 2008.

Air Force, "Reaper moniker given to MQ-9 Unmanned Aerial Vehicle," *Official Website of the United States Air Force*, http://www.af.mil/news/story.asp?storyID=123027012, 2006.

Air Force Pamphlet [AFPAM] 110-31, *International Law—The Conduct of Armed Conflict and Air Operations*, pp. 15–16, Nov. 1976.

Allen, C., Wallach, W., and Smit, I., "Why Machine Ethics?" *IEEE Intelligent Systems*, pp. 12–17, July/August 2006.

Amodio, D., Devine, P., and Harmon-Jones, E., "A Dynamic Model of Guilt," *Psychological Science*, Vol. 18, No. 6, pp. 524–530, 2007.

Anderson, K., "The Ethics of Robot Soldiers?" *Kenneth Anderson's Law of Jaw and Just War Theory Blog*, July, 4, 2007, http://kennethandersonlawofwar.blogspot.com/2007/07/ethics-of-robot-soldiers.html (accessed 9/11/08).

Anderson, M. Anderson, S., and Armen, C., "Towards Machine Ethics," *AAAI-04 Workshop on Agent Organizations: Theory and Practice*, San Jose, CA, July 2004.

Anderson, M., Anderson, S., and Armen, C., "Towards Machine Ethics: Implementing Two Action-based Ethical Theories," *2005 AAAI Fall Symposium on Machine Ethics*, AAAI Technical Report FS-05-06, pp. 1–7, 2005.

Anderson, M., Anderson, S., and Armen, C., "MedEthEx: Towards a Medical Ethics Advisor," *Proc. AAAI 2005 Fall Symposium on Caring Machines: AI in Elder Care*, AAAI Tech Report FS-05-02, pp. 9–16, 2005.

Anderson, M., Anderson, S., and Armen, C., "An Approach to Computing Ethics," *IEEE Intelligent Systems*, July/August, pp. 56–63, 2006.

Anderson, S., "Asimov's 'Three Laws of Robotics' and Machine Metaethics," *AI and Society*, Springer, published online March 2007b.

Aquinas, T., "Summa Theologica," in *The Morality of War: Classical and Contemporary Readings* (Eds. L. May, E. Rovie, and S. Viner 2005), Pearson-Prentice Hall, pp. 26–33, ca. 1265.

ARDEC-WVU Spiral 1 Network Lethality Demo brochure, Armament Research and Development Center (ARDEC), July 25, 2007.

Argy, P., "Ethics Dilemma in Killer Bots," *Australian IT News*, June 14, 2007.

Arkin, R.C., "Neuroscience in Motion: The Application of Schema Theory to Mobile Robotics," chapter in *Visuomotor Coordination: Amphibians, Comparisons, Models, and Robots*, ed. P. Evert and M. Arbib, Plenum, pp. 649–672, 1989.

Arkin, R.C., "Modeling Neural Function at the Schema Level: Implications and Results for Robotic Control," chapter in *Biological Neural Networks in Invertebrate Neuroethology and Robotics,* ed. R. Beer, R. Ritzmann, and T. McKenna, Academic Press, pp. 383–410, 1992.

Arkin, R.C., *Behavior-based Robotics*, MIT Press, 1998.

Arkin, R.C., "Moving Up the Food Chain: Motivation and Emotion in Behavior-based Robots," in *Who Needs Emotions: The Brain Meets the Robot*, Eds. J. Fellous and M. Arbib, Oxford University Press, pp. 245–270, 2005.

Arkin, R.C. and Balch, T., "AuRA: Principles and Practice in Review," *Journal of Experimental and Theoretical Artificial Intelligence*, Vol. 9, No. 2, pp. 175–189, 1997.

Arkin, R.C., Collins, T.R., and Endo, T., "Tactical Mobile Robot Mission Specification and Execution," *Mobile Robots XIV*, Boston, MA, Sept. 1999, pp. 150–163.

Arkin, R.C., Fujita, M., Takagi, T., and Hasegawa, R., "An Ethological and Emotional Basis for Human-Robot Interaction," *Robotics and Autonomous Systems*, 42 (3–4), March 2003.

Arkoudas, K., Bringsjord, S., and Bello, P., "Toward Ethical Robots via Mechanized Deontic Logic," *AAAI Fall Symposium on Machine Ethics*, AAAI Technical Report FS-05-06, 2005.

Armstrong, M., "Combat Robots and Perception Management," *Serviam*, May/June 2008.

Asaro, P., "What Should We Want From a Robot Ethic?" *International Review of Information Ethics*, Vol. 6, pp. 9–16, Dec. 2006.

Asaro, P., "How Just Could a Robot War Be?" *5th European Computing and Philosophy Conference*, Twente, NL, June 2007.

Asimov, I., *I, Robot,* New York: Doubleday, 1950.

Asimov, I., *Robots and Empire*, New York: Doubleday, 1985.

ATSC (Army Training Support Center), "Apply the Ethical Decision-Making Method as a Commander Leader or Staff Member," 158-100-1331, http://www.au.af.mil/au/awc/awcgate/army/ethical_d-m.htm, 2007 (accessed 9/11/2008).

Aviles, W.A., et al., "Issues in Mobile Robotics: The Unmanned Ground Vehicle Program TeleOperated Vehicle (TOV)," SPIE Vol. 1388, *Mobile Robots V*, Boston, MA, pp. 587–597, November, 8–9, 1990.

Bains, S., "Feeling Robots' Pain," Brains and Machines Blog, May 22, 2007, http://sunnybains.typepad.com/blog/2007/05/anthropomorphiz.html (accessed 8/31/2008).

Baker, J., "Judging Kosovo: The Legal Process, The Law of Armed Conflict, and The Commander in Chief," in *Legal and Ethical Lessons of NATO's Kosovo Campaign*, International Law Studies (Ed. A. Wall), Naval War College, Vol. 78, 2002.

Balch, T. and Arkin, R.C., "Behavior-based Formation Control for Multi-robot Teams," *IEEE Transactions on Robotics and Automation*, Vol. 14, No. 6, pp. 926–939, December 1998.

Baldor, L., "Military Declined to Bomb Group of Taliban at Funeral," Associated Press article, Washington, D.C., Sept. 14, 2006.

BBC Online, "What happened at Haditha?" December 21, 2006, news.bbc.co.uk/2/hi/middle_east/5033648.stm (accessed 9/11/2008).

Berger, J.B., Grimes, D., and Jensen, E. (Ed.), *Operational Law Handbook*, International and Operational Law Department, The Judge Advocate General's Legal Center and School, Charlottesville, VA, 2004.

Best, S.J., Krueger, B.S., *Internet Data Collection*, Sage, 2004.

Bill, B. (Ed.), *Law of War Workshop Deskbook*, International and Operational Law Department, Judge Advocate General's School, June 2000.

Borenstein, J., "The Ethics of Autonomous Military Robots," *Studies in Ethics, Law, and Technology*, Vol. 2, Issue 1, Article 2, Berkeley Electronic Press, 2008.

Bourke, J., *An Intimate History of Killing*, Basic Books, 1999.

Bourne, J., *A Catechism of the Steam Engine*, Gutenberg eBook, 1856, http://www.gutenberg.org/files/10998/10998-h/10998-h.htm (accessed 9/4/08).

Brandt, R., "Utilitarianism and the Rules of War," in *The Morality of War: Classical and Contemporary Readings*, (Eds. L. May, E. Rovie, and S. Viner 2005), Pearson-Prentice Hall, pp. 234–245, 1972.

Bring, O., "International Humanitarian Law After Kosovo: Is Lex Lata Sufficient?" in *Legal and Ethical Lessons of NATO's Kosovo Campaign*, International Law Studies (Ed. A. Wall), Naval War College, Vol. 78, pp. 257–272, 2002.

Bringsjord, S., Arkoudas, K., and Bello, P., "Toward a General Logicist Methodology for Engineering Ethically Correct Robots," *Intelligent Systems*, July/August, pp. 38–44, 2006.

Brooks, R., "The Behavior Language," A.I. Memo No. 1227, MIT AI Laboratory, April 1990.

Butler, A. and Wall, R., "Navy: Unmanned Combat Squadron by 2025," *Aviation Week's DTI*, March 12, 2008.

Calhoun, L., "The Strange Case of Summary Execution by a Predator Drone," *Peace Review*, 15:2, pp. 209–214, 2003.

Canning, J., Riggs, G., Holland, O., and Blakelock, C., "A Concept for the Operation of Armed Autonomous Systems on the Battlefield," *Proc. AUVSI 2004*, Anaheim, CA, Aug. 2004.

Canning, J., "A Concept of Operations for Armed Autonomous Systems," Presentation at *NDIA Disruptive Technologies Conference*, 2006.

Canning, J., "Weaponized Unmanned Systems: A Transformational Warfighting Opportunity, Government Roles in Making it Happen," preprint to appear in *American Society of Naval Engineers Journal*, 2008.

Card, J., "Killer Machines," *Foreign Policy*, May/June 2007. http://www.foreignpolicy.com/story/cms.php?story_id=3813 (accessed 9/1/08).

Cervellati, M., Esteban, J., and Kranich, L., "Moral Values, Self-Regulatory Emotions, and Redistribution, Working Paper, Institute for Economic Analysis, Barcelona, May 2007.

CLAMO (Center for Law and Military Operations), *Rules of Engagement (ROE) Handbook for Judge Advocates*, Charlottesville, VA, May 2000.

CLAMO (Center for Law and Military Operations), *Deployed Marine Air-Ground Judge Advocate Handbook*, Judge Advocate Generals' School, Charlottesville, VA, 15 July 2002.

Clausewitz, C. Von, "On the Art of War," in *The Morality of War: Classical and Contemporary Readings* (Eds. L. May, E. Rovie, and S. Viner 2005), Pearson-Prentice Hall, pp. 115–121, 1832.

Cloos, C., "The Utilibot Project: An Autonomous Mobile Robot Based on Utilitarianism," *2005 AAAI Fall Symposium on Machine Ethics*, AAAI Technical Report FS-05-06, pp. 38–45, 2005.

[CMU 07] Carnegie Mellon Robotics Institute Projects Website, "Gladiator," http://www.ri.cmu.edu/projects/project_566.html, Version January 2007 (accessed 9/11/2008).

CNN, "Armchair Pilots Striking Afghanistan by Remote Control," July 9, 2008, http://www.cnn.com/2008/TECH/07/09/remote.fighters/index.html (accessed 9/11/08).

Coleman, K., "Android Arete: Toward a Virtue Ethic for Computational Agents," *Ethics and Information Technology*, Vol. 3, pp. 247–265, 2001.

Collins, T.R., Arkin, R.C., Cramer, M.J., and Endo, Y., "Field Results for Tactical Mobile Robot Missions," *Unmanned Systems 2000*, Orlando, FL, July 2000.

Cook, M., *The Moral Warrior: Ethics and Service in the U.S. Military*, State University of New York Press, 2004.

Danyluk, S., "Preventing Atrocities," *Marine Corps Gazette*, Vol. 8, No. 4, pp. 36–38, June 2000.

DARPA (Defense Advanced Research Projects Agency) Broad Agency Announcement 07-52, *Scalable Network Monitoring*, Strategic Technology Office, August 2007.

Davis, D., "Who Decides: Man or Machine?" *Armed Forces Journal*, 2008.

Defense Update, "Low Cost Autonomous Attack System," Issue 4, Year 2004, http://www.defense-update.com/products/l/locaas.htm (accessed 9/11/08).

Defense Update, "Harpy Air Defense Suppression System," http://www.defense-update.com/directory/harpy.htm (accessed 9/11/08).

Del Giorno, M., Personal Communication, General Dynamics Robotics Systems, August 2008.

Devine, M., and Sebasto, A., "Fast-Track Armaments for Iraq and Afghanistan," *Defense AT&L*, pp. 18–21, May–June 2004.

Dennett, D., "When HAL Kills, Who's to Blame?" in *HAL's Legacy: 2001's Computer as Dream and Reality* (Ed. D. Stork), MIT Press, 1996.

Dillman, D.A., *Mail and Internet Surveys: The Tailored Design Method*, John Wiley & Sons, Inc., Hoboken, NJ, 2007.

Dinstein, Y., "Legitimate Military Objectives Under the Current Jus in Bello," in *Legal and Ethical Lessons of NATO's Kosovo Campaign*, International Law Studies (Ed. A. Wall), Naval War College, Vol. 78, pp. 139–172, 2002.

DOD (Department of Defense), *Unmanned Systems Safety Guide for DOD Acquisition*, June 27, 2007a.

DOD, *Unmanned Systems Roadmap: 2007–2032*, 2007b.

DOD (Department of Defense) Joint Publication 1-02, *Dictionary of Military and Associated Terms*, April 2001, Amended through June 2007.

DOD CIO Department of Defense Global Information Grid Architectural Vision, Version 1.0, June 2007.

Downes, A., *Targeting Civilians in War*, Cornell University Press, Ithaca, NY, 2008.

Endo, Y., MacKenzie, D., and Arkin, R.C., "Usability Evaluation of High-level User Assistance for Robot Mission Specification," *IEEE Transactions on Systems, Man, and Cybernetics*, Vol. 34, No. 2, pp. 168–180, May 2004.

Erwin, S., "For the First Time, Navy will Launch Weapons from Surveillance Drones," *National Defense*, June 2007.

Eshel, D., "Israel Intercepts Two Attack UAV Launched by Hezbollah," *Defense Update*, Aug. 14, 2006, http://www.defense-update.com/2006/08/israel-intercept-two-attack-uav.html (accessed 8/31/2008).

Feldman, Y., "The Transformers," Haaretz.com, http://www.haaretz.com/hasen/spages/1000981.html (accessed 7/17/08).

Fellous, J.-M. and Arbib, M. (Eds.), *Who Needs Emotions? The Brain Meets the Robot*, Oxford University Press, 2005.

Fielding, M., "Robotics in Future Land Warfare," *Australian Army Journal*, Vol. 3, No. 2, pp. 99–108, Winter 2006.

Fieser, J. and Dowden, B., "Just War Theory," *The Internet Encyclopedia of Philosophy*, http://www.iep.utm.edu/j/justwar.htm, 2007 (accessed 9/11/08).

Foss, M., "What are Autonomous Weapon Systems and What Ethical Issues do they Raise," June 27, http://marekfoss.org/works/Autonomous_Weapons.pdf (accessed 8/30/08), 2008.

Foster-Miller Inc., "Products & Service: TALON Military Robots, EOD, SWORDS, and Hazmat Robots," http://www.foster-miller.com/lemming.htm, 2008 (accessed 9/11/08).

Gazzaniga, M., *The Ethical Brain*, Dana Press, 2005.

Gibson, J.J., *The Ecological Approach to Visual Perception*, Houghton Mifflin, Boston, MA, 1979.

Gilmore, G., "Report Reflects Future for Military's Unmanned Systems," American Forces Press Service News Article, Department of Defense, Dec. 18, 2007.

Government Accountability Office (GAO), "Patriot Missile Defense: Software Problem Led to System Failure at Dhahran," Feb. 4, 1992, http://www.fas. org/spp/starwars/gao/im92026.htm (accessed 8/31/2008).

Grau, C., "There is no 'I' in 'Robot': Robots and Utilitarianism," *IEEE Intelligent Systems*, July/August, pp. 52–55, 2006.

Grossman, D., *On Killing: The Psychological Cost of Learning to Kill in War and Society*, Little, Brown and Company, Boston, 1995.

GT MRL (Georgia Tech Mobile Robot Laboratory), Manual for *MissionLab* Version 7.0, http://www.cc.gatech.edu/aimosaic/robot-lab/research/Mission Lab/ mlab_manual-7.0.pdf, 2007.

Guarini, M., "Particularism and the Classification and Reclassification of Moral Cases," *IEEE Intelligent Systems*, July/August, pp. 22–28, 2006.

Guetlein, M., "Lethal Autonomous Systems—Ethical and Doctrinal Implications," Naval War College Joint Military Operations Department Paper, February 2005.

Gulam, H. and Lee, S., "Uninhabited Combat Aerial Vehicles and the Law of Armed Conflict," *Australian Army Journal*, Vol. 3, No. 2, pp. 123–136, 2006.

Haidt, J., "The Moral Emotions," in *Handbook of Affective Sciences* (Eds. R. Davidson et al.), Oxford University Press, 2003.

Hartle, A., *Moral Issues in Military Decision Making*, 2nd Ed., Revised, University Press of Kansas, 2004.

Hauser, M., *Moral Minds: How Nature Designed Our Universal Sense of Right and Wrong*, ECCO, HarperCollins, NY, 2006.

Hersh, S., "A Reporter at Large. The Reprimand," *The New Yorker*, October 9, p. 119, via [Bourke 99], 1971.

Hightower, J.D., Smith, D.C., and Wiker, S.F., "Development of Remote Presence Technology for Teleoperator Systems," *Proceedings of the 14th Meeting of the UJNR/MFP*, September 1986.

Himma, K., "Artificial Agency, Consciousness, and the Criteria for Moral Agency: What Properties Must an Artificial Agent Have to be a Moral Agent?" *7th International Computer Ethics Conference*, San Diego, CA, July 2007.

Horty, J., *Agency and Deontic Logic*, Oxford University Press, 2001.

Hosken, G., Schmidt, M., and du Plessis, J., "9 Killed in Army Horror," *Independent Online*, Oct. 13, 2007, http://www.int.iol.co.za/index.php?set_id=1&click=_i d=13&art+id=vn20071013080449804C939465 (accessed 8/31/2008).

Hoyle, C., "UK Reaper Releases Weapons for First Time," *Flight International*, June 12, 2008. http://www.flightglobal.com/articles/2008/06/12/224507/uk-reap-er-releases-weapons-for-first-time.html (accessed 9/11/08).

Hsieh, M., Cowley, A., Keller, J., Chaimonwicz, L., Grocholsky, B., Kumar, V., Taylor, C., Endo, Y., Arkin, R.C., Jung, B., Wolf, D., Sukhatme, G., and Mackenzie, D., "Adaptive Teams of Autonomous Aerial and Ground Robots for Situational Awareness," *Journal of Field Robotics*, Vol. 4, No. 11–12, pp. 991–1014, Nov.–Dec. 2007.

Human Rights Watch, "International Humanitarian Law Issues in the Possible U.S. Invasion of Iraq," *Lancet*, Feb. 20, 2003.

Hussain, Z. and Dreazen, Y., "Strike Kills Militant tied to Europe Attacks," *The Wall Street Journal Online*, May 20, 2008.

iRobot Press Release, "iRobot and Boston Univ. Photonics Unveil Advanced Sniper Detection for iRobot Packbot," Oct. 3, 2005.

iRobot Press Release, "iRobot and TASER Team to Deliver New Robot Capabilities for Military, Law Enforcement," June 28, 2007.

Isaacson, W., *Einstein: His Life and Universe*, Simon and Schuster, 2007.

Jean, G., "Unmanned Bombers at Sea?" *National Defense*, pp. 42–44, September 2007.

Jewell, M., "Taser, iRobot team up to arm robots," Associated Press News Wire, June 2007.

Johnstone, J., "Technology as Empowerment: A Capability Approach to Computer Ethics," *Ethics and Information Technology*, Vol. 9, pp. 73–87, 2007.

Joy, B., "Why the Future Doesn't Need Us," *Wired*, Issue 8.04, November 2000.

Kaelbling, L., and Rosenschein, S., "Action and Planning in Embedded Systems," in *Designing Autonomous Agents*, ed. P. Maes, MIT Press, Cambridge, MA, pp. 35–48.

Kant, I., *Perpetual Peace and Other Essays on Politics, History, and Morals*, trans. T. Humphrey, Hackett, Indianapolis, 1985.

Kim, H.-J., "South Korea Struggles to Probe Tourist Death," Associated Press, July 25, 2008a.

Kim, H.-J., "North Korea Rejects Probe into Tourist's Death," Associated Press, July 15, 2008b.

Kira, Z. and Arkin, R.C., "Forgetting Bad Behavior: Memory Management for Case-based Navigation," *Proc. IROS-2004*, Sendai, JP, 2004.

Klein, J., "The Problematic Nexus: Where Unmanned Combat Air Vehicles and the Law of Armed Conflict Meet," *Air & Space Power Journal, Chronicles Online Journal*, July 2003.

Koehl, S., "A Milestone in the Annals of Air Warfare," *The Weekly Standard*, November 26, 2007, http://www.weeklystandard.com/weblogs/TWSFP/2007/11/a_milestone_in_the_annals_of_a.asp (accessed 9/11/08).

Kolodner, J., *Case-Based Reasoning*, San Mateo: Morgan Kaufmann, 1993.

Krotkov, E., and Blitch, J., "The Defense Advanced Research Projects Agency (DARPA) Tactical Mobile Robotics Program," *International Journal of Robotics Research*, Vol. 18, No. 7, pp. 769–776, 1999.

Kumagai, J., "A Robotic Sentry for Korea's Demilitarized Zone," *IEEE Spectrum*, March 2007. http://www.spectrum.ieee.org/mar07/4948 (accessed 9/11/08).

Lazarski, A., "Legal Implications of the Uninhabited Combat Aerial Vehicle—Focus: Unmanned Aerial Vehicles," *Aerospace Power Journal*, Summer 2002.

Lee, J.B., Likhachev, M., and Arkin, R.C., "Selection of Behavioral Parameters: Integration of Discontinuous Switching via Case-based Reasoning with Continuous Adaptation via Learning Momentum," *2002 IEEE International Conference on Robotics and Automation*, Washington, DC May 2002.

Likhachev, M., Kaess, M., and Arkin, R.C., "Learning Behavioral Parameterization Using Spatio-Temporal Case-based Reasoning," *2002 IEEE International Conference on Robotics and Automation*, Washington, DC May 2002.

Lockheed-Martin, NLOS-LS Non-Line of Sight Launch System, Fact Sheet, 2006.

Lockheed-Martin, Mule/ARV-A(L), Fact Sheet, 2007, http://www.missilesandfire-control.com/our_news/factsheets/Product_Card-MULE.pdf.

Loyd, A., "Remote-Controlled RAF Reaper Targets the Taleban," *The Times*, July 23, 2008.

MacKenzie, D., Arkin, R.C., and Cameron, J., 1997. "Multiagent Mission Specification and Execution," *Autonomous Robots*, Vol. 4, No. 1, pp. 29–57, Jan. 1997.

Magnuson, S., "Robo Soldiers," *National Defense*, pp. 36–40, September 2007.

Maksel, R., "Predators and Dragons," *Air & Space Magazine*, Smithsonian, July 1, 2008.

Maner, W., "Heuristic Methods for Computer Ethics," *Metaphilosophy*, Vol. 33, No. 3, pp. 339–365, April 2002.

Marshall, S.L.A., *Men Against Fire: The Problem of Battle Command in Future War*, New York: William Morrow, 1947.

Martins, M.S., "Rules of Engagement For Land Forces: A Matter of Training, Not Lawyering," *Military Law Review*, Vol. 143, pp. 4–168, Winter 1994.

Matthias, A., "The Responsibility Gap: Ascribing Responsibility for the Actions of Learning Automata," *Ethics and Information Technology*, Vol. 6, pp. 175–183.

May, L., Rovie, E., and Viner, S., *The Morality of War: Classical and Contemporary Readings*, Pearson-Prentice Hall, 2005.

May, L., "Superior Orders, Duress, and Moral Perception," in *The Morality of War: Classical and Contemporary Readings* (Eds. L. May, E. Rovie, and S. Viner, 2005), pp. 430–439, 2004.

McLaren, B., "Extensionally Defining Principles and Cases in Ethics: An AI Model," *Artificial Intelligence Journal*, Vo. 150, pp. 145–181, Nov. 2003.

McLaren, B., "Lessons in Machine Ethics from the Perspective of Two Computational Models of Ethical Reasoning," *2005 AAAI Fall Symposium on Machine Ethics*, AAAI Technical Report FS-05-06, 2005.

McLaren, B., "Computational Models of Ethical Reasoning: Challenges, Initial Steps, and Future Directions," *IEEE Intelligent Systems*, July/August, pp. 29–37, 2006.

McLoughlin, R., "Fourth Generation Warfare and Network-Centric Warfare," *Marine Corps Gazette*, 2006, http://www.mca-marines.org/GAZETTE/06mcloughlin.asp (accessed 9/11/08).

Moll, J., Zahn, R., de Oliveira-Souza, R., Krueger, F., and Grafman, J., "The Neural Basis of Human Moral Cognition," *Nature Reviews/Neuroscience*, Vol. 6, pp. 799–809, Oct. 2005.

Moor, J., "The Nature, Importance, and Difficulty of Machine Ethics," *IEEE Intelligent Systems*, July/August, pp. 18–21, 2006.

Moshkina, L. and Arkin, R.C., "Human Perspective on Affective Robotic Behavior: A Longitudinal Study," *Proc. IROS-2005*, Calgary, CA, September 2005.

Moshkina, L. and Arkin, R.C., "On TAMEing Robots," *Proc. 2003 IEEE International Conference on Systems, Man and Cybernetics*, Washington, DC October 2003.

Moshkina, L. and Arkin, R., "Lethality and Autonomous Systems: Survey Design and Results," Georgia Tech GVU Center Technical Report GIT-GVU-07-16, 2008a.

Moshkina, L. and Arkin, R.C., "Lethality and Autonomous Systems: The Roboticist Demographic," *Proc. IEEE International Symposium on Technology and Society*, Fredericton, CA, June 2008b.

Mount, M., "Army Suicide Rate Could Top Nation's This Year," CNN.com, Sept. 9, 2008, http://www.cnn.com/2008/HEALTH/09/09/army.suicides/ (accessed 9/24/08).

Norman, R., *Ethics, Killing and War*, Cambridge University Press, Cambridge, UK, 1995.

NSA National Security Agency Website, "Global Information Grid," http:www. nsa.gov/ia/industry/gig.cfm (accessed October 4, 2008).

O'Brien, J., "Killer Robots Could Replace Soldiers," *Fortune Magazine*, pp. 49–53, December 4, 2007.

Opall-Rome, B., "Israel Wants Robotic Guns, Missiles to Guard Gaza," Defensenews. com, 2007, http://www.defensenews.com/story.php? F=2803275& C= mideast.

OPFOR Battle Book, ST 100-7, http://www.fas.org/man/dod-101/army/docs/ st100-7/index.html (accessed 9/11/08), March 1998.

OSD FY 06.3 SBIR Solicitation Topics, "Affect-Based Computing and Cognitive Models of Unmanned Vehicle Systems," http://www.acq.osd.mil/osbp/sbir/ solicitations/sbir063/index.htm (accessed 9/11/08), p. 73, 2006.

Pappalardo, J., "Shift on Future Combat Systems will Rush High-Tech Gear to Iraq," *Popular Mechanics*, June 26, 2008.

Parks, W.H., "Commentary," in *Legal and Ethical Lessons of NATO's Kosovo Campaign*, International Law Studies (Ed. A. Wall), Naval War College, Vol. 78, pp. 281–292, 2002.

Parks, W.H., "Crimes in Hostilities. Part I," *Marine Corps Gazette*, August 1976.

Parks, W.H., "Crimes in Hostilities. Conclusion," *Marine Corps Gazette*, September 1976a.

Parry, C.P., "The Impact of Proliferation: Current and Projected Future Use of Autonomous Vehicles by Criminal & Terrorist Groups," presentation at *Royal United Services Workshop on The Ethics and Legal Implications of Unmanned Vehicles for Defence and Security Purposes*, London, U.K., Feb. 27, 2008.

People Daily Online (English), "Invisible Sword, China's Pilotless Aircraft Unveiled," October 31, 2006, http://english.peopledaily.com.cn/200610/31/ eng20061031_316839.html (accessed 9/11/08).

Perkowitz, S., *Digital People: From Bionic Humans to Androids*, John Henry Press, 2004.

Perri 6, "Ethics, Regulation and the New Artificial Intelligence, Part II: Autonomy and Liability," *Information, Communication and Society*, 4:3, pp. 406–434, 2001.

Powers, T., "Deontological Machine Ethics," *2005 AAAI Fall Symposium on Machine Ethics*, AAAI Technical Report FS-05-06, pp. 79–86, 2005.

Powers, T., "Prospects for a Kantian Machine," *IEEE Intelligent Systems*, July/ August, pp. 46–51, 2006.

Punch, K.F., *Survey Research: The Basics*, Sage, 2003.

222 ■ Governing Lethal Behavior in Autonomous Robots

QinetiQ, "QinitiQ North America Ships First MAARS Robot," Press Release, June 5, 2008, http://www.qinetiq.com/home/newsroom/news_releases_homepage/2008/2nd_ quarter/qinetiq_north_america0.html (accessed 9/11/ 08), 2008.

Radiance Technologies, WeaponWatch Product Sheet, 2007, http://www. radiancetech.com/products/weaponwatch.html.

Ram, A., Arkin, R.C., Moorman, K., and Clark, R.J., "Case-based Reactive Navigation: A case-based method for on-line selection and adaptation of reactive control parameters in autonomous robotic systems," *IEEE Transactions on Systems, Man, and Cybernetics*, Vol. 27, Part B, No. 3, pp. 376–394, June 1997.

Rawcliffe, J., and Smith, J. (Eds.), *Operational Law Handbook*, International and Operational Law Department, Judge Advocate General's Legal Center and School, August 2006.

Rawls, J., *A Theory of Justice*, Harvard University Press, 1971.

Reuters, "Israel Unveils Portable Hunter-Killer Robot," March 8, 2007.

RUSI (Royal United Services Institute) for Defence and Security Studies, "The Ethics & Legal Implications of Unmanned Vehicles for Defence and Security Purposes," Workshop webpage, held Feb. 27, 2008, http://www.rusi.org/ events/ref:E47385996DA7D3 (accessed 8/31/2008).

Russell, S. and Norvig, N., *Artificial Intelligence: A Modern Approach*, Prentice Hall, 1995.

Sagan, S., "Rules of Engagement," in *Avoiding War: Problems of Crisis Management* (Ed. A. George), Westview Press, 1991.

Samsung Techwin website, http://www.samsungtechwin.com/product/features/ dep/SSsystem_e/SSsystem.html (accessed 9/1/2007).

Sandia Intelligent Systems & Robotics Center, http://www.sandia.gov/isrc/fireant. html (accessed 9/11/08).

Schachtman, N., "Robot + Super Gun = 'Crowd Control', " Wired Danger Room Blog, http://blog.wired.com/defense/2008/05/metal-storm-iro.html (accessed 9/11/08), May 27, 2008.

Schmitt, P., "Gunfire Detection System Protects Troops, Garners Award for ARL Scientist," *RDECOM Magazine*, April, May 2005.

Sevastopulo, D., "US Army Suicide Cases at Record 115," *Financial Times*, May 29, 2008, http://us.ft.com/ftgateway/superpage.ft?news_ id= fto0529 200818023- 92265.

Sharkey, N., "Cassandra or False Prophet of Doom: AI Robots and War," *IEEE Intelligent Systems*, pp. 14–17, July/August 2008.

Sharkey, N., "Automated Killers and the Computing Profession," *IEEE Computer*, November 2007.

ShotSpotter, "Military System Overview," www.shotspotter.com/products/military. html (accessed 9/11/08), 2007.

Slim, H., *Killing Civilians: Method, Madness, and Morality in War*, Columbia University Press, New York, 2008.

Smits, D., and De Boeck, P., "A Componential IRT Model for Guilt," *Multivariate Behavioral Research*, Vol. 38, No. 2, pp. 161–188, 2003.

Sparks, B.W. and Neiss, O., "Psychiatric Screening of Combat Pilots," *U.S. Armed Forces Medical Journal*, Vol. 4, VII.6, June 1956.

Sparrow, R., "Killer Robots," *Journal of Applied Philosophy*, Vol. 24, No.1, 2006.

Sparrow, R., Personal Communication, July 2, 2007.

Sparrow, R., "Building a Better Warbot: Ethical Issues in the design of Unmanned Systems for Military Applications," manuscript, 2008.

SPAWAR, "Force Protection Joint Experiment Evaluates Technology Effectiveness," *SPAWAR Systems Center Pacific Robotics Update*, Vol. 8, No. 1, Summer 2008.

SROE, Joint Chiefs of Staff Standing Rules of Engagement, *Enclosure A, Chairman, JCS Instruction 3121.01 (1 October 1994)*.

Strayer, R., and Ellenhorn, L., "Vietnam Veterans: A Study Exploring Adjustment Patterns and Attitudes," *Journal of Social Issues*, 33, 4, as reported in [Bourke 99] 1975.

Sullins, J., "When is a Robot a Moral Agent?" *International Journal of information Ethics*, Vol. 6, 12, 2006.

Sung-ki, J., "Korea Plans to Develop Unmanned Aircraft," *Korea Times*, July 23, 2008.

Surgeon General's Office, Mental Health Advisory Team (MHAT) IV Operation Iraqi Freedom 05-07, Final Report, Nov. 17, 2006.

Swank, R., and Marchand, W., "Combat Neuroses: Development of Combat Exhaustion," *Archives of Neurology and Psychology*, Vol. 55, pp. 236–47, 1946.

Tancredi, L., *Hardwired Behavior: What Neuroscience Reveals about Morality*, Cambridge University Press, 2005.

Tangney, J., Stuewig, J., and Mashek, D., "Moral Emotions and Moral Behavior," *Annu. Rev. Psychol.*, Vol. 58, pp. 345–372, 2007.

Thiesen, B., "TARDEC Robotics for Convoy Automation," *RDECOM Magazine*, June 2004. http://www.rdecom.army.mil/rdemagazine/200406/in_the_lab.html (accessed 9/11/ 08).

Thurston, R., *A History of the Growth of the Steam Engine*, D. Appleton and Co. 1878.

Toner, J.H., "Military OR Ethics," *Air & Space Power Journal*, Summer 2003.

Tran, P., "Stealth Drone Makes Automated Flight Test," *Defense News*, July 8, 2008.

Turilli, M., "Ethical Protocols Design," *Ethics and Information Technology*, Vol. 9, pp. 49–62, March 2007.

Ulam, P, Endo, Y., Wagner, A., and Arkin, R.C., "Integrated Mission Specification and Task Allocation for Robot Teams—Design and Implementation," *Proc. ICRA 2007*, Rome IT, 2007.

U.N. Document A/810, *Universal Declaration of Human Rights*, G.A., res 217 A(III), December 10, 1948.

U.S. Army, Pamphlet 27-161-2, *International Law, Volume II* (23 October 1962)

U.S. Army Field Manual FM 27-10 *The Law of Land Warfare*, July 1956, (amended 1977).

U.S. Army Field Manual FM 3-24, *Counterinsurgency* (Final Draft), June 2006.

U.S. Army Field Manual FM 7-21.13, *The Soldier's Guide*, February 2004.

U.S. Army SBIR Solicitation 07.2, Topic A07-032 "Multi-Agent Based Small Unit Effects Planning and Collaborative Engagement with Unmanned Systems," pp. 57–68, 2007.

U.S. Navy, "Phalanx Close-in Weapons Systems," United States Navy Factfile, http://www.navy.mil/navydata/fact_display.asp?cid=2100&tid=800&ct=2 (accessed 8/2008).

U.S. Patent Office, "Reconfigurable balancing robot and method for dynamically transitioning between statically stable mode and dynamically balanced mode," U.S. Patent Application No. 20080105481, May 2, 2008.

USM University of Southern Mississippi ROTC MI III Reading Material, http://www.usm.edu/armyrotc/MSIII/302/MSL%20302%20L03a%20ROE%20&%20Law%20of%20Land%20Warfare.pdf (accessed 9/11/08).

Vanden Brook, T., "Drones Supply Short of Demand," *USA Today*, March 28, 2007.

Vanden Brook, T., "Drone Attacks Hit High in Iraq," *USA Today*, April 29, 2008.

Van den Hoven, J. and Lokhorst, G.J., "Deontic Logic and Computer-supported Computer Ethics," *Metaphilosophy*, Vol. 33, No. 3, pp. 376–387, April 2002.

Wagner, A., and Arkin, R.C., "Multi-robot Communication-Sensitive Reconnaissance," *Proc. 2004 IEEE International Conference on Robotics and Automation*, New Orleans, 2004.

Walzer, M., *Just and Unjust Wars,* 4th Ed., Basic Books, 1977.

Walzer, M., *Arguing About War*, Yale University Press, 2004.

Weiner, T., "New Model Army Soldier Rolls Closer to Battle," *New York Times*, Feb. 16, 2005.

Wiegel, V., "Building Blocks for Artificial Moral Agents," *Proc. Artificial Life X,* 2006.

Wiegel, V., Van den Hoven, M., and Lokhorst, G., "Privacy, deontic epistemic action logic and software agents," *Ethics and Information Technology*, Vol. 7, pp. 251–264, 2005.

Wells, D., (Ed.), *An Encyclopedia of War and Ethics*, Greenwood Press, 1996.

Wikipedia, "Laws of War," http://en.wikipedia.org/wiki/Laws_of_war (accessed 9/11/08), 2007a.

Wikipedia, "Rules of Engagement," http://en.wikipedia.org/wiki/Rules_of_engagement (accessed 9/11/08), 2007b.

Woodruff, P., "Justification or Excuse: Saving Soldiers at the Expense of Civilians," in *The Morality of War: Classical and Contemporary Readings* (Eds. L. May, E. Rovie, and S. Viner, 2005), Pearson-Prentice Hall, pp. 281–291, 1982.

World Tribune, "U.S. drone smart bombs an Iraqi car bomb," World Tribune.com, August 25. 2008, http://www.worldtribune.com/worldtribune/WTARC/2008/ss_iraq0464_08_24.asp (accessed 9/4/08).

Yoder, J.H., "When War is Unjust: Being Honest in Just-War Thinking," in *The Morality of War: Classical and Contemporary Readings* (Eds. L. May, E. Rovie, and S. Viner, 2005), Pearson-Prentice Hall, pp. 153–159, 1984.

Zilberstein, S., "Using Anytime Algorithms in Intelligent System," *AI Magazine*, pp 73–83, Fall 1996.

Relevant Laws of War

This appendix contains language drawn directly from a U.S. military manual that prescribes the Laws of War. This serves to illustrate those aspects which are potentially relevant to the use of lethal force by autonomous systems. These regulations are drawn directly from the 1949 Geneva Convention Relative to the Protection of Civilians in the Time of War (GC), 1929 Geneva Convention Relative to the Treatment of Prisoners of War (GPW), 1929 Geneva Convention for the Amelioration of the Condition of the Wounded and Sick of Armies in the Field (GWS), Uniform Code of Military Justice (UCMJ), and 1907 Hague Regulations (HR) and Conventions (HC) (See Figure 1.1). Specifically this material is excerpted directly from *U.S. Army Field Manual 27-10, The Law of Land Warfare* (as amended July 15, 1976).

SECTION I. COMMENCEMENT OF HOSTILITIES

25. Enemy Status of Civilians

Under the law of the United States, one of the consequences of the existence of a condition of war between two States is that every national of the one State becomes an enemy of every national of the other. However, it is a generally recognized rule of international law that civilians must not be made the object of attack directed exclusively against them.

FORBIDDEN CONDUCT WITH RESPECT TO PERSONS

28. Refusal of Quarter

It is especially forbidden * * * to declare that no quarter will be given.
(HR, art. 23, par. (d).)

29. Injury Forbidden After Surrender

It is especially forbidden * * * to kill or wound an enemy who, having laid down his arms, or having no longer means of defense, has surrendered at discretion. *(HR, art. 23, par. (c).)*

30. Persons Descending by Parachute

The law of war does not prohibit firing upon paratroops or other persons who are or appear to be bound upon hostile missions while such persons are descending by parachute. Persons other than those mentioned in the preceding sentence who are descending by parachute from disabled aircraft may not be fired upon.

31. Assassination and Outlawry

HR provides:

> **It is especially forbidden * * * to kill or wound treacherously individuals belonging to the hostile nation or army.** *(HR, art. 23, par. (b).)*

This article is construed as prohibiting assassination, proscription, or outlawry of an enemy, or putting a price upon an enemy's head, as well as offering a reward for an enemy "dead or alive." It does not, however, preclude attacks on individual soldiers or officers of the enemy whether in the zone of hostilities, occupied territory, or elsewhere.

1. FORBIDDEN MEANS OF WAGING WARFARE

33. Means of Injuring the Enemy Limited

a. Treaty Provision

The right of belligerents to adopt means of injuring the enemy is not unlimited. *(HR, art. 22.)*

b. Interpretation

The means employed are definitely restricted by international declarations and conventions and by the laws and usages of war.

34. Employment of Arms Causing Unnecessary Injury

a. Treaty Provision

It is especially forbidden * * * to employ arms, projectiles, or material calculated to cause unnecessary suffering. *(HR, art. 23, par. (e).)*

b. Interpretation

What weapons cause "unnecessary injury" can only be determined in light of the practice of States in refraining from the use of a given weapon because it is believed to have that effect. The prohibition certainly does not extend to the use of explosives contained in artillery projectiles, mines, rockets, or hand grenades. Usage has, however, established the illegality of the use of lances with barbed heads, irregular-shaped bullets, and projectiles filled with glass, the use of any substance on bullets that would tend unnecessarily to inflame a wound inflicted by them, and the scoring of the surface or the filing off of the ends of the hard cases of bullets.

2. BOMBARDMENTS, ASSAULTS, AND SIEGES

39. Bombardment of Undefended Places Forbidden

a. Treaty Provision

The attack or bombardment, by whatever means, of towns, villages, dwellings, or buildings which are undefended is prohibited. (*HR, art. 25.*)

b. Interpretation

An undefended place, within the meaning of Article 25, HR, is any inhabited place near or in a zone where opposing armed forces are in contact which is open for occupation by an adverse party without resistance. In order to be considered as undefended, the following conditions should be fulfilled:

1. Armed forces and all other combatants, as well as mobile weapons and mobile military equipment, must have been evacuated, or otherwise neutralized;

2. no hostile use shall be made of fixed military installations or establishments;

3. no acts of warfare shall be committed by the authorities or by the population; and,

4. no activities in support of military operations shall be undertaken.

The presence, in the place, of medical units, wounded and sick, and police forces retained for the sole purpose of maintaining law and order does not change the character of such an undefended place.

40. Permissible Objects of Attack or Bombardment

a. Attacks against the Civilian Population as Such Prohibited

Customary international law prohibits the launching of attacks (including bombardment) against either the civilian population as such or individual civilians as such.

b. Defended Places

Defended places, which are outside the scope of the proscription of Article 25, HR, are permissible objects of attack (including bombardment). In this context, defended places include:

1. A fort or fortified place.

2. A place that is occupied by a combatant military force or through which such a force is passing. The occupation of a place by medical units alone, however, is not sufficient to render it a permissible object of attack.

3. A city or town surrounded by detached defense positions, if under the circumstances the city or town can be considered jointly with such defense positions as an indivisible whole.

c. Military Objectives

Military objectives—i.e., combatants, and those objects which by their nature, location, purpose, or use make an effective contribution to military action and whose total or partial destruction, capture or neutralization, in the circumstances ruling at the time, offers a definite military advantage—are permissible objects of attack (including bombardment). Military objectives include, for example, factories producing munitions and military supplies, military camps, warehouses storing munitions and military supplies, ports and railroads being used for the transportation of military supplies, and other places that are for the accommodation of troops or the support of military operations. Pursuant to the provisions of Article 25, HR, however, cities, towns, villages, dwellings, or buildings which may be classified as military objectives, but which are undefended (para. 39 *b*), are not permissible objects of attack.

41. Unnecessary Killing and Devastation

Particularly in the circumstances referred to in the preceding paragraph, loss of life and damage to property incidental to attacks must not be excessive in relation to the concrete and direct military advantage expected to be gained. Those who plan or decide upon an attack, therefore, must take all reasonable steps to ensure not only that the objectives are identified as military objectives or defended places within the meaning of the preceding paragraph but also that these objectives may be attacked without probable losses in lives and damage to property disproportionate to the military advantage anticipated. Moreover, once a fort or defended locality has surrendered, only such further damage is permitted as is demanded by the exigencies of war, such as the removal of fortifications, demolition of military buildings, and destruction of military stores *(HR, art. 23, par. (g); GC, art. 53).*

42. Aerial Bombardment

There is no prohibition of general application against bombardment from the air of combatant troops, defended places, or other legitimate military objectives.

43. Notice of Bombardment

a. *Treaty Provision*

The officer in command of an attacking force must, before commencing a bombardment, except in cases of assault, do all in his power to warn the authorities. *(HR, art. 26.)*

b. *Application of Rule*

This rule is understood to refer only to bombardments of places where parts of the civil population remain.

c. *When Warning Is to Be Given*

Even when belligerents are not subject to the above treaty, the commanders of United States ground forces will, when the situation permits, inform the enemy of their intention to bombard a place, so that the noncombatants, especially the women and children, may be removed before the bombardment commences.

44. Treatment of Inhabitants of Invested Area

a. *General Population*

The commander of the investing force has the right to forbid all communications and access between the besieged place and the outside. However, Article 17, *GC* (par. 256) requires that belligerents endeavor to conclude local agreements for the removal from besieged or encircled areas of wounded, sick, infirm, and aged persons, children and maternity cases, and for the passage of ministers of all religions, medical personnel, and medical equipment on their way to such areas. Provision is also made in Article 23 of the same Convention (par. 262) for the passage of consignments of medical and hospital stores and objects necessary for the religious worship of civilians and of essential foodstuffs, clothing, and tonics intended for children under 15, expectant mothers, and maternity cases.

Subject to the foregoing exceptions, there is no rule of law which compels the commander of an investing force to permit noncombatants to leave a besieged locality. It is within the discretion of the besieging commander whether he will permit noncombatants to leave and under what conditions. Thus, if a commander of a besieged place expels the noncombatants in order to lessen the logistical burden he has to bear, it is lawful, though an extreme measure, to drive them back, so as to hasten the surrender. Persons who attempt to leave or enter a besieged place without obtaining the necessary permission are liable to be fired upon, sent back, or detained.

45. Buildings and Areas to Be Protected
a. Buildings to Be Spared
In sieges and bombardments all necessary measures must be taken to spare, as far as possible, buildings dedicated to religion, art, science, or charitable purposes, historic monuments, hospitals, and places where the sick and wounded are collected, provided they are not being used at the time for military purposes.

It is the duty of the besieged to indicate the presence of such buildings or places by distinctive and visible signs, which shall be notified to the enemy beforehand. *(HR, art. 27.)* (See also *GC, arts. 18 and 19; pars. 257 and 258* herein, dealing with the identification and protection of civilian hospitals.)

47. Pillage Forbidden
The pillage of a town or place, even when taken by assault, is prohibited. *(HR, art. 28.)*

3. TREATMENT OF PROPERTY DURING COMBAT
56. Devastation
The measure of permissible devastation is found in the strict necessities of war. Devastation as an end in itself or as a separate measure of war is not

sanctioned by the law of war. There must be some reasonably close connection between the destruction of property and the overcoming of the enemy's army. Thus the rule requiring respect for private property is not violated through damage resulting from operations, movements, or combat activity of the army; that is, real estate may be used for marches, camp sites, construction of field fortifications, etc. Buildings may be destroyed for sanitary purposes or used for shelter for troops, the wounded and sick and vehicles and for reconnaissance, cover, and defense. Fences, woods, crops, buildings, etc., may be demolished, cut down, and removed to clear a field of fire, to clear the ground for landing fields, or to furnish building materials or fuel if imperatively needed for the army. (See *GC, art. 53*; par. 339b; herein, concerning the permissible extent of destruction in occupied areas.)

57. Protection of Artistic and Scientific Institutions and Historic Monuments

The United States and certain of the American Republics are parties to the so-called *Roetich Pact,* which accords a neutralized and protected status to historic monuments, museums, scientific, artistic, educational, and cultural institutions in the event of war between such States. (For its text, see *49 Stat. 3267; Treaty Series No. 899.*)

58. Destruction and Seizure of Property

It is especially forbidden * * * to destroy or seize the enemy's property, unless such destruction or seizure be imperatively demanded by the necessities of war *(HR, art. 23, par. (g).)*

4. PERSONS ENTITLED TO BE TREATED AS PRISONERS OF WAR; RETAINED MEDICAL PERSONNEL

60. General Division of Enemy Population

The enemy population is divided in war into two general classes:

- a. Persons entitled to treatment as prisoners of war upon capture, as defined in Article 4, *GPW* (par. 61).

- b. The civilian population (exclusive of those civilian persons listed in *GPW, art. 4),* who benefit to varying degrees from the provisions of GC.

Persons in each of the foregoing categories have distinct rights, duties, and disabilities. Persons who are not members of the armed forces, as defined in Article 4, *GPW,* who bear arms or engage in other conduct hostile to the enemy thereby deprive themselves of many of the privileges attaching to the members of the civilian population.

62. Combatants and Noncombatants

The armed forces of the belligerent parties may consist of combatants and noncombatants. In the case of capture by the enemy, both have a right to be treated as prisoners of war. *(HR, art. 3.)*

63. Commandos and Airborne Troops

Commando forces and airborne troops, although operating by highly trained methods of surprise and violent combat, are entitled, as long as they are members of the organized armed forces of the enemy and wear uniform, to be treated as prisoners of war upon capture, even if they operate singly.

64. Qualifications of Members of Militias and Volunteer Corps

The requirements specified in Article 4, paragraphs A *(2) (a)* to *(d), GPW* (par. 61) are satisfied in the following fashion:

a. *Command by a Responsible Person*

This condition is fulfilled if the commander of the corps is a commissioned officer of the armed forces or is a person of position and authority or if the members of the militia or volunteer corps are provided with documents, badges, or other means of identification to show that they are officers, noncommissioned officers, or soldiers so that there may be no doubt that they are not persons acting on their own responsibility. State recognition, however, is not essential, and an organization may be formed spontaneously and elect its own officers.

b. *Fixed Distinctive Sign*

The second condition, relative to the possession of a fixed distinctive sign recognizable at a distance is satisfied by the wearing of military uniform, but less than the complete uniform will suffice. A helmet or headdress which would make the silhouette of the individual readily distinguishable from that of an ordinary civilian would satisfy this requirement. It is also desirable that the individual member of the militia or volunteer corps wear a badge or brassard permanently affixed to his clothing. It is not necessary to inform the enemy of the distinctive sign, although it may be desirable to do so in order to avoid misunderstanding.

c. Carrying Arms Openly

This requirement is not satisfied by the carrying of weapons concealed about the person or if the individuals hide their weapons on the approach of the enemy.

d. Compliance with Law of War

This condition is fulfilled if most of the members of the body observe the laws and customs of war, notwithstanding the fact that the individual member concerned may have committed a war crime. Members of militias and volunteer corps should be especially warned against employment of treachery, denial of quarters, maltreatment of prisoners of war, wounded, and dead, improper conduct toward flags of truce, pillage, and unnecessary violence and destruction.

5. PERSONS NOT ENTITLED TO BE TREATED AS PRISONERS OF WAR

74. Necessity of Uniform

Members of the armed forces of a party to the conflict and members of militias or volunteer corps forming part of such armed forces lose their right to be treated as prisoners of war whenever they deliberately conceal their status in order to pass behind the military lines of the enemy for the purpose of gathering military information or for the purpose of waging war by destruction of life or property. Putting on civilian clothes or the uniform of the enemy are examples of concealment of the status of a member of the armed forces.

80. Individuals Not of Armed Forces Who Engage in Hostilities

Persons, such as guerrillas and partisans, who take up arms and commit hostile acts without having complied with the conditions prescribed by the laws of war for recognition as belligerents (see *GPW, art. 4;* par. 61 herein), are, when captured by the injured party, not entitled to be treated as prisoners of war and may be tried and sentenced to execution or imprisonment.

81. Individuals Not of Armed Forces Who Commit Hostile Acts

Persons who, without having complied with the conditions prescribed by the laws of war for recognition as belligerents (see *GPW, art. 4;* par. 61 herein), commit hostile acts about or behind the lines of the enemy are not to be treated as prisoners of war and may be tried and sentenced to execution or imprisonment. Such acts include, but are not limited to, sabotage, destruction of communications facilities, intentional misleading of troops by guides, liberation of prisoners of war, and other acts not falling within Articles 104 and 106 of the Uniform Code of Military Justice and Article 29 of the Hague Regulations.

82. Penalties for the Foregoing

Persons in the foregoing categories who have attempted, committed, or conspired to commit hostile or belligerent acts are subject to the extreme penalty of death because of the danger inherent in their conduct. Lesser penalties may, however, be imposed.

6. GENERAL PROTECTION OF PRISONERS OF WAR

85. Killing of Prisoners

A commander may not put his prisoners to death because their presence retards his movements or diminishes his power of resistance by necessitating a large guard, or by reason of their consuming supplies, or because it appears certain that they will regain their liberty through the impending success of their forces. It is likewise unlawful for a commander to kill his prisoners on grounds of self-preservation, even in the case of airborne or commando operations, although the circumstances of the operation may make necessary rigorous supervision of and restraint upon the movement of prisoners of war.

89. Humane Treatment of Prisoners

Prisoners of war must at all times be humanely treated. Any unlawful act or omission by the Detaining Power causing death or seriously endangering the health of a prisoner of war in its custody is prohibited, and will be regarded as a serious breach of the present Convention. In particular, no prisoner of war may be subjected to physical mutilation or to medical or scientific experiments of any kind which are not justified by the medical, dental or hospital treatment of the prisoner concerned and carried out in his interest.

Likewise, prisoners of war must at all times be protected, particularly against acts of violence or intimidation and against insults and public curiosity.

Measures of reprisal against prisoners of war are prohibited. *(GPW, art. 13.)*

90. Respect for the Person of Prisoners

Prisoners of war are entitled in all circumstances to respect for their persons and their honor.

Women shall be treated with all the regard due to their sex and shall in all cases benefit by treatment as favorable as that granted to men.

Prisoners of war shall retain the full civil capacity which they enjoyed at the time of their capture. The Detaining Power may not restrict the exercise, either within or without its own territory, of the rights such capacity confers except in so far as the captivity requires. *(GPW, art. 14.)*

7. WOUNDED AND SICK

215. Protection and Care

a. Treaty Provision

Members of the armed forces and other persons mentioned in the following Article, who are wounded or sick, shall be respected and protected in all circumstances.

They shall be treated humanely and cared for by the Party to the conflict in whose power they may be, without any adverse distinction founded on sex, race, nationality, religion, political opinions, or any other similar criteria Any attempts upon their lives, or violence to their persons, shall be strictly prohibited; in particular, they shall not be murdered or exterminated, subjected to torture or to biological experiments; they shall not willfully be left without medical assistance and care, nor shall conditions exposing them to contagion or infection be created.

Only urgent medical reasons will authorize priority in the order of treatment to be administered.

Women shall be treated with all consideration due to their sex.

The Party to the conflict which is compelled to abandon wounded or sick to the enemy shall, as far as military considerations permit, leave with them a part of its medical personnel and material to assist in their care. *(GWS, art. 12.)*

216. Search for Casualties

At all times, and particularly after an engagement, Parties to the conflict shall, without delay, take all possible measures to search for and collect the wounded and sick, to protect them against pillage and ill-treatment, to ensure their adequate care, and to search for the dead and prevent their being despoiled.

Whenever circumstances permit, an armistice or a suspension of fire shall be arranged, or local arrangements made, to permit the removal, exchange and transport of the wounded left on the battlefield.

Likewise, local arrangements may be concluded between Parties to the conflict for the removal or exchange of wounded and sick from a besieged or encircled area, and for the passage of medical and religious personnel and equipment on their way to that area. *(GWS, art. 15.)*

8. GENERAL PROTECTION OF POPULATIONS AGAINST CERTAIN CONSEQUENCES OF WAR

255. General Protection of Wounded and Sick

The wounded and sick, as well as the infirm, and expectant mothers, shall be the object of particular protection and respect.

As far as military considerations allow, each Party to the conflict shall facilitate the steps taken to search for the killed and wounded, to assist the shipwrecked and other persons exposed to grave danger, and to protect them against pillage and ill-treatment. *(GC, art. 16.)*

257. Protection of Hospitals

Civilian hospitals organized to give care to the wounded and sick, the infirm and maternity cases, may in no circumstances be the object of attack, but shall at all times be respected and protected by the Parties to the conflict.

States which are Parties to a conflict shall provide all civilian hospitals with certificates showing that they are civilian hospitals and that the buildings which they occupy are not used for any purpose which would deprive these hospitals of protection in accordance with Article 19.

Civilian hospitals shall be marked by means of the emblem provided for in Article 38 of the Geneva Convention for the Amelioration of the Condition of the Wounded and Sick in Armed Forces in the Field of August 12, 1949, but only if so authorized by the State.

The Parties to the conflict shall, in so far as military considerations permit, take the necessary steps to make the distinctive emblems indicating civilian hospitals clearly visible to the enemy land, air and naval forces in order to obviate the possibility of any hostile action.

In view of the dangers to which hospitals may be exposed by being close to military objectives, it is recommended that such hospitals be situated as far as possible from such objectives. *(GC, art. 18.)*

258. Discontinuance of Protection of Hospitals

a. *Treaty Provision*

The protection to which civilian hospitals are entitled shall not cease unless they are used to commit, outside their humanitarian duties, acts harmful to the enemy. Protection may, however, cease only after due warning has been given, naming, in all appropriate cases, a reasonable time limit, and after such warning has remained unheeded.

The fact that sick or wounded members of the armed forces are nursed in these hospitals, or the presence of small arms and ammunition taken from such combatants and not yet handed to the proper service, shall not be considered to be acts harmful to the enemy. *(GC, art. 19.)*

b. Meaning of Acts Harmful to the Enemy

Acts harmful to the enemy are not only acts of warfare proper but any activity characterizing combatant action, such as setting up observation posts or the use of the hospital as a liaison center for fighting troops.

260. Land and Sea Transport

Convoys of vehicles or hospital trains on land or specially provided vessels on sea, conveying wounded and sick civilians, the infirm and maternity cases, shall be respected and protected in the same manner as the hospitals provided for in Article 18, and shall be marked, with the consent of the State, by the display of the distinctive emblem provided for in Article 38 of the Geneva Convention for the Amelioration of the Condition of the Wounded and Sick in Armed Forces in the Field of August 12, 1949. *(GC, art. 21.)*

261. Air Transport

Aircraft exclusively employed for the removal of wounded and sick civilians, the infirm and maternity cases, or for the transport of medical personnel and equipment, shall not be attacked, but shall be respected while flying at heights, times and on routes specifically agreed upon between all the Parties to the conflict concerned.

They may be marked with the distinctive emblem provided for in Article 38 of the Geneva Convention for the Amelioration of the Condition of the Wounded and Sick in Armed Forces in the Field of August 12, 1949.

Unless agreed otherwise, flights over enemy or enemy-occupied territory are prohibited.

Such aircraft shall obey every summons to land. In the event of a landing thus imposed, the aircraft with its occupants may continue its flight after examination if any. *(GC, art. 22.)*

9. PROVISIONS COMMON TO THE TERRITORIES OF THE PARTIES TO THE CONFLICT AND TO OCCUPIED TERRITORIES

270. Prohibition of Coercion

a. Treaty Provision

No physical or moral coercion shall be exercised against protected persons, in particular to obtain information from them or from third parties. *(GC, art. 31.)*

b. Guides

Among the forms of coercion prohibited is the impressment of guides from the local inhabitants.

271. Prohibition of Corporal Punishment, Torture, Etc.

The High Contracting Parties specifically agree that each of them is prohibited from taking any measure of such a character as to cause the physical suffering or extermination of protected persons in their hands. This prohibition applies not only to murder, torture, corporal punishment, mutilation and medical or scientific experiments not necessitated by the medical treatment of a protected person, but also to any other measures of brutality whether applied by civilian or military agents. *(GC, art. 32.)*

272. Individual Responsibility, Collective Penalties, Reprisals, Pillage

No protected person may be punished for an offence he or she has not personally committed. Collective penalties and likewise all measures of intimidation or of terrorism are prohibited.

Pillage is prohibited. Reprisals against protected persons and their property are prohibited. *(GC, art. 33.)* (See also pars. 47 and 397.)

273. Hostages

The taking of hostages is prohibited. *(GC, art. 34.)*

10. CRIMES UNDER INTERNATIONAL LAW

498. Crimes under International Law

Any person, whether a member of the armed forces or a civilian, who commits an act which constitutes a crime under international law is responsible therefore and liable to punishment. Such offenses in connection with war comprise:

a. Crimes against peace.

b. Crimes against humanity.

c. War crimes.

Although this manual recognizes the criminal responsibility of individuals for those offenses which may comprise any of the foregoing types of crimes, members of the armed forces will normally be concerned, only with those offenses constituting "war crimes."

499. War Crimes

The term "war crime" is the technical expression for a violation of the law of war by any person or persons, military or civilian. Every violation of the law of war is a war crime.

502. Grave Breaches of the Geneva Conventions of 1949 as War Crimes

The Geneva Conventions of 1949 define the following acts as "grave breaches," if committed against persons or property protected by the Conventions:

a. GWS and GWS Sea

Grave breaches to which the preceding Article relates shall be those involving any of the following acts, if committed against persons or property protected by the Convention: wilful killing, torture or inhuman treatment, including biological experiments, wilfully causing great suffering or serious injury to body or health, and extensive destruction and appropriation of property, not justified by military necessity and carried out unlawfully and wantonly. *(GWS, art. 50; GWS Sea, art. 51.)*

b. GPW

Grave breaches to which the preceding Article relates shall be those involving any of the following acts, if committed against persons or property protected by the Convention: wilful killing, torture or inhuman treatment, including biological experiments, wilfully causing great suffering or serious injury to body or health, compelling a prisoner of war to serve in the forces of the hostile Power, or wilfully depriving a prisoner of war of the rights of fair and regular trial prescribed in this Convention. *(GPW, art. 130.)*

c. GC

Grave breaches to which the preceding Article relates shall be those involving any of the following acts, if committed against persons or property protected by the present Convention: willful killing, torture or inhuman treatment, including biological experiments wilfully causing great suffering or serious injury to body or health, unlawful deportation or transfer or unlawful confinement of a protected person, compelling a protected person to serve in the forces of a hostile Power, or wilfully depriving a protected person of the rights of fair and regular trial prescribed in the present Convention, taking of hostages and extensive destruction and appropriation of property, not justified by military necessity and carried out unlawfully and wantonly. *(GC, art. 147.)*

503. Responsibilities of the Contracting Parties

No High Contracting Party shall be allowed to absolve itself or any other High Contracting Party of any liability incurred by itself or by another High Contracting Party in respect of breaches referred to in the preceding Article. *(GWS, art. 51; GWS Sea, art. 52; GPW, art. 131; GC, art. 148.)*

504. Other Types of War Crimes

In addition to the "grave breaches" of the Geneva Conventions of 1949, the following acts are representative of violations of the law of war ("war crimes"):

a. Making use of poisoned or otherwise forbidden arms or ammunition.

b. Treacherous request for quarter.

c. Maltreatment of dead bodies.

d. Firing on localities which are undefended and without military significance.

e. Abuse of or firing on the flag of truce.

f. Misuse of the Red Cross emblem.

g. Use of civilian clothing by troops to conceal their military character during battle.

h. Improper use of privileged buildings for military purposes.

i. Poisoning of wells or streams.

j. Pillage or purposeless destruction.

k. Compelling prisoners of war to perform prohibited labor.

l. Killing without trial spies or other persons who have committed hostile acts.

m. Compelling civilians to perform prohibited labor.

n. Violation of surrender terms.

11. DEFENSES NOT AVAILABLE

509. Defense of Superior Orders

    a. The fact that the law of war has been violated pursuant to an order of a superior authority, whether military or civil, does not deprive the act in question of its character of a war crime, nor does it constitute a defense in the trial of an accused individual, unless he did not know and could not reasonably have been expected to know that the act ordered was unlawful. In all cases where the order is held not to constitute a defense to an allegation of war crime, the fact that the individual was acting pursuant to orders may be considered in mitigation of punishment.

    b. In considering the question whether a superior order constitutes a valid defense, the court shall take into consideration the fact that obedience to lawful military orders is the duty of every member of the armed forces; that the latter cannot be expected, in conditions of war discipline, to weigh scrupulously the legal merits of the orders received; that certain rules of warfare may be controversial; or that an act otherwise amounting to a war crime may be done in obedience to orders conceived as a measure of reprisal. At the same time it must be borne in mind that members of the armed forces are bound to obey only lawful orders (e.g., *UCMJ, Art. 92*).

510. Government Officials

The fact that a person who committed an act which constitutes a war crime acted as the head of a State or as a responsible government official does not relieve him from responsibility for his act.

Acronyms

AI	Artificial Intelligence
ALV	Autonomous Land Vehicle
ARDEC	Armament Research, Development, and Engineering Center
ARL	Army Research Laboratory
ARO	Army Research Office
ARV	Armed Robotic Vehicle
AWS	Autonomous Weapons Systems
CBR	Case-Based Reasoning
CONOPS	Concept of Operations
DARPA	Defense Advanced Research Projects Agency
DMZ	Demilitarized Zone
DOD	Department of Defense
DSP	Design Safety Precept
FCS	Future Combat Systems
GATERS	Ground-Air Telerobotic Systems
GC	Geneva Convention Relative to the Protection of Civilians in the Time of War
GDRS	General Dynamics Robotic Systems
GIG	Global Information Grid
GPS	Global Positioning System
GPW	Geneva Convention Relative to the Treatment of Prisoners of War
GUI	Graphical User Interface
GWS	Geneva Convention for the Amelioration of the Condition of the Wounded and Sick of Armies in the Field

HC	Hague Conventions
HR	Hague Regulations
HMMWV	High-Mobility, Multipurpose Wheeled Vehicle
IED	Improvised Explosive Device
IFF	Identification Friend or Foe
INS	Inertial Navigation System
LOCAAS	Low Cost Autonomous Attack System
LOW	Laws of War
LTM	Long-Term Memory
MDARS	Mobile Detection Assessment and Response System
MOUT	Military Operations over Urban Terrain
NLOS-LAM	Non-Line of Sight, Loitering Attack Munition
PTF	Permission to Fire
ROE	Rules of Engagement
RUF	Rules for the Use of Force
SAIC	Science Applications International Corporation
SPAWAR	Space and Naval Warfare Systems Center
SROE	Standing Rules of Engagement
STM	Short-Term Memory
SUAV	Small Unmanned Aerial Vehicle
SUGV	Small Unmanned Ground Vehicle
TARDEC	Tank Automotive Research, Development, and Engineering Center
TUGV	Tactical Unmanned Ground Vehicle
UAV	Unmanned Aerial Vehicle
UCAV	Unmanned Combat Aerial Vehicle
UGV	Unmanned Ground Vehicle
UMS	Unmanned System
UV	Unmanned Vehicle

Notation

C.1 GENERAL BEHAVIORAL NOTATION

β behavior

B   vector of all active behaviors β_i at a given time t

s   stimulus

S domain of all interpretable stimuli

S   vector of all stimuli $\mathbf{s}_i$ relevant for each behavior β_i at a given time t (perceptual situation)

r instantaneous response

r' instantaneous response scaled by gain g

R range of responses

R   vector of all responses $\mathbf{r}_i$ generated by the set of active behaviors **B**

R'   response vector **R** scaled by gain vector **G**

ρ overall (overt) robotic response

P the set of all overall (overt) robotic responses (read as capital rho)

ø   null response

g scalar gain value (strength multiplier)

G   vector encoding the relative strength or gain g_i of each active behavior β_i

C   behavioral coordination function

p perceptual class

λ strength of stimulus

τ threshold for a given perceptual class

C.2   ETHICAL AND LETHAL BEHAVIOR NOTATION

C	the set of specific ethical constraints derived from the LOW and ROE
c	an individual ethical constraint derived from the LOW and ROE
β_{lethal}	a potentially lethal behavior
$\mathbf{B}_{lethal}$	the set of all potentially lethal behaviors
$\mathbf{r}_{lethal}$	a lethal response for a behavior
ρ_{lethal}	an overall (overt) lethal response for a robot
$\rho_{l\text{-}unethical}$	an unethical overall (overt) lethal response for a robot
$\rho_{permissible}$	an ethically permissible overall (overt) response for a robot
$\mathbf{P}_{lethal}$	the set of all overall (overt) lethal responses for a robot
$\mathbf{P}_{l\text{-}ethical}$	the set of all overall (overt) lethal responses for a robot that are ethical
$\mathbf{P}_{permissible}$	the set of all ethically permissible overall (overt) responses for a robot
$\mathbf{P}_{l\text{-}unethical}$	the set of all unethical overall (overt) lethal responses for a robot
V_{guilt}	the variable representing the current scalar value of the affective state of guilt
Max_{guilt}	the threshold constant for V_{guilt}

C.3 DEONTIC AND ACTION LOGIC NOTATION

C	a specific ethical code
L	a particular computational logic
Φ_C^L	the formalization of C in a particular computational logic L
STIT	"See to it that" operator
O	"it is obliged that" operator
$\forall$	for all (universal) operator
$\exists$	there exists (existence) operator
$\wedge$	and (conjunction) operator
$\rightarrow$	if-then (implication) operator

Index